D1200863

John Wesley Hardin TEXAS GUNMAN

John Wesley Hardin

Texas Gunman

BY LEWIS NORDYKE

CASTLE BOOK**S**

This edition published in 2001 by Castle Books,
A division of Book Sales Inc.
114 Northfield Avenue, Edison, NJ 08837

Reprinted by arrangement with and permission of
William Morrow, an imprint of
HarperCollins Publishers
10 East 53rd Street, New York, New York 10022-5299

Library of Congress Catalogue Card No. 57–6085

ISBN 0-7858-1317-9

to Dottie with appreciation

Contents

Foreword

After watching John Wesley Hardin shoot down five armed and wildly firing men in about a minute, Fred Duderstadt, a cowman on the Chisholm Trail, remarked: "With either hand or both hands at the same time, that boy can handle a pistol faster than a frog can lick flies."

This was scarcely an exaggeration. Hardin probably killed more men in personal combat than any other man in the nation. He was easily the most sensational gun-fighter of the gun-fighting Old West; compared to him, the renowned Billy the Kid was an apt apprentice. Yet this is the first time the Hardin story has been told in full.

This book is not intended to vindicate or accuse, to defend or condemn any person, family, or group, but simply to tell the story of a high-mettled human being who lived, loved, and killed during the most troublous era of the wild Texas frontier. Hardin and his associates were people caught in the firm clutch of the circumstances of their time; they had their own ideals of right and wrong and the shining, starry thing they called honor. Perhaps the reader should also be reminded that passages on the Negro and the Indian and on the sectional bitterness in the United States reflect attitudes of that time and not of the present; like the frontier, and like life itself, these things are ever changing.

Lewis Nordyke

Amarillo, Texas,
July 27, 1956.

John Wesley Hardin TEXAS GUNMAN

1

Desperate Decision

On a sunny September afternoon in 1871, young John Wesley Hardin halted his horse beside a shallow lake near the edge of the small town of Smiley, Texas. He loosened slightly the blue bandanna knotted under his chin, pushed back his broad-brimmed black hat. With each hand resting lightly on a holstered revolver, he looked searchingly all around.

Puffs of wind from the southwest sent ripples racing like sudden chills across the water. A straggling herd of lanky long-horn cattle from the open range browsed nearby, lazed in the shade of giant live oaks, or stood knee-deep in the cool lake. But the lean, tanned youth had no eye for pastoral beauty. Every move and every glance, even the way he sat in the saddle, indicated expectancy and hard experience. He looked first at the herd to make sure no cunning enemies, ready to level down with rifles, lurked among the cattle. Then his gaze fastened on the familiar village. Located on the frontier some fifty miles to the east of old San Antonio, Smiley was a weather-beaten little place in the center of a vast, sunburned territory known far and wide as rough fighting and feuding country.

Hardin eyed intently the cluster of unpainted houses and the few business buildings with their wooden galleries and hitching rails. He studied every horse in sight, for he knew the mounts of his friends and, therefore, could determine whether friends or strangers were in town; every stranger was a potential foe. Moreover, by watching and listening, almost by sensing as a hounded coyote would, he could detect the presence of danger.

There was a deadly serious reason for this lad's extreme caution. Two weeks before, a band of fifty men had threatened to raid the region to kill him. Then a few days later, troops from the Reconstruction Era state police had slipped into Smiley to try to get the drop on him.

Hardin was now eighteen years old. He was the good-looking, intelligent son of a Methodist minister, but he had wandered far from his father's fold. Temporarily he was living out on Elm Creek at the ranch home of a cousin, Manning Clements.

Earlier in the day Clements, knowing well what a few hours spent in the wrong place could bring forth, had warned his cousin against doing any visiting and thus exposing himself to trouble. Then Clements had ridden north to Salty Creek to see a friend about trading for a high-stepping strawberry roan.

Despite his admiration for his older cousin, Hardin depended more on his own judgment and premonitions than he did on the advice of others. He wanted to ride into Smiley because he had it in his head to do so. And there was a compelling question in his mind: Could he spend a few hours on Saturday afternoon in this isolated little town and not become embroiled in a shooting scrape? The answer was of utmost importance, for in the cool of the day he intended to ride on to Coon Hollow and see pretty Jane Bowen—if all went well in Smiley.

Hardin's reconnaissance satisfied him that he could risk going into town and he touched his black horse, Old Bob, with his spurs. Just before reaching the first house he again stopped and listened. The drumming clatter of hoofbeats echoed in the air. A moving trace of dust rose a few hundred yards north of town. Instantly Hardin saw several men run out into the narrow street and look in the direction of the galloping horse. When the rider came into view, Hardin recognized Manning Clements on a fine roan—and knew that violence was upon him. He knew his cousin wouldn't run his new horse on a hot afternoon otherwise.

Hardin spurred Old Bob to a fast pace and met Clements on the rutted main street in front of the general store; they pulled their horses to quick stops. Half-a-dozen armed men gathered around them. Hardin took a swift look at them and then turned his gray eyes on Clements.

"Wes," Clements said excitedly, "it looks like all hell's to pay. I just struck up with a feller out here north of town. Told me a mob of around fifteen are on their way down here to get you. Coming from Austin and Gonzales."

"Is that so?" Wes said. His voice had a soft drawl. A trace of a smile played across his sun-browned face. Again he pushed his hat far back on his head and then hooked his thumbs in his holster belt.

Clements quickly related in detail what he had heard. About a dozen men in Austin had sworn to kill Hardin because of his recent battles with the state police. They had formed themselves into a posse, armed with rifles and revolvers, and had ridden sixty-five miles from Austin to Gonzales; there they had rested, mapped their plans, and picked up two

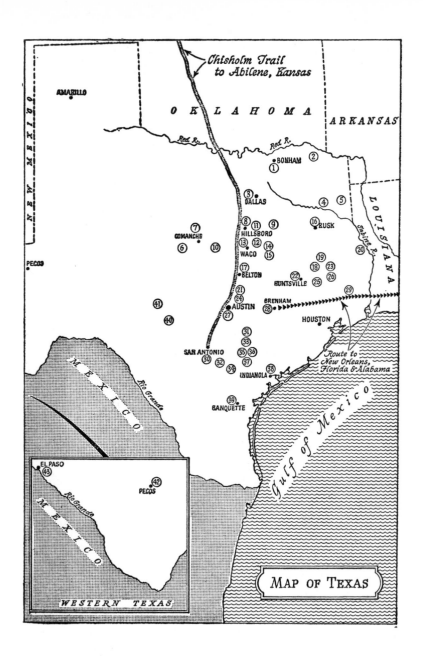

Chisholm Trail
to Abilene, Kansas

AMARILLO

NEW MEXICO

OKLAHOMA

ARKANSAS

Red R.

Red R.

① ② BONHAM

③ DALLAS

④ ⑤

LOUISIANA

Sabine R.

⑦ COMANCHE
⑥

⑧ ⑪ ⑨
HILLSBORO
⑩

⑯ RUSK

⑬ ⑫
WACO ⑭
⑮

⑲
⑱ ㉓
⑰ ㉒ ㉖
BELTON HUNTSVILLE ㉕ ㉑

PECOS

㉑
⑪ ㉔ AUSTIN
㉗ BRENHAM ㉙
㉘

⑪
⑩

㉛
㉝
㉟ ㊱
㉜ ㉟
SAN ANTONIO ㉚ ㉜ ㉞
INDIANOLA ㊳

HOUSTON

Route to
New Orleans,
Florida & Alabama

MEXICO

Rio Grande

㊴
BANQUETTE

Gulf of Mexico

EL PASO ㊸

Rio Grande

MEXICO

㊷
PECOS

WESTERN TEXAS

MAP OF TEXAS

Key to map

1. Bonham, Hardin's birthplace.
2. Bennett Station, Jane lived here with Ma Hardin.
3. Dallas.
4. Longview, Hardin once arrested here.
5. Marshall, here Hardin bought pistol while in jail.
6. Brown County, here Hardin brothers took possession of disputed cattle.
7. Comanche, Deputy Sheriff Webb killed here.
8. Hillsboro, state police declared martial law here.
9. Corsicana, here Hardin and Simp Dixon rode together.
10. Hamilton, here Hardin-Taylor herd was stopped in aftermath of Webb killing.
11. Towash, scene of Bradly killing.
12. Mt. Calm, Hardin family lived here several years.
13. Waco.
14. Horn Hill, circus hand killed here.
15. Kosse, jealous lover killed here.
16. Rusk, here Hardin, near death, surrendered to sheriff.
17. Belton, here Hardin killed three men.
18. Trinity City, Hardin wounded here.
19. Sumpter, Hardin's boyhood home.
20. Hemphill, here Hardin lectured a judge.
21. Brushy Creek, here Hardin met the fortune-teller.
22. Huntsville, the state prison here.
23. Moscow, near here Hardin killed his first man.
24. Round Rock, the Hardin brothers attended school here.
25. Evergreen, here Hardin met Bill Longley.
26. Livingston, center of Polk County.
27. Austin.
28. Brenham, Uncle Bob Hardin lived on farm here.
29. Hardin County, here the Hardins first settled in Texas.
30. San Antonio.
31. Gonzales.
32. Albuquerque, here Jack Helm was killed.
33. Smiley.
34. Asher Cemetery.
35. Coon Hollow, here Hardin wooed Jane.
36. Mustang Mot.
37. Cuero, DeWitt County seat.
38. Indianola, here Bill Sutton died.
39. Banquette, from here Hardin made a 100-mile, horse-killing ride to see Jane.
40. Kerrville, Hardin lived here while trying to reconcile his second wife.
41. Junction, Hardin lived here after leaving Gonzales County.
42. Pecos, Hardin's first stop on the way to El Paso.
43. El Paso, here Hardin died.

or three recruits. They had also boasted a little of their intentions, and word of their proposed raid had seeped out in Gonzales and then spread by word of mouth into the country.

Clements figured that the men were probably no more than fifteen miles north of Smiley.

"This makes me just a little bit mad," Wes said coolly. He lifted and examined one revolver and then the other.

"We can outdistance 'em easy, Wes." Clements patted his roan's neck.

"Outdistance 'em—hell!" Hardin said, yanking at his belt. "I'll go get 'em."

"You? By yourself?"

"Yes, Manning."

"But, Wes, this is a mob. Might be fifteen of 'em. You ain't got that many balls in your guns."

"I think I've got enough to take care of this situation," Wes replied. He gathered his reins and nudged Old Bob with his knees.

"Wes, wait a minute," Clements urged. "You know I'm ready."

The other men surged in more closely; in a chorus they volunteered to join in any fight.

"This is my fight!" Hardin interrupted. The statement, which had the flinty sound of finality, meant that he expected Clements and the others to keep hands off. He reached over and gave Manning a warm clasp on his shoulder. "Thanks, anyway," he said and grinned. "I like your pony!"

Then he was gone like the wind. Clements had no chance to argue, but he wouldn't have tried anyhow; he knew Wes Hardin better than any other man—so well, in fact, that he could sense the lad's feeling. Clements knew that when Wes made up his mind he was mule-headed, determined, and that nothing short of killing could change it.

However, Clements' point on the number of shots a man might need in fighting a posse was a sound one, at least for the ordinary man. Hardin's weapons were the cap-and-ball sort, and reloading was a chore that took time. At the most, he had twelve shots in his two pistols. But he rode out eagerly to meet more than a dozen heavily armed men who sought his blood.

He set his horse to an easy lope over the open range. After crossing Clear Creek a short distance out of the village, he came to a stretch of alternate low hills, streams, woods, and grassy glades. Here he could see far ahead and on either side and, therefore, had a chance to spot any possible ambush. There was only a wide scatter of small farms and ranch houses, and no fences to impede a cross-country ride. Anxious to find the posse before dark, he rode now at a swift clip, but he knew how to make time and also spare his horse so it would remain fresh enough despite the sultry heat and with sufficient reserve strength for any necessary burst of speed.

Wes slowed down when he approached Salty Creek. Hackberries, pecans, and tall cottonwoods bordered the winding stream, and the trail across it was narrow and dark. Wes rode with extreme caution, scrutinizing both sides of the trail. Birds flitted from the lower branches of the trees. Old Bob twisted a little when a cottontail bounced up and thudded off through the underbrush.

At the top of a slight rise to the north of Salty, Wes stopped, almost as if by instinct. Far ahead, where a broad, treeless strip separated two large patches of timber, he detected movement. He centered his gaze on this strip and presently saw horsemen riding two abreast at an easy trot.

Wes turned his horse to the left. He sat there a minute or two as if looking for cattle; then he dismounted and pretended to adjust his saddle rigging. Thus inconspicuously he studied the riders and counted fourteen—about the right number for the posse. With his practiced eyes he saw that the men were armed with rifles, which had far greater range than his pistols. He had no doubt that here were the men who had sworn to kill him.

Here, too, was an excellent chance for an ambush. Wes could angle off to the right, circle back, hide in the woods of Salty Creek and pick off the possemen as they rode into the stream. But if the thought of ambush crossed his mind he didn't show it. He knew he had the advantage of surprise: he recognized the posse, but the men had no idea that he would ride out to meet them.

Wes remounted and rode forward at a slow trot, acting as if he didn't see the men—or, at least, as if he didn't mind meeting a group of strange riders. The possemen showed their wariness. They slowed their pace. They were now erect in their saddles and watchful, but they kept coming.

Wes held his casual gait until he approached effective pistol range; then he leaned on the horse's neck and rammed the spurs to him. Old Bob lunged into a dead run straight toward the bristling guns of the posse. The men stopped. A warning shot whined a few feet from Wes's left ear. He straightened in the saddle, with the same movement drew his right-hand pistol, and fired.

One of the lead men pitched almost backward off his horse, a bullet in his head. Bodies made broader targets than heads, but Wes didn't shoot to wound. A split second later, a pistol ball ripped through the head of the second lead man and he plunged off his rearing horse.

The man just behind was taking aim with a rifle. Wes fired. The bullet cut through the horse's ear and hit the man's right arm; the rifle fell without firing. Wes swept out his left-hand pistol and shot the rider in the head. As the victim tumbled off, a foot caught in the stirrup. The wounded horse screamed and spun around with such speed that the dead man's body flew straight out.

The whirling horse, with the man sailing through the air, blocked somewhat Wes's view of the posse, which was scattering wildly. Unable to get a clear shot, he wasted no bullets. Finally the stirrup leather broke and the dead man rolled across the grass like a log downhill. The frenzied horse, freed of its frightening burden, raced after the retreating men.

Shocked by the audacity of the charge and the deadly shooting, the men had fired only the warning shot. By the time the third man was hit, the others had turned tail and fled, darting like frightened rabbits into the nearby timber.

Wes rode a short distance past where two of the bodies were sprawled close together on the prairie. He listened a brief moment to the retreating rumble of hoofs; then he whirled his horse and headed back southward at a swift gallop, angling for the nearest trees. Old Bob shied slightly when he passed the body with the stirrup leather wrapped around the legs; it had ended its long roll in a crumpled heap far from the others. Wes only glanced sidewise at it and rode on.

This man was the twenty-seventh Hardin had killed in the past three years; the fifteenth in the past twelve months.

Dare-devil young John Wesley Hardin was the fightingest killer, the most unreconstructed rebel and the most wanted man in Texas. Likewise he was the most paradoxical.

He was the most hunted, yet the most feared.

He was both detested and admired.

He had hoped to avoid trouble that afternoon, but three men had his bullets in their heads.

He had charged a posse of fourteen men, but now that the posse had been defeated and dispersed, he was in the role of the pursued. Yet this young man, once again on the dodge and running for cover, had decided some time ago to quit his wild ways. The reason was a girl, Jane Bowen, who lived in Coon Hollow. Jane and Hardin had been engaged for several months, and in his immaturity he had thought it possible to marry and lead a peaceful life. It was clear to him now, though, that the state police and others who yearned for retaliation weren't ready to holster their guns and call it quits. He was positive that when news of his surprise attack on the riders reached Austin, where nearly all the survivors lived and also where the state police had headquarters, efforts to kill him would be intensified.

Wes knew that a man of his reputation and perilous circumstances could drag a girl down to a life of danger, anxiety, and sorrow. He did not ride to Coon Hollow that night.

Instead he rode to the Clements' house, and it was dark when he reached it. There he told his cousin of the quick attack on the posse. Manning Clements was too accustomed to Wes's exploits to do more than pose a question which Wes had already asked himself many times:

"What can you do now, Wes?"

"Just one thing to do this time," Wes said. "Get out of this part of the country for two or three months."

Before daybreak, Wes was several miles east of the Clements' home, out on the open range in a land of wide grassy stretches and frequent clumps of timber. Spanish moss hung from huge oaks in long, frowzy beards. Wes staked Bob out to graze and curled up under a tree to sleep. At noon when the sun penetrated his hiding place, he awoke and rode on eastward.

He could have been any young lad of the region searching for stray cattle in out-of-the-way places, or a happy-go-lucky cowboy riding on a Sunday afternoon to a neighbor's house to do a little courting with a fair-haired county belle, for Wes didn't look like a killer. Indeed there was nothing sinister or

brutal about him. Rather he had the mild manner of one
wanting to please. He was of medium build: five feet, ten
inches tall, and solid with a weight of 155 pounds. Thick
brown hair—almost curly—showed under his stiff hat brim.
His eyes were a fathomless gray, especially when he suspected
danger or was in a gun fight, but when he was in a good humor or his face was lighted up with laughter, they had a warm
brown sheen. His mouth was straight and firm with no hint of
cruelty. All this gave Wes the appearance of a bashful country
boy who might be secretly in love with a young schoolma'am.
Still there was an air of audacity about him, and he sat his saddle with a jaunty, rhythmic ease that made him almost a part
of the horse he rode.

About sundown that Sunday he made camp on the shore of a
river and unpacked some food he had brought along. He soon
had coffee boiling on a small fire. The fragrance steaming out
of the blackened pot heartened him. As darkness gathered, he
put out the blaze so there would be no telltale night glow.

The next morning Wes resumed his hunted, haunted ride.
In the early afternoon he pulled Old Bob to a halt between
two large trees and watched four uniformed state policemen,
one an extremely large Negro, pass along a narrow road a few
yards away. He eased out his right-hand pistol, ready to shoot
if a man noticed him or turned his way. The men rode on,
never knowing that the motion of a head would have meant
death for all four.

A few days later and a hundred or so lonely miles farther
into deep Eastern Texas, Wes stopped at a small store at a
crossroads. When he stepped outside he met a man armed
with two low-hanging revolvers and wearing a deputy sheriff's
badge.

Wes turned to jump on his horse.

"Say," the man called, "don't I know you?"

Wes whirled with both hands flashing to position.

"I'm sure I know you," the man said.

"I'm John Wesley Hardin," Wes told him bluntly. "Do you have papers for my arrest?"

The man laughed. "I thought you were Wes Hardin," he said. "I have no papers for you and wouldn't use 'em if I had." He offered his hand.

Wes never shook hands with an armed stranger since this could give the other an advantage in the draw. "There is no difference between us," he said simply. "You have my good wishes."

The new acquaintance was insistently friendly. "You may not remember it, but I saw you in Abilene last summer, and I think the way you made old Wild Bill Hickok swaller crow was mighty good."

Occasionally Wes stopped in the homes of relatives—he had a host of kinfolks and he loved them all—but mainly he was alone on the dim trails and little-used roads. Day after day he rode, going no place in particular, and night after night he camped under the stars. He saw autumn color the prairies, the pine-clad hills, the dense forests, and the dark, swampy river bottoms; and overhead he heard the honking of wild geese going south. Just after Christmas he rode, still cautiously, back to Elm Creek, his mind made up on future action.

He would ride to the mountains of the wild, unsettled Big Bend Country of Southwestern Texas, where he had never been. He would establish himself in the cattle business and start life all over; then he would return and marry Jane Bowen.

On the day of his return there was a big to-do. Gip Clements, a cousin Wes's age, and Annie Tenelle were married in the bride's home. Wes was with Jane at the wedding and later at the supper and dance. Gip looked a bit abashed and somewhat uncomfortable in a tight collar, but Annie was radiant. So was Jane—in her neat Sunday dress of white dimity and ruffled lace. Her wavy brown hair was tied back with a ribbon. There was a touch of dreaminess in her brown eyes. The small dangling earrings in the pierced lobes of her ears sallied in little circles when she talked. Jane's features were doll-like and dainty, but at sixteen years of age she was a fully developed young woman.

A wedding seems to give people a certain license—especially to speculate on other weddings. This time Wes Hardin and Jane caught the knowing looks, the winks, and the sly questions about when wedding bells could be expected to ring again. Jane smiled and blushed and held on to Wes's arm. There was unmistakable tenderness in her eyes when she gazed at him. Wes smiled wryly, his face very red.

For two or three weeks, Wes considered telling Jane's brother, Brown Bowen, of his plan and asking him to break the news to Jane. He discarded this idea, however, because he had never quite trusted Brown.

It was not until March of 1872 that Wes finally broached the subject to Jane himself. The night was warm with the scent of spring in the air. The early-rising moon shed a soft glow over the wide prairie draw that was known as Coon Hollow. Leading Old Bob, they strolled from the Bowen house to a live oak a short distance away. Wes and Jane stopped in its shadow. For a little while they didn't speak but stood close together and looked and listened. The beauty of the night and the peacefulness of the valley were in brutal contrast to the storms that raged around and within them.

From a nearby creek came the croupy sound of frogs and the occasional call of a screech owl. In and near the tree was a monotonous drone of night insects. Old Bob strayed off a few steps, lowered his head, and nibbled the new grass.

"Jane," Wes said, "I've got something important to tell you."

"Yes. What, Wes?" There was a slight quiver in her voice.

"I've got to go away for a while."

"Again? Why, Wes, you've just barely got back. Where this time?"

"To the mountains near El Paso."

"But why, Wes?"

"To live. I mean, to stay for a while, anyhow."

"But why, Wes?" Jane was insistent.

"Let's sit down," Wes said, "and I'll tell you."

They spread Jane's fascinator on the ground at the base of the tree and sat on it. Wes explained the desperateness of his situation and his plan to go to the mountains and live six months, a year, or two years—whatever time it took for things to blow over. And then return and marry Jane.

The moon through the live oak leaves barely lighted their faces. Jane looked straight into Wes's eyes and said:

"Be honest, Wes. Don't you love me any more?"

"You know I do, Jane. That's the reason I've got to leave. I don't want to hurt you or drag you down."

"But, Wes, wouldn't it be dangerous in the mountains? Couldn't you be killed out there and never come back?"

"You know there's always a chance I'll get killed, wherever I am. That's the reason—"

"But Wes," Jane was crying softly. "I couldn't stand it if you didn't come back. I love you so much I'd be miserable the rest of my life if you were never my husband."

Wes was silent a moment. He picked up a small dead branch and dug in the ground between his knees. "Jane," he finally said, "if you knew I'd be killed tomorrow, would you marry me tonight?"

She placed a hand on his arm. "You know I would, Wes."

"If that's the way you feel," Wes said, "then we should no longer live apart. Could we get married soon?"

Wordlessly, Jane moved into his arms.

They sat there for a long time. The light in the house had been extinguished. They had to themselves the night and the wide landscape. Jane did not know that one day not too far in the uncertain future she would weep bitterly because of an occurrence under the gnarled branches of the very tree where she sat now, warm and safe in the loving embrace of Wes Hardin.

Wes had thrown aside his decision and lost the argument, if such a discussion between a girl and a boy in the spring moonlight could be called an argument. But doubt still filled his mind. Should a man with such enemies marry a girl like Jane?

Of course, Jane knew of his past—Wes had never tried to hide that—and she didn't hold it against him, but perhaps she had no idea of what life could be like with a man who felt he could live only by his guns.

"Jane," he said, "you know I love you all there is, but I don't want to hurt you."

"If you love me like you say you do, Wes, don't talk like that. We've settled it, haven't we?"

"Yes, darling, but you know I've got a lot of enemies and they're strong as can be."

"They're cowards and midnight murderers," Jane stormed. "I hate them for their bloody crimes."

"But you know they try to kill me every day and even every hour." Wes was being perfectly honest.

"I know, Wes," Jane replied, without giving ground. "I know your troubles. I know they're honorable. Why can't I share your troubles in everything?"

It was past midnight when Jane and Wes walked to the

house and he rode out of Coon Hollow on Old Bob. A new day had dawned for them. Jane had pleaded with her heart and not with reason and Wes had yielded against what obviously was his better judgment. But one thing was certain: Jane Bowen was the only person on God's green earth who had ever changed the mind of Wes Hardin once he had set his head. Even his parents, with their love and hope, persuasion and prayer, had failed to solve the complex puzzle that was their son.

2

Preacher's Boy

It was never intended for Wes Hardin to ride the trail that had led him to Coon Hollow. He was supposed to have been a preacher. That was the hope of his father, the Reverend James Gipson Hardin, the hour the lad was born on May 26, 1853, at the village of Bonham in Northern Texas. The Hardins already had one son, Joe, who was three years old at the time, but it was the second son on whom the father pinned his ambitions and the name he considered the greatest in Christendom, the name of the founder of Methodism.

Little John Wesley was not born to any great estate, but he did inherit all a child could wish in the way of family esteem and mettlesome ancestors.

His mother, Mary Elizabeth, had been reared as a young lady of culture; she was the daughter of Dr. William Dixon, who had emigrated from the bluegrass of Kentucky to the red clay hills and black bottom land of Texas, and Elizabeth Cartwright Dixon, a devout Methodist herself. Mary Elizabeth had been a lovely girl with long, golden hair and a soft, Southern voice; her life had been sheltered, filled with reading, Bible study, music, and parties in hooped skirts and frills.

On the paternal side, the Hardins had tried for generations to stay one jump ahead of civilization. They were early settlers of Georgia; they moved from there to Tennessee, and then in 1825, just four years after Stephen F. Austin had established the first Anglo-American colony in Texas, the Hardins loaded their belongings on wagons and headed for Texas, where they found a frontier to their liking. Having found it, they promptly threw all their energy into making something of it and were soon recognized as makers of the Republic of Texas and the State of Texas.

Preacher Hardin's uncle, Augustine Hardin, signed the Texas Declaration of Independence, but previously he had drafted a plan (known as the Separation of Texas and Coahuila) designed to give Texas colonists more freedom. Stephen F. Austin had taken this proposal to Mexico City and had been thrown in jail, an incident which was not ignored by those at home and which led to the Texas Revolution.

Another uncle, Franklin Hardin, had fought with the Texas Army in the Battle of San Jacinto, the decisive struggle that avenged the tragedy of the Alamo and won freedom from Mexican rule. Hardin County, Texas, had been named for another uncle, William B. Hardin, a noted judge. Preacher Hardin's father, a brother of these other famed Texans, was Benjamin Hardin, who had served in the Texas Congress which worked out details for the annexation of Texas by the United States.

Preacher Hardin had grown up under the rule of Mexico and then the Republic of Texas. One of his first assignments as a clergyman was in Dallas. He was the second Methodist minister to preach there, and his name was carved in the cornerstone of the First Methodist Church in Dallas. He had then taken the circuit at Bonham, across Red River from the Indian Territory. In those days, he, like John the Baptist, went about preaching and teaching in the wilderness—in cabin homes, in tents, on camp grounds, and in the first little churches.

Hardin was a positive, straight-laced man and a kindly, but strict father; yet, understandably, because his circuit was thinly settled with people who did well to scratch out a bare living, he was not a good provider. The frugal offerings that dropped into the hat scarcely met the basic needs. Therefore, Hardin took weekday work as a schoolteacher to add to his income, and in spare time he studied law. Within a few years he was admitted to the bar.

In 1855, when John Wesley (his mother called him Johnny) was two years old, the minister moved his family to Moscow in Polk County in Southeastern Texas near where the Hardins had settled originally. For several years the family lived alternately in Moscow and in Sumpter, in neighboring Trinity County, the father plying all three of his professions.

This part of Texas was backwoods country. Vast forests of pine dotted the uplands, and the valleys were timbered with oak, walnut, magnolia, sweetgum. The plantation system had begun to take hold there and some families had acquired slaves; but there were many more small farmers who lived in log cabins in clearings in the forests, their small fields enclosed by stake-and-rider rail fences. Nearly all these pioneering people had come west to new country from the Old South.

It was only natural, then, that even in the isolation of these deep woods, rivers, and swamplands, talk of impending secession and war was on all lips.

Little John Wesley had heard of these issues by the time he was acquainted with Santa Claus, and he heard about them over and over. At home and on the street corners, wherever he happened to be, Preacher Hardin talked strongly against the forces that were pressing toward secession and its consequences. His argument was many-sided and by no means narrow. He opposed human slavery; yet his heart and voice were with the cause of Southern rights, though he battled with all his might any decision or blunder that could lead to a dissolved Union. He took the stand that time, cool-headedness, and unprejudiced statesmanship could settle the grave issue to the satisfaction of all.

When the question of dissolving the Union came to decision in Texas, the minister cast his vote against secession, realizing that he was one of a small minority. But when war came, he cast his lot with Texas and the South. He dropped all other duties and recruited a company of volunteer soldiers. However, his health had become frail and his neighbors insisted that he, in his threefold capacity of minister, lawyer, and teacher, was needed more at home than on the battlefields of Virginia. Hardin gave in and took his stand on the home front.

This was good news for the family. It was said of the Hardins that every time there were events of great import some Hardin was having a baby. There was a new one in the preacher's family, the third son and fifth child. Elizabeth had been born in 1855 and Martha Anne (Matt) in 1857. There was no difficulty in selecting a name for the third son: he was Jeff Davis Hardin.

As a good-sized chunk of a boy living in a cultured, religious home, John Wesley saw and felt both the excitement and despair of the war. With his brother Joe, he stood at the edge of the little town and gazed at herds of bawling longhorn cattle plodding eastward—food for the boys in gray. The Hardin lads saw remudas of frisky horses, requisitioned from Texas families, heading toward Confederate encampments, their destination the Southern cavalry. At Moscow and at Sumpter the boys stood at the collection places for food and clothing for the soldiers and also the relief depots for the wives, widows, and children of those who were away fighting for the Southern cause.

Joe and Wes took over men's work—guarding the home at a time when police protection was almost nonexistent, and helping provide food. These jobs called for the use of firearms, and it was a necessity for small boys to know how to shoot guns. Wes was carrying a pistol by the time he was nine years old. From the first he displayed a talent for handling a revolver; it came naturally to him, just as playing a musical instrument might be natural for another child. He was fast on the draw, and his marksmanship was deadly; it was no trick at all for him to pop out the eye of a squirrel on a swinging limb high in a tree.

Whenever Wes could get his hands on powder and lead he practiced shooting. He and his friends frequently fashioned scarecrowlike effigies of President Lincoln, swung them in trees, and riddled them with bullets. Wes always aimed at the head, saying that was the place that counted. Realizing that he was an excellent marksman, Wes wanted to shoot real Yankees. He mentioned this to his father and received only a good scolding for even thinking such a thing. Thereupon he schemed to run away and join the Confederate Army. He included a cousin, Barnett Jones, in his plans. The boys got together some muskets, pistols, and enough food to last them a few days. They hid their war materials in the woods near town and were ready to slip off that night.

Preacher Hardin, aware that John Wesley was acting peculiarly, questioned him so sharply that the boy revealed the plan. The father thanked him for his honesty in admitting his intentions, praised him for his patriotism—and whipped hell out of him for disobedience.

Poverty was so close to the door that the Hardins moved to the country, where they could grow food and cotton for home spinning. Their home there was makeshift, little more than a camp, but Wes liked it immensely. He roamed the forests and swamps, often wandering into the woods with his dog, Old Watch. The boy loved nature. He was extremely fond of horses and could ride well, with or without a saddle, but he detested mules. One time he confided in his mother that he had whipped a mule named Kit with a fence rail and that the long-eared animal had reared on its hind feet, showed its teeth, and cursed him.

On one occasion, the Hardins' saddle horse—named Stonewall Jackson, but called Jack for short—strayed and turned up at the home of a neighbor four miles away. Taking a bridle and lead rope, and also Old Watch, Wes hiked out across a dense forest to get the horse. The fall day was cold and muggy, with a light fog hanging over the creek bottoms. The fog had turned into a drizzle by the time Wes was on the way home with Old Jack. He was afraid of the dark and the stormy weather, and he prodded the horse along in order to get to the house before night. When he was halfway home he heard Old Watch baying as if he had treed something special.

The dog was easily a mile off the route home and in the heart of the dark woods, but Wes couldn't resist an urge to see what his faithful dog had found. He rode toward the barking. Watch was yapping and gnawing at a large whiteoak. The boy searched the tree, which was about seventy feet high, and spotted four coons on a limb very near the top.

The first branches of the giant oak were some fifteen feet from the ground, and the trunk was so large that it was impossible to climb. Wes found some chunks of wood and threw them with all his might, but the chunks were at once too bulky and too light to be hurled more than halfway to the coons.

The sharp-eyed animals looked down at the boy. They showed no fright and didn't even move. Wes gazed for a long time at the complacent-looking coons; he measured the tree with his eyes. Obstinacy and the will always to win, which were native to his make-up, stiffened within the lad. He wouldn't give up or retreat; he would get the coons at the risk of his own neck.

He mounted Jack and rode close to the tree. Standing on the horse's back, he tossed his lead rope over the lowest limb and caught the dangling end; then he snaked up the rope with his bare feet walking up the trunk. When he reached the first limb, he stood on it and pitched his rope to the next limb above. In this way he reached the place where the trunk was smaller, with numerous branches forking off.

Wes broke off a good-sized dead limb for a club and smoothed a handhold with his pocket knife; then he climbed slowly toward the coons, with Old Watch dancing around the base of the tree, whining and barking. When he was within a few feet of the long-clawed, sharp-toothed animals they rushed at him as if he were a hound. He struck the lead coon, a large boar, and his club shattered; then he fought the growling, scratching, biting animals with his bare hands. One by one he knocked the coons off their perch, and each dropped the long distance to the waiting dog.

The boy's clothing was torn to shreds. His hands, arms, chest, and face were lacerated and bleeding, but he proudly climbed down and claimed his coons from Old Watch. By now, darkness enveloped the forest. Wes took off his galluses, tied two coons to one end and two to the other; then he started to throw his string of game across Jack's back. The horse, excited by the noise and the smell of fresh blood, threw a walleyed fit.

It took the boy almost an hour to calm the horse and persuade him to carry the coons. Wes arrived home long after dark. His worried mother almost fainted when she saw his torn clothes and skin. "Why did you do it, Johnny?" she cried.

"I thought some coon stew would be mighty good for supper, Ma," he replied.

In the latter days of the war the Hardins moved back to Sumpter, and soon Joe and Wes and the two girls were in school. The family was crowded in the tiny house, and Preacher Hardin built a room at the rear so the boys could have a quiet place to study. He had a strict philosophy with which no one could argue—honor, honesty, bravery, and chivalry were its main principles—and he preached it tirelessly. He taught his sons that women were inviolate, that men should fight for womanhood and virtue, regardless of whether mother, sister, or total stranger was involved. In preaching bravery to the boys, the father warned them against violence, but told them over and over that self-preservation was the first law of nature.

Joe was dutiful; he liked his books and the lectures, too. But Wes was restless. All his life he had been told that he was marked for the ministry; he was twelve now, and he wanted some fun while he had the chance.

He crawled out the back window one night to join some neighborhood Negro and white boys wrestling and shooting craps. Hearing the commotion, his father walked out and caught him. Preacher Hardin led the lad into the house and gave him a hard whipping with a stout piece of rawhide he kept handy for that purpose. He topped the whipping with a lecture. Nonetheless, Wes continued to slip out to frolic with the boys. In this way, he learned a great deal about the art of wrestling and the thrill of earning pennies, nickels, and pocket knives by throwing dice.

Despite the truancy, Wes had no trouble standing at the head of his class in school. He had a brilliant mind, and his bright personality was attractive to both teacher and pupils. On the playground, at recess, and the noon hour, Wes excelled at play—wrestling, boxing, running, jumping, playing ball. Any time two sides chose up to play town ball the one privileged to make the first choice always picked Wes because he could bat, throw, and field a ball better than anyone else. This was not due to huskiness or strength. Wes was not a large boy, but he used his head and he practiced endlessly; he had a desire to excel in everything he attempted.

Wes was often heedless of the teachings of his father but some of them stuck; either by nature or by teaching, he was thoughtful of others, especially those he considered unfortunate. One such was a girl named Sally. She was very plump, slightly cross-eyed, and, therefore, self-conscious. In a thoughtless way, nearly all the youngsters were cruel to Sally; they poked fun at her plumpness and called her "Sal." Wes was kind to her; he never called her by the detested nickname, and he often came to her defense on the playground.

This gave his chief rival—a lad named Charles Sloter—a chance to try to even accounts. One Friday at noon, Charles slipped into the schoolhouse and wrote a naughty verse on the wall about Sally. It started: "I love Sal, and Sal loves mutton." It ended with an ugly slur at Sally's personal attractions.

When the other pupils saw the verse and tittered over it, Sally was so embarrassed that she ran to her seat, sobbing. Charles accused Wes of writing the verse.

Wes stood up in school and denied it; he accused Charles, saying he had seen him sneak into the schoolhouse during the noon recess.

Shouting, "You're a liar!" Charles rushed at Wes, socked him in the nose and drew a pocket knife.

Wes came out of his seat snarling. He yanked out his pocket knife, flipped it open and drove the long blade into Charles' chest. He pulled it out, reached behind Charles, and rammed the blade up to the hilt in his rival's back.

Charles sagged to the floor, blood spurting from both wounds. For ten days it looked as though he would die, but he recovered and saved the Hardin boy from an accusation of murder.

When news of the fight spread, tempers flared. Men called on the trustees, demanding that Wes be expelled. His father, distressed because of the use of the knife, was critical of his son and joined in demands for a full investigation. The trustees met and heard the whole story. They decided that Wes had been in the right. Then the boy's father—though still unhappy about the knife—praised him for his bravery, chivalry, and the defense of his life.

On a day in April, a few months after the knife episode, Preacher Hardin loped his horse all the way from town. He was pale and short of breath when he reached the house. He had heard that General Lee had surrendered and that the war was over. Moreover, the backwoods town was rife with stories that Governor Murrah, many other state officials, and all the Confederate generals stationed in Texas had fled to Mexico, fearful of the wrath of the approaching victors. The preacher at once predicted a reign of terror.

Not long thereafter, Wes and Joe Hardin saw their first Confederate veterans on the streets of Sumpter. Gaunt and tattered survivors of the conflict, they were straggling home. Eyes wide with wonder, Wes stood with groups of men and heard the tales of the soldiers—of bloody action in far-off Pennsylvania, Virginia, Mississippi, and Georgia.

Then there were other soldiers—in strange blue uniforms —passing through Sumpter, and some of them stationed there. Many of them were former slaves who had recently joined the army that had made them free. By raising and by instinct, little Wes Hardin hated the soldiers in blue. Not long afterward he and his family would have tragic personal reason to fear them.

A man from Northern Texas, where Mrs. Hardin's family lived, moved to Sumpter to reside with relatives. He struck up acquaintance with the Hardins and told them that the family of one of Mrs. Hardin's brothers—a mother, daughter, and son named Dixon—had been brutally killed and their home burned by Yankee soldiers. The women, he said, had been tortured and ravaged. Another son, Simp Dixon, had been away from the house at the time. When he returned he found the bodies piled in the yard near the smouldering ruins of the home. Months later, the Hardins had confirmation of this report through letters from their relatives.

Rumors of tragedy like this swept the town nearly every day. Before long, nearly every heinous crime committed against a Texan was attributed to occupying soldiers or to freed slaves; on the other hand, every act of outlawry against the military rule and the Negro people—and there were many —was blamed on former Confederate soldiers and rebels in general, and confusion and insurrection remained in Texas.

Preacher Hardin fumed when, in April of 1866, he heard that President Johnson had declared the rebellion at an end in all Confederate states except Texas. But if the preacher was angry at what looked like an insult to the State of Texas, his rage was boundless when he went to vote that year. The polls were manned by white and colored soldiers and strange people known as scalawags and carpetbaggers. Only citizens approved by the soldiers were permitted to vote. Preacher Hardin was denied that right because he had recruited a company for the Confederate Army.

However, the election didn't count for a great deal, for in July of 1867 Congress passed a law giving military commanders the authority to remove any public official at will. General Philip Sheridan, who was in command in Texas, promptly ousted Governor Throckmorton and installed a man of his own choosing. Of course, every other public official was subject to the will of the military commander who could remove a sheriff or judge and replace him with anyone he wanted.

It was in this time of doubt and fear that the Hardin boys grew into their 'teen years, each according to his make-up— Joe displaying the obedient, diplomatic, studious side of his inheritance, and John Wesley, the impetuous, self-reliant, and pioneering spirit. Wes still detested lectures, but he never tired of hearing his father retell the stories of the Hardins, who seemed to have been cut from a heroic mold.

Their mother seldom had a great deal to say, that being left to the father, but her cheerful love of life was contagious, and all her children caught it. Hardships hadn't dimmed her optimism. To each of her succeeding humble homes she had tried to bring beauty. True to the Hardin tradition of babies in critical times, Mrs. Hardin was now nursing little Nannie, who brought her brood to six. Even with a house filled with children the mother seemed to have an especially warm spot in her heart for her second son, who was to be a minister. It may have been because of his good looks, his bright personality, and his clever way of getting what he wanted.

The mother lost a friendly argument with him on an autumn day in 1868—when the Union military had been in complete command in Texas for a year. Wes, then fifteen years old, saddled his pony, Old Paint, to ride several miles to visit his uncle, Barnett Hardin, as he often did. This uncle differed from Preacher Hardin in that he was a true son of the soil. His farm prospered. Cotton picking was over, the corn was in the crib, and it was time to harvest the cane crop to make sugar. Wes wanted to be in on this fine occupation, for nothing else tasted sweeter than fresh, ripe sugar cane, the outer bark peeled off and the grainy core oozing a tangy syrup. It was just to a boy's taste—especially at a time when money was never spent for candy. Only at Christmas did a boy have a chance to get his hands sticky with anything except molasses—then and when the sugar cane was ripe.

John Wesley's mother asked him not to take his pistol on the trip. He wouldn't need it, she told him, since he was not going hunting. With smiles and boyish argument, he wheedled her into granting him permission to carry the gun, and he galloped away into an experience that neither he nor his mother could ever forget.

3

The First Law of Nature

Wes was now a well-built, quick-moving boy. His hair was on the long side and a bit ragged at the edge, especially on the back of his neck. Fuzz with only a tinge of color showed on his chin and upper lip. His face and hands were as brown as an autumn nut. He wore grayish homespun pants, a blue shirt open at the neck, and a battered black hat pushed far back. His pistol belt was a piece of home-tanned rawhide an inch wide. The holster, also of rawhide, was a crude thing that Wes had made himself. Wes sat with ease on his pony, a slow-gaited chestnut with large white spots.

He rode along the wooded trail watching the birds dart through the low-hanging branches. Occasionally he pulled out his pistol, twirled it and drew down on a bird. He didn't shoot. Powder and lead were scarce, and Wes had been taught not to kill wild things except for food or to protect himself or others.

On this autumn morning Wes seemed simply a carefree

youngster riding through the woodland. He was the picture of rugged health and brimming with energy. He was riding a horse he loved dearly and carrying a pistol which gave him a sense of self-reliance. He was going visiting—to an uncle's plantation for the sugar harvest, always an exciting event. He appeared to be impervious to the troubles of the nation and of his backwoods Texas community. But was he? Could an autumn day excursion to the cane harvest change a preacher's boy into a man with a deadly mission?

Wes was perhaps more serious and thoughtful than he looked. In his time he had never heard of compromise as anything but evil; he had known only black and white, right and wrong. The Bible was right. Honesty, chivalry, fair play, and courage were right, and anything to the contrary, regardless of circumstances, was wrong. Murder was wrong, but it had been all right to kill Yankee soldiers. Wes had been taught to live peacefully and to avoid trouble, yet personal bravery and standing up for one's rights, no matter what the odds, were virtues that had been ingrained in him; self-preservation was the first law of nature and almost the supreme law of the troubled land that Wes knew. It was up to each individual to decide, perhaps on short notice, when that law should be invoked.

Being a preacher's son—and being further set apart, or singled out, by the fact that he bore the name of a renowned man of God—Wes knew that exemplary behavior was expected of him. How many times he had heard that from his family and playmates! Therefore, his mind was burdened with the thought that he had to be all the stronger and braver and more daring to avoid being considered a sissy. So Wes played hard. Other boys might test the water before jumping in, but Wes dived in head first. In a wrestling match, it wasn't sufficient to throw the opponent, but to throw him hard. This came easy for Wes. His native obstinacy and his penchant for going all the way, however violent, seemed as natural as his smile. He liked excitement and rugged contests, and he looked forward to plenty of action that mellow day.

At the Barnett Hardin plantation Wes found Barnett Jones, the cousin with whom he had once plotted to run away and join the Confederate Army. Wes's uncle was firmer than his mother had been; before he would permit the boys to start on whatever adventure awaited them he insisted that Wes leave his .44-caliber pistol at the house.

After spending an hour or so in the cane field and loading their pockets with small pieces of the sweet stalks, Wes and Barnett chased each other about the place, stopping now and then to wrestle. In running and wrestling the boys were about even, either a good match for any man.

After an hour of horseplay, Barnett had an idea that promised real sport. Working on the plantation was a swarthy, muscular Negro man named Mage. He had been the slave of Clabe Holshousen, a brother of Barnett Hardin's wife. Like many of the freed slaves who had quit the plantations and farms and congregated in the towns, Mage had left the Holshousens. He had heard the talk that he didn't have to work, that the government which had freed the slaves would take care of them and shift to them a great deal of the property that had been owned by their masters. One of these promises was that the government would give each Negro forty acres of land and a mule.

Mage, looking forward to fulfillment of these promises, had moved into Moscow, but he retained a sort of belligerent loyalty to his former master and the neighboring white people he had known most of his life. He grew lonesome for the fields and forests he had tramped, and occasionally, at cotton-picking or cane-cutting time, he wandered back to work.

The boys watched with enthusiastic admiration as the big Negro sliced through the cane. It was then that Barnett Jones suggested to Wes that they match a wrestling bout with Mage. Wes gaily welcomed the idea and Barnett propositioned Mage. Looking down at the two boys, Mage grinned and accepted, remarking that he hoped he didn't hurt them.

Wes and Barnett locked arms with Mage and the bout was on. The boys quickly overbalanced the Negro and he tumbled to the ground with Wes and Barnett on top. Several men, black and white, stopped their work and gathered to watch the fun. Mage immediately wanted to try again, and the boys, gleeful in victory, were eager. This time Mage was careful to keep his balance and he put up a terrific fight. However, the boys tripped him and down he went again. Wes let his fingernails scrape across Mage's face as he went down, and the scratch brought a trickle of blood. That quick flip of Wes's hand as it passed Mage's face was typical of some force within him that had always made him go just a little further at whatever he did. He went the second mile, but often it seemed to be in the wrong direction.

When Mage wiped his face with a hand, looked at it and saw the blood, his countenance clouded with rage and his eyes blazed. Mumbling, "No white boy can draw blood from Mage and live," the Negro dived at Wes.

Barnett and the men and boys who had gathered to watch the wrestling rushed between Wes and the menacing man.

Mage swore he would get a gun and kill Wes.

His eyes big and round, the boy dashed to the house to find his pistol. There he ran headlong into his uncle, and his words tumbled over one another as he told what had happened. Barnett Hardin instructed Wes to keep his hands off his pistol and to stay inside the house; then the uncle found Mage and ordered him off the place.

Early the next morning, Wes mounted his horse and started home; he had forgotten about the trouble with Mage. In every direction the trees were putting on their autumn color, and there was a fresh, almost frosty crispness in the air. Wes whistled between his teeth and kicked at the sides of Old Paint, urging him to hit a lope.

Near a bend in the road Wes saw Mage striding toward him with a stout stick in his hand. Mage cursed the boy and yelled a threat: "Mage is going to kill you!"

Wes turned in his saddle but kept kicking the sides of his pony. "Look, Mage," he called, "I was only playing when I scratched you."

Mage moved rapidly toward him, brandishing his stick. "Just wait 'til I get my hands on you. I'll kill you and throw you in the creek."

Instead of running, Wes stopped; it was not brave to run from danger. Mage rushed at him with the stick and barely missed him; then the man grabbed the horse's bridle.

"Get back, Mage," Wes cautioned, "or I'll shoot." He pulled his pistol.

Mage swung his stick. Wes fired straight into his chest. The shot forced the man loose from the bridle, but he bounded back. Wes fired again, knocking the man down. Mage jumped up and rushed at the horse. The boy fired his third shot, and Mage fell to the ground, bleeding and moaning.

Wes galloped Old Paint to the Holshousen home, which was nearby, and told Judge Holshousen about his fight. Holshousen and one of his neighbors hurried with Wes back to the scene. Mage lay in the dirt, writhing in pain, but he still had fight in him. He cursed the boy. Wes pulled out his pistol. Holshousen ordered him to put the gun back in the scabbard and Wes obeyed.

"This man will probably die, Wes," Holshousen said, turning serious eyes on the youth. "You'd better go home as fast as you can and tell your pa what's happened. My advice to you is to keep a sharp lookout for Yankee soldiers. They'll be snooping into this as sure as the world."

Wes rode home to his parents, his heart pounding as heavily as Old Paint's feet.

Preacher Hardin and his wife listened in silence to Wes's account of his fight. His mother's face paled and she bit her lips, but there was a show of fire in her eyes.

"Maybe he won't die," Wes Hardin's mother said, in a prayerful tone.

"Maybe not," the preacher agreed.

Not long later, on a day in November of 1868, the news came. Mage had died. Wes Hardin had killed a man.

If conditions had been normal—even as normal as they had been during the war—the father would have insisted that the boy give himself up and stand trial; self-defense would have been an honorable plea.

But now there were other serious considerations which the father contemplated as a lawyer and as a Southern minister. The Union military was in charge in Texas; every judge had to answer to the wishes of the commanders. Juries could be hand-picked with virtual instructions in advance.

Could a boy, or man, get a fair trial for killing a Negro under any circumstances? Would it look as if the real motive were the rebel cause? After secession, the Hardins had been rebels to the core, and Wes had been raised a rebel. And there was the question—had the Union soldiers tortured and killed the Dixons?

The mother and father looked long at each other, misery in their eyes. The father could well ask: "How about John Wesley's chance to become a minister?" The mother could well remember that she had permitted her fifteen-year-old boy to take the pistol. But what might have happened to him if he hadn't had the gun? There was no way to call back the boy's impulse, be it a mean streak or not, to scratch Mage. The parents couldn't take up their problem with their older son, Joe, for he was teaching school at Logallis Prairie some twenty-five miles away.

The father reached the conclusion that no white Texan would have a chance if he were tried for trouble with a former slave. He reasoned that if his son were caught he would probably be shot or hanged by sundown. The mother agreed. There seemed only one decision: to send the boy away to become a fugitive.

Preacher Hardin had some close friends named Morgan near Logallis Prairie. He believed they would shelter John Wesley for a short time, and they perhaps could stay in cautious touch with Joe. He wrote a letter to his friend, asking that he take in John Wesley, listen to his story, and protect him. He gave the letter to the boy for delivery and instructed him to keep in hiding and to do everything possible to avoid being caught.

The parents emphasized to Wes that if he were caught he would very likely be killed or, at the very best, thrown into prison. He was to stay at Logallis Prairie only a short time; the father would join him there and take him far to the north where the Dixons and other relatives lived.

Sending a fifteen-year-old boy into hiding with the admonition that if he were caught he would be killed was not an easy task for a minister-father, but Hardin, still believing implicitly in "the first law of nature," went another step; he handed the lad a shotgun and told him he might need it as well as his pistol, to protect himself.

As the late fall dusk settled on the heavily wooded country

around Sumpter, Wes Hardin left home on the back of Old Paint, headed for Logallis Prairie. He arrived before dawn, but waited until daybreak to ride up to the house.

The Morgans took him in. Morgan managed to get word of John Wesley's arrival to Joe, and he also arranged a sort of grapevine communications system with the older brother. The Morgans and other families living in that vicinity had been rebels and hadn't changed their attitudes.

Within a few days, Joe Hardin reported to Morgan that he was being spied on. Apparently the soldiers investigating the death of Mage had deduced that Wes might have been sent to his brother. Joe's message to Wes warned him to watch sharply; the soldiers in the vicinity might show up at any time.

Two mornings later, Wes saw three strange horsemen—a good way on the opposite side of the creek—riding toward the Morgan farm. He soon saw that they were uniformed soldiers and he figured he would be dead within a few hours. Morgan advised him to get on his horse and get away fast if he didn't want to put up a fight.

Grabbing his shotgun and pistol, Wes raced out the back door. He saddled and mounted his horse and headed into the nearby woods. When he was well out of sight of the house he stopped. There were several courses of action open to him; he could try to escape, fight the soldiers, or give up. If he fled, there was no place to go except back to Sumpter and he didn't consider that a safe refuge. If he got away this time, he might be caught later.

The shooting of Mage had been a thing of hot blood, but in Wes's mind it had been a pure and simple case of self-defense which could be proved in any court of justice. Wes had been told by his parents that, although he had acted within his rights, he could not get a fair trial, and therefore he had become a fugitive. The soldiers had come to capture and perhaps kill him for doing a thing he had been forced to do.

Could Wes retreat in the face of such danger—three men against one boy? It wasn't in him to do so; it was against every fiber in him, against the teachings of his father about bravery and standing up for one's rights, and against his heritage. He had been raised a rebel.

And here were soldiers wearing the uniform of the Union Army. These were the men who had bled and ravaged the South and sent Confederate men back to Sumpter looking like walking skeletons; these were the men who had raped and killed his mother's relatives, the Dixons. As far back as Wes could remember, men in these uniforms had been his enemies. He had yearned to run away and fight them.

Now here were Yankees coming to him, closing in on him. Everything within him—his savage intensity, his instinctive aversion to giving quarter or retreating, the teachings of his father, his embittered feeling toward Yankees—fused into a mood of intense hatred. In that moment, completely unaware of consequences, he was simply obsessed with the need and desire to shoot them down.

Other boys of his age, even Joe Hardin, might have fled terror-stricken or have fallen down and begged for mercy, but neither alternative entered Wes's mind. He wouldn't wait for the soldiers; he would ride to meet them and kill them.

Wes decided the men would follow the road across the creek toward the house. His best chance, accordingly, was to beat them to the crossing. Urging Old Paint forward at a fast trot, he followed a sharp bend in the creek and carefully approached the crossing at right angles to the road. Staying close to the bank, he saw the soldiers riding in single file across the creek, the polished buttons of their blue garb glinting in the sun. Two of them were white men and the third, the man riding behind, was a Negro.

Wes opened up with his shotgun, firing straight down the creek—two shots almost simultaneously. The two white men crumpled off their horses. The Negro whirled his horse and fled. Wes pursued him, shouting for him to "surrender in the name of the Southern Confederacy." The soldier turned and fired, and the ball nicked Wes in the left arm. He drew his pistol and killed the fleeing soldier. His aim was steady and sure.

Then the boy whipped his horse with the end of the reins and raced to the house, where he met Morgan, who had run outside when he heard the shooting. Wes was pale and his hands shook violently. He told Morgan what had happened.

Morgan was more frightened than the boy, fearing that other scouts might find the slain soldiers and blame him and perhaps his neighbors. He recruited two of the latter and they concealed all evidence of the shooting. This was a relatively easy chore since the woods and brush were dense along some sections of the creek.

That night Wes rode stealthily home to Sumpter, carrying his shotgun and pistol, both fully loaded, and awakened his parents. How many times this would happen they had no idea. When Wes told them about the triple slaying, they were grave, grief-stricken, nearly beside themselves. His mother sobbed as she dressed the slight flesh wound in her boy's arm with fresh, clean bandages torn from an old sheet.

Wes was satisfied in his own mind that he had killed in self-defense, that the soldiers wanted his life and that he had the right to take theirs. His parents reluctantly agreed with him. But there, towering up before them, was the awful question of what to do now.

Wes had killed four men. Sooner or later the fate of the soldiers would be known; a thing like that simply couldn't be kept quiet forever. When the shooting of the soldiers was added to the death of Mage, Wes certainly wouldn't have a ghost of a chance if he were caught. Surrendering him, then, was out of the question.

Before dawn Preacher Hardin took Wes to the home of a friend who promised to keep the boy hidden. Moving surreptitously for the first time in his life, Hardin arranged for two good horses and saddles.

On a stormy winter night a few days later, the solemn preacher and his young son rode northward through the dense, cold timberlands of Southeastern Texas.

4

Rebel at Large

Riding by night and hiding by day until they were many miles from home, the father and son headed for Navarro County not far to the south of Dallas. They had many relatives in the vicinity of Corsicana, where Mrs. Hardin had grown up; among them was Simp Dixon, who had neither forgiven nor forgotten what had happened to his mother, brother, and sister at the hands of occupying soldiers.

At this point in his son's life, Preacher Hardin didn't in the least consider Wes a wayward boy, but rather he thought him a victim of circumstances in a savage time. The father still held tenaciously to the hope that if Wes could find a place of safety and walk the straight and narrow, he might yet be a Methodist minister. Wes was now halfway across Texas, far from the scene of his shootings, and the people in Navarro County, having about the same Reconstruction heartaches as those in Polk and Trinity Counties, weren't likely to find too much fault with a lad who had killed under the circumstances young Hardin had faced.

The father was well acquainted all over the county and his standing as a minister commanded respect. Because of his influence, Wes was offered the highly respectable position of teacher in a small community school. Advising his son that this was perhaps his real chance to make good as his brother Joe was doing in Logallis Prairie, the preacher with his arm around the boy's shoulder told him to forget his experiences as a fugitive. Then the father turned his horse back toward Sumpter and his family.

Wes had two dozen girls and boys as pupils, several of them as old as their teacher. He managed the school well and soon became a model in the community. When the three-month term was finished the trustees offered him the school for the next year.

But spring had greened the blackland valleys and reddish hillsides, and something great and thrilling was taking place before the young teacher's eyes. Great herds of longhorn cattle were passing by—plodding up the northbound trail to market. Cowboys on dashing horses followed the cattle; at night they camped out under the stars, on a creek or near a spring, and sat by their glowing fire. Never had there been anything with the lure, the exciting promise, of the cattle trails—a free and easy life in the open with new adventures every day, and a stack of gold and a big celebration at the end. This was the beginning of the era when every boy longed to be a cowboy and more especially a trail driver.

A writer in *The Galveston News* had seen, almost with horror, how Texas boys were heeding the alluring call of the cow camp and the trail. "So far as I can learn," he complained, "there is not a boy of American parentage learning a trade or reading for a profession west of the Colorado River in Texas.

. . . The little children, as early as they can walk, pilfer their mother's tape to make lassos to rope the kittens and the ducks; the boys, so soon as they can climb on a pony, are off to the prairie to drive stock. . . ."

Like other boys, Wes, who detested restraint, was fascinated by the lumbering cattle and the trail outfits; he visited the camps and met some of the men and boys. He found an easy-going comradeship among them for which he had been hungry—and the same exhilaration that had kept him climbing out his bedroom window at home, while Joe turned up the wick in the lamp and kept his nose buried in books.

With his sixteenth birthday, Wes decided to be his own man in the way he chose, regardless of his father's advice and the pattern of good behavior Joe was stamping out. He told the trustees he couldn't take the school again. With the money he had earned he bought a shining black horse and a fine saddle and became a cowboy.

Now Wes drove stock and rode wild mustangs and met many rough characters. He counted himself as tough a fighter as any of them. Occasionally he used some of the tricks he had learned from the Negro crapshooters and tried his hand at a little gambling. He had a knack for almost any game. It seemed, in fact, that Lady Luck had her arm around his shoulder. He loved the element of chance and he loved winning. There was no halfway business about it with him— he would push his hat back, his eyes would shine brown, and since this taste for gambling at campfires enlarged into gambling in barrooms and saloons, Wes had a chance to acquire a taste for whiskey, too. However, he usually had no more of this than he could handle. There was no element of daring in draining a glass, and he had been born with the feeling of competence and joy that most men drink to acquire.

He learned to play seven-up and poker. He liked fast horses

and couldn't resist wagering on them. Soon he would bet on any kind of contest—a chicken fight, a dog fight, or the ability of a bewhiskered pioneer to squirt tobacco juice at a crack in a floor or a mark on the ground.

Shooting matches were popular. Wes really opened eyes at these events. With either hand he could draw a pistol, twirl it and hit any mark, moving or still, and the swiftness of it was unbelievable. Consequently, his renown as "the fastest thing on earth with a gun" spread over the countryside. Rumors of his resisting the Yankees leaked out and there was wide speculation about his past. He became a boy of mystery. The gossip of his troubles with soldiers won him a certain respect, for even among people who shunned all manner of serious entanglements, there was admiration for anyone who had the rebel spirit and the courage to show it. So it was that Wes heard his name mentioned with awe, and he liked this, for it gave him the notion that he was a man with a mission and that he was appreciated and respected. Therefore, his cockiness grew and he liked to hobnob with men who had the name of being ready fighters and hard to whip.

Among the cowboys and gaming men Wes met was Frank Polk, who had killed a man and was wanted by the military. Wes was often in the company of Polk; he had found someone else who faced the uncomfortable uncertainty of being "wanted." One day a detachment of soldiers made a quick pass to surround Polk while Wes was with him in Corsicana; Polk was caught, but Wes was too fast and slipped away. So in Navarro, as in Polk and Trinity Counties, he had to start keeping a sharp eye peeled for soldiers.

Wes heard a great deal about a young man named Bill Longley. Longley, then eighteen, was the son of a genteel farmer, Campbell Longley, who lived at Evergreen in Southern Texas. The story was to the effect that one day when Bill was sixteen years old, a Negro sat on a horse in Evergreen and cursed white men. He knew he had the protection of soldiers and he laid it on thick. When he got around to cursing Campbell Longley, young Bill yanked out his pistol and shot the Negro. He threw his rope on the dead man, dragged him into a ditch and covered him. This was the start of one of the most sensational careers in the West.

Wes heard good men speak well of Longley—men who had never met him, but had heard and discussed his story—and he was impressed.

When Wes heard talk that a burly Negro in a nearby village often insulted disabled Confederate veterans and, sometimes, white women, he decided to take the matter into his own capable hands. He rode into the town, disguised as a cripple, and went hobbling along a road frequently used by the Negro.

Soon the man came by in a wagon drawn by two oxen. He made no attempt to pull out of the road for the cripple. Instead, he stopped and turned loose with abusive language.

Wes told him he was an old soldier and didn't want to be bothered. The man popped his whip at Wes and finally hit him. Wes jerked off his mask and pointed his pistol straight into the man's face.

Speaking in a slow drawl, with a trace of a smile on his face, Wes told him he intended to kill him for his cruelty, but that first he would give him a chance to pray and make things right with his Maker.

The terrified man dropped to his knees in the wagon, raised his face, and clasped his hands. He poured out such a fervent prayer, petitioning for his life, that his words rolled like thunder. Hearing their master's voice, the oxen started again to plod along. Wes walked beside the slowly moving wagon with pistol pointed. He fired, and a bullet whizzed within a quarter-inch of the man's head. The victim crumpled over, apparently thinking he had been shot. When he realized he was still alive, he inched up, stopped the oxen and made guarantees for his future behavior, with the Lord as his witness. Wes let him go.

The boy then returned to his cow camp unmolested by the military. Word of his action spread in various versions, and men spoke of Wes as "a game kid."

In general, there were two ways in which Southern white men felt compelled to cope with the complex racial situation —the way of the outright rebels like Wes Hardin and Bill Longley, or the way of the men who donned white robes and hoods and rode with their friends and neighbors in the Ku Klux Klan. Honest, sincere men made such rides only when some outrage occurred that could not be endured—for if the wearers were caught, or even the robe and hood found in a man's home, hanging was certain.

Simp Dixon tried both ways—the way of Wes and the way of the white-clad men. Wes admired his cousin Simp and saw eye to eye with him in his resentment of the brutal mistreatment of his family. One day Simp and Wes were riding together on Richland Creek near Corsicana when they ran into a small detachment of soldiers. They decided the time was ripe for them to take the fight directly to the Yankees. Simp opened fire. So did Wes, and so did the soldiers. In the hot skirmish, two soldiers were killed. Wes claimed one and Simp the other. Immediately the boys were prime targets of all the officials in Texas; they were not fugitives on the dodge but rebels asking for a fight.

Not long afterwards, soldiers surprised Simp when he was alone and he was shot to death. Wes was left to carry the colors for the family.

Then in the hot days of the scorching summer of 1869, news that greatly affected the life and actions of Wes Hardin came from Washington and Austin. Edmund J. Davis, a Texan who had fought with the Union forces, was running for governor of Texas on the Republican ticket. In July of 1869, the national Republican organization recognized the Davis ticket. President Grant immediately issued a proclamation postponing the election in Texas nearly a month from the usual time until November 30 so that Davis could have extra time to organize.

Then started a systematic removal of all Texas public officials who were not lined up with Davis. Soon there was no civil government in the state. The military took over, and General J. J. Reynolds became absolute dictator. He ordered the registration lists of voters revised, and he named new registrars. Registration places were guarded by troops, mainly Negro soldiers. The only way anyone could register was to pass through lines of these troops. The same thing happened when the election was held—more lines of troops. Wes was now old enough to realize why his father had been so outraged when a thing like this had happened soon after the war.

Although the election was held on November 30, the results were not announced until January 8 of the next year. Of course, Davis won. He was committed to the proposition of forcing former rebels to knuckle under.

All this, especially the troops at the polls, embittered Wes more than ever, and he became a sort of one-man Confederacy. He rode town and country virtually daring anyone in authority to contest him; he knew full well that there existed a genuine respect for his ability and willingness to handle guns. His relatives around Corsicana were sorely worried about what might happen to him, and also to them if he continued his bold ways. They wrote his parents, telling them that Simp had been killed and that Wes thought he was Robin Hood. They urged the parents to try their best to do something about Wes.

This was indeed bad news, and gloom and a feeling of help-lessness spread over the Hardin household. The parents decided to move immediately to Navarro County and do all they could to take charge of Wes and control him. That would take time, however, and something had to be done at once; so Joe was sent on a hurried ride to Navarro County to get Wes away before he was killed.

Upon his arrival, Joe persuaded Wes to leave Navarro County. The brothers traveled to neighboring Hill County to visit relatives while their parents were in the process of moving. They stayed awhile with an uncle and then went on down the Brazos River to see other kinsmen at Towash, a one-time Indian community which had become a trading center with a cotton gin.

Wes liked Towash, for nearby was the Boles Race Track where fast quarter horses were run. Wes struck up with another young racing enthusiast, John Collins, who had married one of the Hardin cousins, and the two went often to Boles Track. Wes won enough to keep money jingling in his pockets.

By this time the parents had made their move to Navarro County, and Joe, seeing that he couldn't manage his younger brother, went to his new home. Wes now seemed the older of the two boys. Deep down, they were much alike, but the generations of energetic, daring blood seemed to have been concentrated in Wes's veins. A fury burned within him. He knew he could not go home and ever again be a boy in his father's house, as Joe could so easily do. So he stayed at Towash, asking Joe to give his love to the family.

Joe reported sorrowfully to his parents that Wes had turned to gambling.

"Why is this?" the father said, asking the question as much of himself as of anyone else.

"I don't know, Pa," Joe replied. "He's grown up. He's good-looking and friendly and people like him a lot, and he wants his own way."

"I'll go to him myself," the preacher said, "and see what I can do."

That afternoon the father sat in the house trying to compose a letter to his wayward son. Late in the day, Mrs. Hardin and her daughter Matt started into the room and stopped. They saw Preacher Hardin on his knees with his hands clasped before his face. He was praying. Before his wife and daughter could tiptoe away, they overheard a part of the supplication:

"Oh, Lord, it must be my fault and my failure. Have I been too hard on the boy? Did I use the rod too often instead of reason?"

This touched Mrs. Hardin very deeply, for she knew well the lofty ambition the father had for John Wesley, yet that ambition scarcely matched her pride in the good-looking, high-spirited boy. That evening she joined her husband in a heart-to-heart discussion of their problems, and together they wrote a long letter imploring their son not to "be a law unto himself." They appealed to his intelligence and his loyalty to home and loved ones, a strong tradition in this family. Christmas was near at hand and they wanted Wes back home. They told him again that the time would come when there would be courts of justice in which he could stand fair trial and clear his name; that until that day they stood ready to love, help, and protect him. Home with family was the place for a boy.

But Wes did not go home.

On Christmas Eve, Preacher Hardin rode to Towash on a fine horse. Like the Good Shepherd who left His ninety and nine, he had come seeking his lost sheep. Wes was happy to see his father and to have news from home. On Christmas Day, the preacher visited with relatives a few miles away. While he was gone, Wes borrowed his horse. He and John Collins decided that the animal had all the marks of a quick-running quarter horse and they matched him in a race. He won and paid off handsomely, and Wes had about three hundred dollars in his pockets. A nice Christmas present in a roundabout way from his unknowing father.

At the race track that day was a man named Bradly, who was known as something of a desperado and killer, and who had recently migrated hurriedly from Arkansas to Texas. Bradly had heard of young Wes Hardin and he sized him up, apparently hoping for an excuse to shoot the boy or get his money.

Wes eyed the stranger, who was important enough to have half a dozen friends hanging around him, doing his bidding. After the races, Bradly invited Wes to a poker game, and Wes was elated because a man of reputation had apparently recognized him as an equal. He quickly accepted the invitation, and John Collins went along.

The poker game took place in a box house no more than ten feet square and with only a single opening. The little house, which stood off a way from the cotton gin, was cold, although crowded. This was Wes's first experience in what he considered the big time and he assumed an attitude of nonchalance in order to hide the fact that he was something of a new hand.

At the start of the game, Bradly took off his holster belt and dropped his guns in a corner, explaining that a man wanted to be comfortable when playing a friendly game. In a little while, Wes decided he needed more comfort also. He took off his pistol and handed it to one of the men to drop in a corner; moreover, his boots were pinching a little because of heavy wool socks and he slipped off the boots and pitched them into the corner, too.

Wes had improved his game, and luck was with him that Yuletide night. Within an hour or so he had won all the money—nearly six hundred dollars. Bradly still owed him five dollars. Wes asked for it. Bradly reached in his pocket. He pulled out a Bowie knife.

He cursed Wes, calling him a dirty coward and a crook, and he forced him to hand over all the money.

Wes whirled and leaped toward the corner where his gun had lain. One of Bradly's confederates was standing there with a drawn revolver. Wes stopped short, instantly realizing that he had been duped and that his money, gun, and boots were gone.

Bradly lunged at him with the knife. John Collins leaped between them and shoved Wes toward the entrance. "Get to hell out of here," he shouted.

Wes and Collins jumped through the door and ran over the rough, frozen ground toward their horses.

Bradly and some of his confederates came out laughing and walked toward the grocery; they had really taken the bold Wes Hardin and chased him out barefooted into the frost. Some of the other men remained in the little house, yelling and laughing.

Wes stopped and stood behind a tree, fearing the men might shoot in that direction.

"Let's go, Wes," Collins insisted. "We're in a hell of a mess."

"I won't go, John," Wes said. "I won't go and face my father in this condition."

He talked Collins into going back to the little house to bargain for his boots and pistol. Collins returned with the boots, but told Wes the man with his pistol had gone to a boarding-house. Wes pulled on his boots and went to the boardinghouse. He found the man and asked for his pistol, saying that his money was enough to lose.

"Can't do it, son," the man said, "unless it's all right with Mr. Bradly. I'll go over to the store and ask him."

The man headed for the store. Knowing it was not safe to face Bradly without a gun, Wes stayed in the house. John Collins managed to borrow a pistol in the boardinghouse, on the promise that he would get Wes out of there, and he and Wes headed for the store.

Meanwhile, when Bradly heard that the boy was still hanging around, his anger swelled and he started for the boardinghouse to finish the job.

They approached each other on the frost-covered ruts of the street. Bradly was cursing loudly and proclaiming his intention to "kill that fool boy."

He yanked out his pistol and fired. The careless shot missed. With two quick shots, Wes put a bullet in Bradly's heart and another in his head. Bradly crumpled to the street.

Wes and Collins raced to their horses and galloped out of town under the Christmas stars.

At two o'clock in the morning, Wes arrived at the home where his father was staying. He awakened him and said bluntly: "Pa, I've had to kill another man." And then he told his story.

"I was counting on taking you home with me, John," the father said sorrowfully.

"I'll go anyhow, Pa," Wes said, "for a visit."

However, Wes decided he would hide out a day or so, just in case Bradly's friends stirred up something. This was a wise decision, for the next day a score of armed men searched the countryside for Wes. Having learned where the father was staying, they watched the place so closely that the preacher had to slip away and then ride his fleet horse like a wild

Comanche to outdistance the mob—a sorrowful ending to a Christmas trip to rescue his son.

A couple of days later, Wes rode home and found himself in his mother's arms for the first time in a year. But he also faced a stern father.

5

Young Seven-up

The Hardins had moved from deep Southeastern Texas to Navarro County so they could get Wes home again; now the plan was to send him away. Still chagrined by the memory of his undignified sprint to escape the mob, and still appalled at his son's behavior, Preacher Hardin laid down the law. He had forgiven Wes for killing in self-defense; he had even forgiven him for shooting Bradly under the circumstances, but he couldn't forgive the circumstances. He couldn't forgive gambling or race betting (especially with a minister's mount). These things were not connected with the boy's real troubles; they weren't forced on him.

Therefore the father wrote to a brother, Bob Hardin, a farmer near Brenham deep in Texas, to make arrangements for Wes to live there and become a farm hand—and to behave himself.

When the word came that Bob Hardin would be happy to have his nephew on the farm, the preacher arranged for Alec

Barrickman, one of Wes's cousins, to ride with Wes some fifty miles to make certain that he arrived safely in fresh country, where he had not been in trouble. Late in January of 1870, when the new administration of E. J. Davis was gathering steam, Wes and Alec started toward Brenham on horseback.

The boys covered about twenty-five miles the first day and stopped in the small town of Horn Hill in Limestone County for the night. They attempted to get a room in the hotel, but there was a circus in the village and show people had taken all the space. While wandering around town Wes and Alec heard that there had been a fight between some local citizens and circus people that afternoon. So the young travelers decided to go out to the circus grounds and see whether anything was still going on. The night was cold and several of the hands sat around a roaring fire. Wes and Alec joined them. In the center of the group was a large, muscular man who had been involved in the afternoon trouble. Those around him were friends who were verbally patting him on the back for his action. The big fellow asked questions that indicated he thought Wes and Alec might be spies from town, planning trouble. They assured him they were travelers.

Within a few minutes the big man picked up a fagot and raised it to light the stub of his cigar. Wes accidentally nudged the man's elbow, and the glowing fagot raked across the fellow's upper lip.

He spluttered out the cigar stub and turned on Wes. "Why, you—you—you—"

"Sorry," Wes apologized. "I didn't intend to. It was an accident."

"You rusty little devil," the circus man growled. "I'll cave you in."

Wes bristled. "Just cave," he dared. "I'm a sort of smasher myself."

The circus man let go with a haymaker to the nose which brought the blood spurting. He pulled his pistol.

But Wes had practiced his draw too many times to be caught napping, especially with a bloody nose; he whipped out his pistol and shot the man between the eyes.

Wes and Alec ran to their horses and left Horn Hill behind. They camped in the woods a few miles away. The next morning Alec rode about fifteen miles more with Wes and then returned home.

Wes rode on alone through the blackland farming belt, passing the homes of farmers and the cabins of Negroes. The smoke of burning wood rose from the rock chimneys of every house, filling the air with a heart-warming odor. Men worked at clearing land, felling the giant white oaks, red oaks, hickory, and hackberry trees in the rich river bottoms. At times, Wes rode through dark forests out of sight and sound of civilization, and he grew lonely.

After his long ride across Limestone County, Wes decided a little town life would be pleasant, and he stopped a few days in Kosse. There he met a pretty girl he liked. She seemed to be attracted to him, for she mentioned that he might come to see her that evening.

Soon after Wes arrived at the girl's house, and the two were comfortably seated before a roaring fireplace, there was a banging on the door. The girl jumped up and warned Wes that evidently her regular beau had come and would be furious to find a stranger with her.

A young man came blustering into the room. He threatened to kill Wes there and then if the boy didn't hand over one hundred dollars and leave. Wes was inexperienced with girls but he knew he was being rolled. He stuttered that he had only about fifty dollars and would have to get the rest of the money out of his saddle pocket. Acting as if he were badly frightened, Wes started toward the door, saying he would go get the money. The man demanded that he hand over what he had and then go after the remainder. Wes gave him a pile of money and carelessly let some of it drop to the floor.

When the man straightened from picking it up, to the point where his head was directly in line with the boy's holster, Wes whipped out his pistol and pulled the trigger. As at Horn Hill, the ball hit the man squarely between the eyes. Wes grabbed his money, and soon the dim lights of Kosse faded behind him as he urged his galloping horse toward Brenham.

It was apparent now that young Hardin's pistols were becoming a part of him—to be used as others used their hands. Wes had reached the point where he himself realized that he could draw quicker and shoot straighter than most men— even those who had been handling guns twice as long. This was dangerous knowledge for a boy.

At the Bob Hardin home near Brenham, Wes discovered that his uncle and his cousins—Bill, Aaron, and Joe—were improving their farm and clearing some land of timber so that the rich soil could be used for growing cotton and corn. Uncle Bob treated Wes as a son and partner on the farm; he would get his board and room and a share of the crop. Wes felled trees and grubbed stumps; he split rails and helped build stake-and-rider fences; he plowed corn and hoed cotton.

It was about this time that big, misbehaving, impoverished Texas was admitted back into the United States—on March 20, 1870. The per capita wealth was $194.31, the smallest of all the states. For the five long, hectic years since the end of the Civil War, Texas had been considered in a state of rebellion. Wes had known little else but war and its devastating repercussions in his part of the state and in his life. But all of Texas was not like the woods and hills and small open glades of Central and Eastern Texas; to the northwest stretched the great open spaces of the Panhandle, and to the southwest lay the mountains and the mesquite-dotted vastness of the Big Bend Country, as wild as the Panhandle.

From all this territory the Union Army started withdrawing. There had been a concentration of troops in the central part of the state, for it was there that the unreconstructed rebels found the largest batch of trouble. In the outlying stretches there were only the border bandits and Indians. The army never had been quite successful in coping with all its many varied duties as the strong arm of the victor.

The time at Brenham was an almost peaceful interlude in Wes's turbulent life. His excess of spirit was worked off in the fields. The uncle and his family were thrifty, salt-of-the-earth folks, and for a while Wes savored their steady, uneventful way of life. He and his aunt added a little spice to daily living by their discussion of Wes's finances. When he had first arrived, his aunt had learned that her nephew had more than $100. She was aghast that he had ridden through the country with so much money and had suggested firmly that he leave it all with her for safekeeping. With a grin that made his eyes turn brown, Wes handed over the gold coins.

But there were complications. On wet days and Saturdays Wes and some of his cousins usually rode into Brenham, and then Wes wanted his money. His aunt, however, had definite ideas about how many jingling coins a boy should carry. She was proud that her handling of Wes's finances was keeping his spending at a reasonable figure. She, in her trustfulness and innocence, didn't know that within four months after his arrival, her nephew was known in Brenham as Little Seven-up. Phil Coe, the elegant gambler who was famous from one side of the country to the other and whom Wes admired for his immaculate attire, which at times included a gold-headed cane, a pearl-handled six-shooter, and always a natty derby hat, was whiling away some time in Brenham. He had given Wes that nickname because the kid was so good at gambling.

Wes had been sufficiently adept as a gambler to parlay the pittance his aunt doled out into a pocket stuffed with money. Once at roulette he won more than fifty dollars, took it home, and left it in his Sunday pants. In putting away the boys' clothes, Mrs. Hardin found the winnings. She demanded that Wes tell her where he got the huge sum, which was an amount that was pretty hard to come by until cotton-picking time in the fall.

It was difficult—impossible—to explain to his aunt that the coins she had found were his winnings at roulette. Wes mumbled rebelliously that he had had the money a long time. Mrs. Hardin triumphantly took possession of this new treasure to add to the hoard. Financially as well as physically, it was a stable time for Wes.

But when the summer sun began to beat down and the rows of cotton seemed to simmer and melt into interminable lengths as he hoed them, Wes looked forward more and more to the Saturday afternoon trips into Brenham and the dark coolness and the restful green of the gambling spots. It was on one of these trips to town that he learned of the organization of the newest threat to the pursuit of happiness in Texas— Governor E. J. Davis' state police.

The governor had demanded that the legislature create the force so that he would have means with which to enforce law and order. The legislature was obedient to his will. The state police organization consisted of a chief, four captains, eight lieutenants, twenty sergeants, and one hundred and twenty-five privates; the force was under the direct command of the governor and answered to his beck and call.

Thunderous reaction reverberated throughout the state.

Many Texans felt that Davis had set himself up as a dictator and that the new force would be his private army.

About one-third of the personnel were Negroes. Davis, looking forward to perpetuating himself in office, was depending on this diplomatic move to insure the Negro vote and he also might have deemed it a bitter dose for Texas rebels to swallow.

The main purpose of the state police was to rub out young rebels like Wes Hardin and suppress the Ku Klux Klan; however, the force could police elections, pass on the qualifications of voters, take over a town or county, and levy taxes on the local population to pay the costs of "martial law," and do by force anything else the governor wished.

This police arm was a frightening threat to the majority of the 818,579 residents of Texas, and it didn't look very good to Wes Hardin, for some of the new state policemen were stationed in the Brenham area. Word was out that Wes was on the wanted list. It would be hard for him to hide out on the neatly kept Hardin farm.

Moreover, he had grown weary of drinking branch water. Farm life was dull, hard work, and not very profitable. A good farm mule or horse was worth from seventy-five to a hundred dollars, and a yoke of gentle oxen could be bought for thirty dollars. A milk cow and calf brought $12, and a beef cow was worth no more than five dollars. The farmers, including Wes's Uncle Bob, grew their own tobacco and seldom had a chew or a smoke of store-bought tobacco from Virginia or Carolina. Wes knew that he could make as much money at cards in a lucky evening as he could earn in six months by the sweat of his brow.

He talked over the future with his uncle and aunt. The decision was that, since he was becoming well known in Brenham, it might be best for him to make tracks to parts unknown. This decision was made mainly because these kindly, trusting people knew that it was what Wes wanted; a restlessness had seized him and he yearned to be on the go. His Uncle Bob was fond of him and so were his aunt and cousins. Without consulting his parents, Wes sold out his interest in the crop to his uncle, collected the money his aunt had been accumulating for him, saddled his horse, and rode away, destination unannounced.

Wes was not too worried about the state police; he was accustomed now to the life-and-death game of hide-and-seek, and he had already decided that the state police would not arrest him.

Actually, Wes was not running from trouble—rather, he was champing at the bit for new adventure. That is the reason he turned his horse toward Evergreen, only forty miles from Brenham, where big Bill Longley lived. This was Bill Longley, the outlaw, whom Wes had admired from stories he had heard.

Except for Phil Coe, Wes had never met a man of really wide reputation, and Phil was a gentleman of gambling and not a gentleman of guns. Wes wanted to know men in the big league, for example, like Bill Longley.

This was the era in our national history when gunmanship —killing—was a profession. Some men were killers just as some were teachers. Economic, social, and political stresses and the growing pains of the westward movement must have been at least partially responsible. To say the least, nearly all the men in the biggest and most colorful crop of noted bad men in the West and the Middle Border—Billy the Kid (born in Manhattan), the James boys of Missouri and their close associates, Bill Longley, Ben Thompson, Sam Bass (born in Indiana)—were born within five to ten years of the birthday of John Wesley Hardin. Most of them were robbers as well as killers, though Bass was a robber and not a killer.

As long as a gunman lived he thrived on reputation. He could achieve this by being quick on the draw and a deadly marksman. Great numbers of notches were impressive in this profession. But the sure way to reputation, and a dubious kind of immortality, was to outfight a professional of equal or greater reputation. Little Seven-up had established something of a reputation as a very fast man with a gun without having met any of the big time boys, and now he was going to look up Bill Longley.

Wes rode boldly into town, which was crowded because of the horse racing. He knew where to find "the boys" and he found them. He was soon recognized, and there was excitement. A good many men liked the idea of having two of Texas' best-known gun artists in the same village at the same time. Wes was speculative about Longley, and Bill was just as speculative about Wes. Bill no doubt wondered what this kid lead-slinger was like. Bill was a big fellow with a black countenance; Wes was a boy who didn't need to shave more than once a week.

Ben Hinds, a friend of Longley, approached Wes and suggested a friendly game of seven-up. This suited Wes, and they found a convenient upended goods box. Evergreen was really wide open, with poker, seven-up, and other games being played on the streets and in the shade of the trees. On that summer day the streets of the small, steamy little town teemed with roughly dressed men—farmers, townsmen, transients, Confederate veterans, Negroes. The quarter horse racing program of the next day was quite an attraction. Many of the men carried arms, although this was now against the law. There wasn't much law in Evergreen, actually; any officers, civil, military, or state police, would have thought a long time before trying to disarm the men who wandered in small clots on the street.

Wes had good luck in his game with Hinds and soon won twenty dollars, but he was not interested in wasting a lot of time on Hinds; he was itching to try his hand with the big boy of Evergreen, Mr. Longley, so he ended the game and pocketed his money. Hinds acted as if he were highly insulted, saying that it wasn't exactly customary for a man to get a bit ahead and then quit the game. "If you was anything but just a boy," he told Wes, "I'd beat you half to death."

"I stand in men's shoes," Wes drawled.

Hinds cursed the boy, ending his string of oaths with, "I'll beat the hell out of you."

Wes's pistol leaped into his right hand, and Hinds gazed down the .44 caliber muzzle. Soon it was obvious that the little game had been a maneuver to feel out the visitor. A dozen men quickly appeared and some of them reached for their guns.

Wes backed against the wall, and his left-hand pistol whipped out. "If any man makes a move or draws a gun, I'll kill him," he said.

Surprised that a strange kid could cover so many so quickly in Evergreen, the men stared at Wes. Then Hinds, apparently deciding that Wes was no baby, broke the tension by apologizing. He promised to be Wes's friend; then, almost as proudly as if he had been introducing the President of the United States, he said: "Bill Longley will be at the races tomorrow. Stop over and we'll have a good time."

Longley didn't wait until the next day. Word of Wes's impressive behavior reached him within a little while. Late in the day big Bill strolled down the main street. He walked up to Wes and introduced himself. Showing his hand quickly—that he intended to get something started in a hurry—he said: "I hear you're a spy for the state police, and I believe it."

For the first time, Wes Hardin was face to face with a

celebrated gunman. Men on the street and others standing barely inside doors and behind posts watched expectantly. The situation was like that of two wild mustangs challenging each other.

Tall, dark, grave Bill Longley looked down on Wes Hardin and studied his mild, but steady, gray eyes. Without apparent tenseness, Wes studied Bill. At this point, Longley couldn't add too much to his fame by shooting down the boy; he could add a notch to his gun, of course, and achieve the recognition that came with outdrawing a man of some reputation. On the other hand, Wes could add instant fame to his name—and no doubt draw a good deal of praise—by making short work of Longley. However, he had admired Longley and many of the things he had heard about the big man. The same force had led both of them to kill their first men. Moreover, Wes was on Longley's stomping ground; he knew that at least a dozen guns would open up on him if he made the first move.

"If you believe I'm a spy for the state police," Wes said calmly, "you believe a lie. All I ask is a fair fight. If your name is Bill Longley I want you to understand that you can't bullyrag or scare me."

Now was the time for Bill to draw if he intended to. He had not bluffed Wes Hardin, and a fight with him would certainly not be a one-sided affair. Bill might shoot later if conditions stacked up right, but he wouldn't try it now.

"I reckon I made a mistake," he said, and the slightest of smiles brightened his dark face. He invited Wes to stay over for the races. On second thought, he suggested an immediate poker game, the traditional come-on. Wes hadn't forgotten his poker game at Towash, but he accepted Bill's invitation.

Bill and Wes headed for a corncrib, or bin, just off the main street. Several men followed them, and before long Wes was playing four-handed poker with Bill Longley and two of his friends. Several other Longley confederates were standing by. Wes had the guts to trust himself. He didn't remove his guns or his boots.

When it came his turn to deal, he caught three jacks to go on and raised five dollars. All stayed in, and in the draw Bill drew three cards, while the other two players drew one apiece. Wes drew two and caught the other jack. Bill filled on aces. One of the other players made a flush and the other filled on queens. The flush man bet five, the man with the full went ten better. Wes studied awhile and said:

"You can't run me out on my own deal. I go ten dollars better."

"Well, stranger," Bill said, "you've got your foot in it now; I go you fifty better."

The man with the flush passed; the man with the queen full said: "Bill, I call a sight."

"All right," Bill said, "how much money you got?" He counted out forty-five dollars and added, "Well, stranger, it's up to you. What do you do?"

"What are you betting—wind or money?" Wes asked.

"Money," Bill replied.

"Put it up," said Wes.

Bill pulled out four twenty-dollar gold pieces and a five-dollar gold piece.

"All right," Wes said. "Here is your fifty and I go two hundred and fifty better."

"I go you," Bill said. "I call you."

Wes told him to put up the money. Bill asked if his word wasn't good, and Wes shook his head. Bill pulled out eleven twenty-dollar gold pieces and asked Wes if he would credit him for the balance. Wes told him, "No."

"Well," Bill said, "I call you for two twenty."

"All right," Wes said. "I reckon you've got me beat."

"I reckon so." Bill grinned. "I've got an ace full."

"Hold on," Wes put in. "I've got two pair."

"They're not worth a damn."

"I reckon two pair of jacks are good," Wes said.

He raked the money to him and pocketed it.

Just to prove that he didn't win and run, Wes remained in Evergreen that night and went to the races next day and won more money. He was not challenged by Longley or his pals. Did he have a charmed life, or was there very great respect for his steady boy nerve and his unerring guns?

He rode aimlessly when he left Evergreen. There was no place he wanted or needed to go, nothing to do but to ride and keep on the move. He had imagined Bill Longley a great hero, but had found that he was not.

Not only was Wes disappointed, he was confused. At seventeen he had killed at least eight men within two years. Stories of his exploits—a boy's fight against the Yankees—had spread by word of mouth over the scattered settlements of Texas, and the name of John Wesley Hardin was becoming known. This notoriety had naturally swelled his head or at least given him a feeling of importance; to some extent, it was encouragement to the boy to go forward with his mission.

But with it went the acquiring of a reputation which made him vulnerable wherever he happened to be. At any time he was apt to be contested by men who desired whatever glory could come from outdrawing a game kid. And there were the state police. There was no place Wes could go without the probability of a fight. He was not spoiling for trouble. Instead of taking a chance on danger, he kept out of sight, riding along through the woods and edging the prairie glades. For weeks he rode every day, going nowhere in particular, and every night he slept on the ground with a gun in his hand. He was trying to decide what to do. He didn't want to be a gunman, but what *could* he do?

One damp, chilly night as he lay under the branches of a towering pine, he decided to go home. If fighting were forced upon him he could fight there as well as anywhere. Perhaps, after all, his father was a wise man and could help him straighten out his troubled life. The next morning he turned his horse toward home. As had been true for two long years he had no idea into what violence he might ride.

6

Terror of Texas

A pall of almost paralyzing fear crept over Texas in the late summer of 1870. No individual, family, or community felt safe day or night. Governor Davis' state police were smashing roughshod over all opposition; the troops had full authority to take over any town or county, to levy taxes as they pleased, to kill without provocation.

Wes Hardin was jolted into a full realization of what this meant to him when he showed up once more at the home of his father, who had moved to the quiet town of Mt. Calm on the line of Hill and Limestone Counties.

Wes was saddle-worn and weary of wandering. He told his father he had come home to stay. But the anxious father wasn't sure he could invite his son to do so.

The state police had just published a list of 2,870 men, described as fugitives and criminals, whom the force was dedicated to capture. Wes Hardin's name was at the top. A reward of $800 was offered for his body, dead or alive.

The reward made him a target for gunmen who didn't know him and who had nothing against him, for there were many men who would kill for that much money—plus the notoriety that would come from dispatching a man of the reputation Wes had acquired.

One thing that added starkness and immediacy to the meaning of all this was a terrifying story his father told him. It was being circulated over Texas and published in many of the enraged newspapers. It was the story of the Kelly boys and the state police.

On an August evening Henry and Bill Kelly of DeWitt County in South-Central Texas had taken their families to a traveling show at the little town of Sweet Home. The brothers considered the show indecent and shot out the lights. Early in the morning two days later, state policemen in the company commanded by Captain Jack Helm appeared at the home of Henry Kelly and informed him they had to take him to the courthouse.

Henry told his family that he reckoned he would be fined for shooting out the lights.

The policemen also picked up Bill Kelly, who lived close by. The brothers' pistols were taken from them at the outset.

Mrs. Henry Kelly was worried. She got in a buggy, picked up her mother-in-law, Mrs. Delilah Kelly, and followed. She was so close she saw Bill Kelly fill his pipe. The group stopped and Bill crawled off his horse, squatted down and struck a match on his boot to light the pipe. A policeman on a horse pointed his gun down at Bill and fired. Bill tumbled over dead. At almost the same instant, another policeman shot Henry Kelly, who fell from his horse. Then the policeman fired a dozen shots into the bodies and dashed into the brush.

The policemen were indicted and quickly tried, but they

were acquitted because they claimed the prisoners were shot while trying to escape. These same policemen were continuing in their official role as the supreme law of Texas.

This story was retold so often as an example of what was happening in Texas that the folks in Mt. Calm spoke of the Kelly boys as if they had known them all their lives.

Many of the braver newspapers in Texas cried out against the savagery and the terroristic methods of the dreaded state police.

Where in Texas, Preacher Hardin asked himself, was there safety for his son? Or for his family?

Joe Hardin was in school at Round Rock near Austin. He was studying to be a lawyer in the school of Professor J. C. Landrum, who had been a teacher and a friend of the Hardins back in Sumpter during the Civil War. Preacher Hardin wondered whether Joe had heard of the Kellys, whether even this older son could escape harm.

His speculation was ended by a letter from Joe and the professor. They knew about the Kellys and the state police list. They were worrying about Wes, and they made a daring suggestion. They thought Wes ought to make his way to Round Rock and enter the professor's school to study for the law or teaching. Round Rock, they pointed out, was near Austin and almost under the nose of state police headquarters. But if the police were searching for Wes perhaps they would never guess that he was in a place of learning and so close.

The letter brought a gleam of hope to Preacher Hardin's eyes and it appealed to Wes. The two sat under a peach tree at the back of the little white house in Mt. Calm and reread the finely written page.

The preacher looked old and austere sitting there with the letter in his hand. He was bulky and slightly stooped in the shoulders. His hair was long and graying and there were flecks of gray in his mustache and short chin whiskers. He wrinkled his eyes as he read.

"Son," he said, "this may be the hand of the Lord. You know I've always hoped you'd be a minister, but maybe I've erred in trying to foreordain a life for you. Maybe you ought to have the right to pick your own profession just as I was called to mine. If you wish to study for law or to be a professor, I'm with you on it." To the father there was no incongruity that he spoke thus to one of Texas' most fiery killers.

The father glanced again at the letter while waiting for an answer.

Wes dug at the ground with the toe of his boot. The warm air hung silent. He was conscious of the mountainous disappointment and anxiety he had brought upon his father.

Wes was deeply sunburned; even the fuzz on his face and the few hairs on his upper lip had been given a reddish tinge by the sun. His legs were slightly bowed from constant riding. He was slim, lithe, and as hard as iron; yet there remained in his face the look of a bashful boy who wanted to please.

From the time Wes had become a fugitive after killing Mage, the Moscow Negro, he had been a youth of double nature—two almost distinct characters. In him, on the one hand, were the instincts of the outlaw and the rebel. He was proud of his ability to handle guns. He was aware of the fact that even influential men looked on him with awe and spoke his name with a certain respect. Wes enjoyed this status and attention. His life on the dodge had led him into gambling, horse racing, and drinking; these things appealed to him because they seemed manly. At times, Wes had considered himself a man with a mission—to ride forth with his two guns blazing and eliminate from the face of the earth the enemies of honor, chivalry, and the nobility of man.

Yet his most violent fight had been within himself. He was still a boy—in years, at least. He adored his mother and respected his father. On his lonely rides over Texas he had longed to be with his family, and to be like Joe. He had yearned for a life of peace. Often he had promised himself when this thing or that thing was settled he would return to his home and forget the lonely but adventuresome life of the fugitive.

Now his father stood ready to help him in his expressed desire to follow the good life. So did Joe and Professor Landrum.

With his decision to study law along with Joe, for the moment his better instincts were in the ascendant.

"I'd like to try it," he said. "I'd like to study law as Joe is doing. And I'd like to be with him again."

The father straightened his shoulders. His advice was for Wes to go as carefully as possible to Round Rock at once.

"I will, Pa," Wes said, "but I've made up my mind never to surrender to the state police. If they catch me, I'll do everything I can to give them trouble."

"I can't say that I blame you, son," the father replied.

On his horseback trip to Round Rock Wes began to realize that the state police were employing hit-and-miss methods no longer. Officers were stopping and questioning all travelers. Three times Wes had to ram the spurs to his horse and use all his resourcefulness and knowledge of the woods to avoid being caught. He made it to Professor Landrum's school, saw Joe, and attended classes all in one day.

Then he discerned that he was being shadowed by state police and also, perhaps, by local reward seekers who had calculated that he might show up there to visit his brother. Wes went into hiding and did his studying away from school. He and Joe managed to get together only on the sly. Deep in the brushy woods of a small stream, but within walking distance of Round Rock, Wes made his secret camp. Piles of tall grasses covered with an old blanket served as a mattress on the hard ground. In a little hollow niche of stones in the densest spot of overhanging hackberry trees he built small fires to cook his food, which Joe brought him at intervals—always on dark nights after all the lights in the little town had disappeared, and always with Joe traveling a different route. Along with the food, Joe brought books and the notes he had made in lectures. The boys huddled close over the glow from a few slow-burning knots of wood and studied together so that Wes could stay up with his class. Wes endured the time between Joe's visits only because life was satisfying when they were together; there was companionship in their whispered conversation and arguments over points of law.

One night when there was no moon and faraway rumbles of thunder echoed, Joe brought disturbing news.

Their father had written, urging them to watch with utmost vigilance for state police activity. He warned Wes not to return to Mt. Calm but to get out of Texas if the state police landed on his trail. The father was very anxious, for state police terrorism had broken out almost at his doorstep in Hill County.

Two Hill County youths, Jim Gathings and Sol Nicholson, had been accused of killing two Negro men in a fight. State police under Lieutenant W. T. Pritchett went to the home of Colonel J. J. Gathings, father of Jim, thinking the accused men might be hiding there. Pritchett went stalking into the house without even knocking. Colonel Gathings asked about a search warrant and Pritchett said he had none.

"Well, get out then," the colonel ordered. "You can't search my house with your damned Negro police."

Pritchett went ahead and virtually wrecked the house. When he came out, without finding the hunted men, he was stopped by Colonel Gathings and a dozen other citizens who had quickly appointed themselves local officers of the law. They arrested Pritchett and several of his men and took them to Hillsboro for trial.

The justice of the peace, who held office only because he was satisfactory to Governor Davis, set bond for the policemen at five hundred dollars.

Colonel Gathings was so shocked he almost suffered a stroke. He rushed up to the justice of the peace and shouted: "By gad, if you don't make the bond stiffer than that I'll rearrest Pritchett and hold him until the day of his trial."

However, the threats gained nothing; the policemen were released under the light bond, which they forfeited. But this didn't settle the issue.

When Austin headquarters heard of the action of Colonel Gathings and his friends, Adjutant General Davidson, the man in charge of the state police department, and fifty picked troopers headed for Hill County. Davidson declared the entire county under martial law. He had Colonel Gathings and seven other men arrested and hauled to the courthouse. All persons except the officers and the prisoners were ordered out of the building. Then Davidson told Colonel Gathings that the only way he and the other seven could escape court martial would be to pay one hundred dollars each per day for each day that martial law was in force. Colonel Gathings said he did not have the means.

Davidson then suggested that perhaps the case could be settled if Colonel Gathings could raise three thousand dollars to pay over to the police. "If you do not do this," he was told, "the troops will be quartered on the people and you will be tried and sent to prison before you have time to appeal."

Moreover, Gathings was refused the right to call in a lawyer, and he was given only fifteen minutes to make up his mind. The colonel and his friends managed to raise $2,765, which Davidson accepted, and martial law was lifted from the county.

At the same time this story of arrogance and graft at Hillsboro was circulating over Texas, many of the newspapers reprinted an editorial from *The Victoria Advocate* which added to the fear in the hearts of Texans. It pointed out darkly that in its early weeks the state police had shot down scores of men, as the Kelly boys had been slain, and the instances closed with the explanation: "Killed in attempting to escape."

At Round Rock, when Joe finished his course and was ready for graduation, Wes slipped in at night and took examinations with him on the prelaw subjects they had studied. Professor Landrum graduated both boys. The brothers had studied the same books, and their diplomas from the little private school were the same, but after that, their paths parted.

Joe rode back to Mt. Calm to teach school with his father; Wes headed for Louisiana to escape the vengeance of the state police.

Late one day near the town of Marshall in deep Eastern Texas a deputy sheriff arrested Wes in a small restaurant, and he was held for a day as a suspect in a shooting. It soon became evident to the sheriff that Wes, who had not given his true identification, was not involved in the case and was ready for release. However, a state policeman had seen him in the Marshall jail and decided he met the description of a man wanted for murder in Waco. So Wes was held, pending state police transfer to Waco.

One of the three other prisoners in jail had somehow managed to pass inspection and get in with a .45 caliber pistol with four of the chambers loaded.

Wes suggested to the others that they break the jail. He would take the pistol. When the jailer came to see about them, he would throw down on him and force him to open the jail or else kill him. When the others shied away from this bold plan, Wes talked the owner of the pistol into selling it to him.

Anticipating transfer to Waco, Wes tied the gun under his left arm with a strong string and put his shirt on over it.

On a cold, blustery January night two men opened the cell door and said they were ready to start the trip with Wes. Wes dressed, putting on another shirt and then his overcoat. The officers, thinking that no man in jail could possibly be armed, and especially not a bashful-looking kid, made no effort to search their prisoner.

Outside the jail, Wes found that he was to ride a black pony with only a blanket as a saddle. He objected loudly and demanded to know where his own horse and saddle were. He was told they were in safekeeping, that he was to ride the pony and no back talk.

The officers lashed his hands and hobbled his feet under the pony's belly. With one man riding ahead and leading the pony and the other in the rear, Wes started on a trip of more than two hundred miles. He knew that if he reached Waco he was sure to be recognized, thereby bringing great joy to the state police. But he was tied hard and fast and all he could do was watch his chances.

On the second night out the two men and their prisoner made camp, and one of the officers went to a farmhouse to get feed for the horses; the other was left on guard. Wes was untied from his pony. The guard cursed the boy and threatened to fill him full of holes if he attempted to run. Wes pretended to be badly frightened. He stood with his head on the pony's back as if he were crying. He eased his right hand under his two shirts, untied the pistol and pulled it out. The guard glimpsed the action and reached for his gun. He was too late. Wes shot him to death, leaped on the best horse in the bunch and dashed away. Before dawn he rode up to his father's Mt. Calm home. He awakened his parents and told them what had happened: he had been forced to kill another man, this time a state policeman.

The next morning the elder Hardin hired a boy to return the horse and turn it loose in the neighborhood from which Wes had ridden home; there might be shooting in the family but no horse stealing.

The father was almost at his wit's end. For a time, Wes, of his own volition, had tried to behave and settle down. The father, fully aware of what was going on in Texas, couldn't blame the boy for doing anything to escape the clutches of the state police.

"Son," he said, "we see that you simply can't live in Texas except by your guns. If you had made it to Louisiana and had ever been picked up, you probably would have been turned over to the Texas police. So I think your only hope is to escape to Mexico. I can't help believing that at the next election this terror will be removed from Texas. Then you can come home, clear up your name and start over."

Wes told his father that he was tired of hiding, running, and shooting and that he was ready to try Mexico.

Hastily, the parents helped Wes prepare for his exile. Early one morning he kissed them and his brothers and sisters time after time, telling them that he might never see them again. Then, with a warning from his father not to use his guns again except to save his life, Wes rode southward, and sadness mingled with hope settled over the Mt. Calm home.

At midnight three nights later, there was a hushed knock on the door of that home. The father opened it and there stood Wes, his clothing torn and his face scratched and bruised.

"Why, son!"

"Pa," Wes said, "I had to kill three more men."

Mrs. Hardin was aroused and the parents listened to the most amazing of the stories their son had brought home in his tempestuous years.

Three men who claimed to be state police had slipped upon Wes while he was asleep in a clump of trees near Waco and had overpowered him. They weren't positive of his identity, but they asked whether he was John Wesley Hardin. He denied his identity, but they started to Austin with him nevertheless and camped for the night near Belton, with the men taking turns guarding him—two sleeping while the third was on watch. Wes feigned sleep, but actually kept a watchful eye on the guard; he had noted where the men left their guns. A few hours before sunup, the man on guard dozed off. Instantly Wes leaped into action. Grabbing the nearest gun, he shot the startled guard; then he turned loose on the other two as they awakened and went for their weapons. Wes recovered his own pistols, mounted his horse, and headed back home.

The father seemed to age before their eyes.

"Son," he said, "never tell a mortal man about this. I don't believe you. I don't see how so many things can happen to one boy. Now I know you must get to Mexico as soon as possible. This time, I'll go a part of the way with you."

The mother and Joe agreed that this was the only thing left to do. Joe was planning to marry a Mt. Calm girl and move to the town of Comanche in the central part of Texas to open a law office. Joe's future looked promising. But for Wes it was different. He slipped into a cellar in the back yard and remained in hiding for two days; then he bade farewell to his family again, and he and his father headed southward. The elder Hardin accompanied his son some seventy miles—a short distance past where Wes had killed the three men. The preacher watched the boy ride out of sight over a wooded ridge;

then, with a heavy heart, he turned his horse and jogged back to Mt. Calm.

This was on January 12, 1871. Wes would be eighteen years old in May. Keeping as usual to unused trails through the woods, he rode toward Mexico.

7

Cowboy Hardin

Gonzales County lay directly on the trail to Mexico, and Wes had relatives there. A few days of rest from the saddle before heading into that unknown land seemed quite appropriate. Wes stopped on the wide, undulating prairie to visit the Clements branch of his big family.

The Clements boys, all big, jovial, and good shots, were Jim, Manning, Joe, and Gipson. And there were two girls, Mary Jane and Minerva. The Clements were cattle people and lived on the open range south of Smiley. They had heard tall tales of John Wesley Hardin and, knowing he was their kinsman, they had long wanted to meet him. His welcome was warm, and that evening the table was loaded with big dishes of good food in honor of his visit.

Wes confided to the family that he was in trouble almost all over the state and that he was heading across the Rio Grande as fast as he could. The Clements listened eagerly to his every word. They thought it was a mistake for him to go as far away as Mexico; he could stop in Gonzales County and live with them. The boys were just starting the work of rounding up herds to be put over the trail to Abilene, Kansas. Wes could join them.

The warmth of their urging made Wes want to stay, especially when Manning clasped him on the shoulder and said: "Be mighty pleased to have you here." Wes agreed to visit a few days and then decide whether to follow his father's advice that he escape from Texas.

He rode the range with Manning and Jim Clements. He stopped at such frontier towns as Gonzales, Smiley, Cuero, and Clinton. He saw the hills and valleys of that region, known as the Sandies, where a series of creeks—Rocky, Elm, Clear, and Salty—which headed in the sandhills to the west wound down to the Guadalupe River. He also saw Coon Hollow.

The Clements girls thought Wes ought to meet some young ladies and they arranged a few country parties and dances. Gip Clements introduced Annie Tenelle to Wes and she told him about a pretty friend, Jane Bowen. Wes met the shy, brown-eyed Jane at one of the parties. He liked her from the first instant. And Jane was interested in him. For her there was an aura of mystery and might about this gray-eyed boy who had seen so much high adventure.

Jane had been a lonely girl. She had received little formal education, but she had always loved to read, and as books in Gonzales County were scarce, she had reread many times the few she owned and the few she could borrow. For hours at a time, Jane delighted in hearing Wes talk. His conversation was filled with the long, alliterative phrases he had learned from his father and from his study with Professor Landrum. His tongue loosened with Jane's appreciation, and when he was with her he felt himself to be a gentleman of letters rather than one of pounding leather and cold steel.

His visit growing into weeks, Wes lived at Manning's house on Elm Creek. Manning was several years older than Wes, but from their first handshake there had been an intangible bond between them; they seemed to be cut from the same rash, unrestrained pattern. Almost every day Manning assured Wes that he would be safe from arrest in Gonzales County and especially on the trail to Abilene.

But no one could minimize to this experienced lad what living in Gonzales County would mean. At the dances and parties he had noticed that the men wore their six-guns or carried rifles and that they posted sentries to watch their horses; no one knew when the state police or a "party" would ride up and open fire.

There was a reason: in all the wide world, which was relatively quiet and peaceful in 1871, there was perhaps no other single spot where violence, real and potential, was so concentrated as in Gonzales County and neighboring DeWitt County. Savage mob vengeance reigned supreme. The conflict, which had grown out of Reconstruction after the Civil War, was known as the Taylor-Sutton Feud.

After the war the sons of old Creek Taylor had remained rebels, much in the manner of John Wesley Hardin. Union soldiers had gone into DeWitt County to tame the Taylors, but the soldiers and not the Taylors were tamed. Finally the military authorities had employed Jack Helm to organize a band of fifty gunmen known as the "Regulators" to whip out the Taylors and their fighting friends. Helm was a man of mystery and local legend. It was said that he had been a Confederate soldier and that one day after the war he had shot a Negro off a rail fence because the former slave was doing nothing more than whistling "Yankee Doodle." He was the man who, as a captain of state police, had aroused all Texas by shooting down the unarmed Kelly brothers and claiming they were killed while trying to escape.

With Helm in the Regulators was William E. Sutton, a handsome, curly-headed, blue-eyed young man with a lot of dandy in him. The Regulators had ridden a wide territory gunning for Taylors and anybody else who opposed them. In their constant raiding they had shot down dozens of men and terrorized nearly everybody else. Gradually the Regulators became known as "the Sutton Party" and all opposition to it was "the Taylor Party."

By the time Wes Hardin arrived in Gonzales County this strife had seethed into a little civil war involving hundreds of men. Helm and Sutton had quit the state police, but they still headed their fighting band. In a wide area it was extremely dangerous to take sides, and it was just as unhealthful to try to remain neutral. About all any man could do was fight or run.

The Clements had done no shooting of record up to the time that Wes arrived, but their sympathy was with the rebel side, the Taylors, and the inclination of Jane's menfolks was likewise there.

If Wes really wanted to keep away from violence until conditions were normal in Texas, the last place he should stop was Gonzales County. But this was the same kind of country that Wes was a man—wild, free, and full of fight—and it was a place in Texas where a talent for shooting was considered a very commendable trait.

One night after visiting Jane, Wes told Manning he had made up his mind to stay with him, help round up cattle and ride the long trail to Kansas.

It didn't take Wes long to show his relatives that his reputation as a man who took no foolishness was genuine, all wool and a yard wide. One day he, Manning, and several others stopped at a Mexican camp where there was a monte game. Wes tried his hand and when he had won he demanded pay. The dealer refused. The dealer went for a long-bladed knife, but he was too slow; Wes cracked his head with a pistol barrel. Two other Mexicans flashed gleaming blades, and in twin flashes Wes shot one in the arm and the other through the chest.

Wes and his friends rode on about their business. A few days later he was pleased when he was told: "Leading people are saying you did a good thing when you shot up the monte game."

Tales of the new Clements cousin spread over the region, and many of the neighboring people knew Wes better by reputation than by sight. One of these was a man named Dreyfus, a San Antonio gambler who was dealing monte in a place in Cuero, over in DeWitt County. Wes and the Clements boys were hunting cattle near the town late one day and rode in for a little fun.

Wes walked up to Dreyfus and asked for a layout. When the man was a little slow, Wes asked him to hurry it up a bit. Dreyfus looked over the two-gunned lad and smiled. "Let's be a little more patient, son," he said. "Looks to me like you're a little too well pistoled, anyway."

Wes smiled. Men scattered in a hurry. One man rushed up to Dreyfus and whispered: "You crazy fool! That's John Wesley Hardin."

The dark, swarthy face of Dreyfus paled. He pivoted and dashed through a door to the back of the place and was never again seen in Cuero. Unperturbed, the boy asked for another dealer and was quickly accommodated.

Wes gloried in recognition. By some force, perhaps his high-spirited personal charm, reputation, or both, he was always up front. Although still a boy and a newcomer to the wide range of Gonzales and DeWitt, he was not regarded as an ordinary cowpuncher; he was made boss of a herd of twelve hundred longhorns that were being gathered for Columbus Carol and Jake Johnson. He was younger than any other hand in the outfit, but he drew a hundred and fifty dollars a month, about five times the pay of a regular cowboy. Jim Clements was his assistant. Manning, Gip, and Joe Clements were to go to Abilene with a herd for Doc Burnett. Barring a mishap, the two herds would be in communication nearly all the way up the Chisholm.

One day when Wes's cattle were about ready for the trail an armed Negro cowboy from another outfit rode over on orders from his boss to determine whether stock of his brand had mingled in the herd.

Wes stopped him and told him that no one could cut the herd without permission of the boss.

"Who's boss?" the cowboy asked.

"I am the man," Wes informed him.

The cowboy wasn't too deeply impressed. He turned and cut a big steer from the herd. Wes hammered the cowboy's skull with a pistol and drove him away. There was no doubt in anyone's mind that the Negro would have been shot if his right hand had moved toward his pistol.

Being the boss, Wes could leave the cattle for a little while, charging the other hands to take care of them. He took advantage of this executive capacity to ride over and tell Jane good-bye. Like all the other women on this frenzied frontier, all Jane could do was admonish Wes to be careful. Like all the other men, Wes promised. But trouble and relatives were always close at hand for Wes.

Even on the Chisholm Trail he had kinsmen. His herd started the long trek toward market in the early days of

March. A week later Wes stopped near the home of a relative, Barnett Young, there to rest and await the approach of the Manning Clements herd. All the hands except Wes and Jim Clements came down with measles, necessitating a ten-day stop.

During this delay, a white steer in the neighborhood seemed to like the transient herd and joined up. Wes didn't want this animal seen in his herd, for it might look as if his outfit had intentionally hooked onto it. Several times he drove the steer away, but always it came back bellowing for company. Wes's patience grew a little thin and he yanked out his pistol and fired. The ball hit the steer in the eye. The animal spun around like a chicken with its head off and alarmed the countryside with its bellows of rage and pain as it died. The owner was not the least happy, and he threatened to go straight to court to collect payment. Wes didn't have any desire to visit any courthouse; moreover, the owner was a neighbor of Wes's relatives, and he didn't want his visit to cause hard feelings. He paid a premium for the steer and told the owner to keep it for beef.

Wes Hardin could soon see that he was a part of something big and great and thrilling. It was like a vast exodus or a mighty migration—the Chisholm in the year of '71. Almost simultaneously, three hundred thousand winter-wooly Texas cattle of assorted shades and hues and of many dimensions of legs and horns snorted and pawed and popped their hoofs on the trail. More than three hundred chuck wagons, their iron tires freshly set and their tarps new and white, rattled along over the unfenced land that greened as spring, with showers and sunshine, eased northward. More than six thousand horses of every color and disposition made up the combined remudas. Some twenty-five hundred men, many of them for the first time, were on the trail, the recruits thrilling expectantly to tales told by the veterans of wild rivers, buffalo, Indians, and Abilene. Nearly all these men were youngsters, ranging from sixteen years old and up. Months of freedom and excitement lay ahead of them; they were free of the bonds and restraints of parents and wives; they had pistols; they had good horses under them; they were men doing men's work and taking men's risks. They were as wild and as free as young men anywhere had ever been.

This was the great year on the trail, the very peak. This was the year that cowboying ceased being a low-rated occupation for men who could find nothing else to do; this was the year when the cowboy started his glorious way toward a place of honor and romance as a character of folklore. The trail— that was the absolute apex of range life.

The year before had brought the first big boom to the western range business. Every owner who delivered a herd in Abilene had come home with big money bulging his saddle bags. Overburdened with an excess of wild, worthless cattle for years, the Texans, by free use of the trail and the co-operation of Joseph G. McCoy, who had started Abilene as a livestock center, had finally found a lucrative market for their longhorns. And now in '71, nearly everyone tried to get a herd together for delivery in Kansas. Enthusiasm was so rampant that no one seemed to realize that there could be too much of a good thing and that the cattle market could have busts as well as booms. There was no time for forecasting; everything went up the trail in '71.

The meandering line of cattle, horses, rattling wagons, and hard-riding men extended almost a thousand miles across Texas from the Rio Grande to the Red River. At no place on that long stretch could a man get out of earshot of the bawling of cattle, the shouting, cursing, and singing of men, the neighing of horses, and the rumble of hoofs. At night the campfires twinkled, one within sight of the next. Simply by telling the boss just ahead or behind him a man could send word all the way up or down the trail.

When halfway across Texas, W. F. Burks of Banquette, near Corpus Christi, a man who had married only recently, decided that it was senseless to be away from his wife for months; so he sent word back down the trail to his bride to hire a man to drive her in a buckboard to his herd. She arrived in due time, and joined the outfit. The Burks had Mexican cowboys. One was a surly, lazy fellow who felt the necessity of a siesta after lunch. This was unheard-of on the Chisholm. Burks had trouble with the man several days and finally fired him and told him to get back to Corpus the best way he could. Then the other hands rode up and told Burks that if he fired the man they would quit, too. Burks could get no other hands, and so he kept the lazy one and permitted a daily siesta.

Word of a row which ended in the killing of Pete Owens, a cowman, near Waco crackled up and down the trail. Several outfits had camped near a place where liquor was to be had. Nearly everybody got a "high lonesome" which lasted until guns flashed.

Rumors came in relays down the trail that the red men in the Indian Nation were unhappy and were levying a head tax on each herd. When Wes Hardin heard this he said to Jim Clements:

"I'm just about as much afraid of an Indian as I am a coon. I'm getting a little anxious to meet some of them on the warpath."

Wes himself was the biggest news on the trail. Every trail boss and cowhand the full length of the Chisholm heard that "the notorious John Wesley Hardin" was bossing a herd to Abilene. And this set off engaging speculation. It was fairly common knowledge in the cow country that Abilene, which had been besieged by wild Texans, now had a new law, the colorful fast-shooting Wild Bill Hickok. Now the question was: what will happen when Wes Hardin and Wild Bill come together in Abilene? Bill Hickok, who had heard that Hardin was riding to Abilene, wondered the same thing. So did Wes.

But that prospective excitement had to wait many long miles. Meanwhile, interest in the booming trail of '71 centered on Wes, who observed his eighteenth birthday on the slow trip between the Sandies and the Abilene prairie. Cowhands with outfits just ahead of or behind the Hardin-Clements herd made it a point to ride into Wes's camp for a glimpse of him or a word from him. Older men, some who had attained the rank of cattle king, were just as curious; they visited Hardin along the way. They made long rides and put themselves to a great deal of trouble for brief visits. One of these was Bill Coran, a well-liked stockman. Another was Fred Duderstadt of DeWitt County.

No man in all the years of the overland movement of cattle —no cattle baron, however rich; no puncher, however efficient; no bronc-buster, however able; no cook, however popular at chuck wagon or Dutch oven—had ever had the attention of this good-looking boy. It was not exactly hero worship, although Wes had many admirers in Texas; perhaps it was curiosity about a preacher's boy who stood up against whatever odds he happened to face and shot it out; a lad who was not afraid of man, fortune, or death.

Whether the attention accorded him on the trail of '71 resulted from curiosity alone or a variety of causes, it was enough to make almost any head swell, and Wes thrived on the attention. But to quite an extent, he was on the spot; if he didn't involve himself in a little fireworks, nearly every man making the trail would be disappointed. Strangely, the state police and the sheriffs of Texas counties through which Wes pushed his herd made no attempt to capture him. Trail drivers were seldom bothered unless they got far out of line; moreover, the relay communications system up and down the trail was virtually limited to the outfits moving north with cattle. Another thing: on the trail it would have been difficult for any man to have maneuvered the drop on a youth with the experience of cowboy Hardin. The men in his outfit were his friends, and they were by no means in the pantywaist classification.

Wes passed within a fairly short ride of his father's home, but he didn't have the time to visit; he stayed with the herd. Like others on the trail, his outfit paused a few days in Fort Worth to lay in provisions and to blow off a little steam.

Fifteen herds stacked up at Red River, which lay between Northern Texas and the Indian Nation. A herd owned by Pleas Butler was among them. Butler's hands maneuvered their cattle just ahead of Wes's outfit because they wished to travel in the company of Wes and Jim Clements. This put a herd bossed and driven by Mexican cowboys immediately behind Wes. The fifteen herds, about forty thousand longhorns, crossed over the Red in one day and entered the virgin country of the Indian Territory.

For most of the Texas boys, including Wes, this was a wild new land; it was a territory in which there was little restraint. Its grass and water were free, and no trail boss had to ask where he could pitch camp; the trail drivers were a law unto themselves. Wes's boys saw more wolves, buffalo, antelope, and wild turkey than they had ever seen before in their young lives. This was an exciting life, especially since every man wondered when the first Indian would come shouting over a ridge. Indians still slipped off the reservations and raided widely scattered borderline Texas communities, and there was little love for the red man.

One morning Wes strayed from camp and stalked a beautiful wild turkey gobbler. Dismounting, he left his horse standing and followed the turkey into the brush. He shot the bird, picked it up, and started back to his horse. The animal was "buggering" and snorting. In a flash Wes realized that the horse was not frightened by the turkey, for it was pointing its ears in another direction. Wes's eyes scanned the terrain in the direction the horse was looking. He saw an Indian. He jerked out his pistol and fired, hitting the Indian between the eyes.

Wes jumped on his horse and raced to camp, yelling to Jim Clements and the others that he had shot an Indian. He swore that at the instant he saw the Indian, the red man was drawing his bow and ready to release the arrow.

Going to the scene with Wes, the men saw that the Indian did have a bow and arrow. The men quickly buried the body, the idea being to get it out of sight and not arouse the ire of other Indians. Wes Hardin had heard that it was Indian custom to bury the personal belongings with a fallen brave; so he insisted that this Indian, whose big mistake in life had been meeting up with Wes, be buried according to custom and take his bow and arrow to the grave with him.

On several occasions groups of Indians visited Wes's herd and demanded a tax of ten cents per head on the cattle; Wes refused and he and his men threatened with their firearms. One day when the herd was nearing the Kansas border, some twenty Indians approached the outfit; their leader rode up and demanded cattle. Wes refused and pulled his pistol. When the Indian failed to depart, Wes hit him over the head. The Indian yelled and his companions joined him. Then the leading Indian rode into the herd and cut out a steer. He threatened to kill the animal if Wes didn't give him beef.

"If you kill the beef, I'll kill you," Wes threatened.

The Indian shot the steer, which was the last thing he did before falling off his horse with a Wes Hardin bullet in his head. The other Indians raced away. Wes's patience was wearing thin again and he decided that it was time to show the Indians that it didn't pay for them to bother Texas cowboys who were crossing their land. With a lasso, he lashed the Indian's body to the dead steer and left him there as a warning.

Of course, these two brushes with the Indians made news along the trail; Wes was living up to what was expected of him.

For a few days before the Hardin herd reached a Kansas area known as the Newton Prairie, the herd behind, the one handled by a Mexican outfit, had been crowding Wes. Several times the herd had overrun his cattle, and it had required a major cutting job to separate them. Wes kept asking the Mexican boss to slow down or else go around him, but the Mexican paid no attention. The Mexican herdsmen were among the few on the trail who didn't know of Wes's career and his high temper. They laughed at Wes as if he were a boy. Ever since the Texas Revolution, Mexicans had not been completely forgiven nor the Alamo forgotten, and the Mexicans had no love for smart young Anglos.

The bickering between Hardin and his men and the Mexican drovers went on for days, increasing in intensity. News of the growing animosity crackled up and down the trail, and several bosses stayed as close as possible to the two herds to watch developments.

Fred Duderstadt, who had met Wes during the early days of the trip, tried to prevent an explosion.

"This boy," he said to some of the drovers, "has got the quickest trigger finger in the world. He can pull a pistol as fast as a frog can lick in a fly. But he's not a bad kid. I've ridden with him for miles and miles, and I'm positive he's a much better man than he's given credit for being. But he's going to start shooting if the *hombres* don't leave him alone."

Duderstadt and some of the others went to the Mexican boss and told him he was tampering with dynamite and advised him to pass the Hardin herd and avoid trouble. The Mexican showed his white teeth in a leering smile and his dark eyes flashed. He waved the men away.

The next day the Mexican herd crowded up again. Wes rode up to the Mexican boss and said: "Hold 'em back. If you crowd up just one more time, there's going to be trouble."

The Mexican's temper flared. He cursed Hardin and swore he would get a gun and kill him. The Mexican galloped away.

For the sake of comfort, Wes was carrying only one pistol. He waited to see whether the Mexican would make good his threat.

The Mexican returned with a pistol in hand. Wes spurred his horse into zigzagging movement. The Mexican fired and missed. Wes swept out his pistol. The firing mechanism failed and he realized that he had no weapon. By some strange coincidence, the Mexican's gun also failed. The two men fell off their horses and charged together like two infuriated bulls.

The Mexican yelled to his men for help. They dashed up and tried to get in a shot at Hardin but were afraid to fire for fear of hitting their boss. Another Mexican came sailing out of the herd, rode up close and tried two shots at Hardin. He missed. By this time, Jim Clements was there and he covered the last Mexican and made him throw up his hands.

Wes and the herd boss grappled, punched, and swatted for

five minutes. Seeing that they were evenly matched, they agreed to postpone the fight until they could get better fire-arms, or otherwise settle their difference. This was Hardin's first fist fight since he had learned to use pistols.

Hardin and Clements rode to their wagon. Wes buckled on his two-gun trappings and filled his holsters with smooth-working .44 caliber pistols. Clements was a one-gun man. Wes's men gathered around. He told them that if there was additional trouble the fight was his and Jim Clements' and that they were to stay out.

Presently the Mexican boss approached the wagon. Wes mounted his horse, rode out, and told the Mexican to return to his herd, that he wanted no more trouble.

The Mexican tauntingly accused him of being a coward and invited him to come on out and fight or else keep quiet. The boss whirled his horse and headed for his five armed com-panions. These men charged Wes and Clements with their guns blazing. Wes and Clements rammed spurs to their mounts and met the charge. Within seconds the prairie roared with gunfire with bullets flying from the pistols of the six Mexicans and the two cowboys.

Wes dashed among the Mexicans with both his guns spout-ing lead. When the battle was over, six *vaqueros* lay dead on the Newton Prairie. With the help of witnesses—nearly fifty cowmen and cowboys had gathered around—Wes and Jim Clements compared notes and it was decided that Hardin had killed five of the men and Clements one.

Everyone knew that word of this would get to Abilene on the double and that Kansas officials might ask Marshal Hickok to arrest Wes on charges of murder in a Kansas county. It was likewise fairly obvious that Texas officials, knowing of Wes's destination and of Wild Bill's reputation, would rush a warrant to Abilene for his arrest.

If Wes thought about these things, he didn't let on. The excitement over the Newton Prairie battle soon died down and the herd humped it over hill and dale for Abilene. Now that the end of the trail was near, the cowboys grew impatient to reach the fabulous marketing center on the Kansas plain; this was to be the climax of the long, long ride.

Wes looked forward to Abilene with perhaps more eagerness than any other man on the trail. He would see his old Brenham friend, Phil Coe, and blustery old Ben Thompson, a famous Texas gunman; both were rumored to be there. And then there was Wild Bill.

Columbus Carol had gone ahead to Abilene to sell the herd and also to "square" Wes in the town—that is, make a deal with Wild Bill not to molest the lad unless he got far out of line. This would put Wes in the class of very important persons in Abilene in '71.

Carol found the market badly depressed and decided not to sell for a while; however, he raised the money to pay off his hands, and he sent word to Wes and Clements to make camp on the North Cottonwood, where the herd was to be held. This meant that only half of the men could be in town at one time, since they had to take turns holding the herd.

On June 1, Wes, Jim Clements, and a few of the other men received word to ride into Abilene and get their pay. Across the prairie they rode in a long lope.

8

Little Arkansaw

Wes and the other boys passed herd after herd of Texas
cattle. An area extending thirty-five miles out from the bus-
tling little Kansas town was covered with milling, lowing
longhorns. Men galloped into town and out of town and all
around, and a thick fog of gray dust hung over Abilene, with
its plank hotels, rooming houses, saloons, and gaming places.
Abilene was the first great cattle marketing center. It was
easily the roughest, toughest town in the nation, but it did not
awe Wes. He rode confidently into town, knowing that he was
to be treated with kid gloves by no less gunman than the noted
Wild Bill Hickok himself.

At eighteen, and still almost beardless, Wes was at his
peak—a kid hero to many in his home state and the most
feared man on the Chisholm Trail. He was aware of the
attention centered on him. He had seen cowboys bend over
backward to be friendly with him. He knew that veteran
cowmen, who had sufficient stature to be called cattle kings,

had treated him as an equal. In conversations around the campfires they had agreed with whatever he had said—about handling cattle and horses and other topics that ordinarily raised a tussle of words. The only men on the trail who had disagreed with him were the *vaqueros*, and they lay under the sod of Newton Prairie. Wes knew of the keen speculation among cowmen and cowboys on what might happen when Wes Hardin and Bill Hickok locked horns. He was confident in his own mind that he had the backing of many of the leading Texas drovers, for they, like Fred Duderstadt, had openly admired him.

This lionizing of Wes was not from fear that he might suddenly disagree with some cowman or cowboy and flash a fast pistol; rather it was a sort of twofold admiration. First, men of this outdoor era, and especially those in the ever-dangerous work of trailing large herds of wild longhorn cattle, liked a man of guts and action. Second, Wes, in battling the occupation forces and the state police, had done things that many a man had yearned to do but had restrained himself from doing because of his family or the possible consequences. Wes had stood up and fought alone for his convictions without weighing the costs.

Now he was a gunman and an outlaw. Yet he was unlike any other killer of reputation in the country. His first killings had been forced upon him—at least, he considered it that way. Once he had acquired a reputation as a fast man with guns and also as a man willing to use them, it was a matter of shooting to stay alive. He differed from other bad men of the West, including Billy the Kid, in that he had never used his gun for gain—that is, he had never robbed. Nor had he ever killed for pay. He had never ambushed a man or shot one in the back. Each of his victims except Mage, the Moscow Negro, had been armed with gun or knife. Wes had never been accused of rustling cattle and had never stolen a horse; on the other hand, he had gone to considerable trouble many times to return saddle animals he had taken or borrowed at times of extreme emergency.

Nearly all the noted outlaws—Jesse James, for example— had gangs. Until he had met his cousins, the Clements boys, Wes had seldom had a partner; he had been a lone wolf. Of the famous bad men of the day, he was perhaps more like Jesse James than any other. Jesse, who was now reaching his prime over in Missouri, was also the son of a minister—a Baptist. Like Wes, he was a rebel and a shining hero in the eyes of many. Early in Jesse's career it was said of him that he robbed rich Yankees and gave money to the poor. Jesse and Wes were about the same size and build; they were personable young men and born leaders. Jesse was ten years older than Wes and therefore had had an opportunity—for which Wes had longed—to fight Yankees. He had ridden with Quantrill's gang of guerrillas and had fought in bitter battles along the Missouri-Kansas border. Like Wes, Jesse had started his career as a mission when he was a fuzzy-faced boy. Jesse was the most youthful member of the gang, but his calm courage, shooting ability, and personality had inspired the respect of much older men, and they often depended on him for leadership. The same had been true of Wes, as was indicated by the admiration of the cowmen.

The careers of both Wes and Jesse had been molded to some extent by public opinion and public acclaim; praise of their deeds had convinced them that they were right and encouraged them on until they reached the point where, because of reputation gained, it was almost impossible to turn back. Each one of these men realized that he was feared and respected—food and a cheering section for the natural ego of man.

But here the similarity of the two outlaws ended. Jesse had

his gang and Wes stood alone; Jesse robbed banks and trains, often killing men while pulling the job or making the getaway, and Wes never took a dime off anyone.

Several of the more noted gunmen, such as Wyatt Earp who was just now getting started, and Ben Thompson, who was in Abilene anxious to see Wes, had been officers of the law, serving in jobs that were given them because of their reputations as lead-slingers. Wes had never aspired to wear the star of authority; he had never had the backing of the law.

Wild Bill was a "legal gunman" because throughout most of his career he had at least appeared to be on the side of law and order; he had worn a badge or uniform or had otherwise been clothed with the authority to kill in the line of duty. He had fought for the Union in the Civil War and had built his reputation as a scout, Indian fighter, sheriff, and town marshal before coming to Abilene, where he again was a legal gun toter. Bill played up to the public as a colorful professional and he dressed and acted the part, decking himself out in gaudy frontier garb and letting his golden curls droop down from under his big hat to his shoulders. This in itself was a challenge to footloose cowpunchers and especially to a youth like Wes, who had only contempt for pretense and ostentatious posing and strutting.

Bill was more widely known and more colorful than Wes. Nevertheless, Bill had heard of this fast-shooting young Texan. Being a Western gunman, Bill knew the breed. He knew that a man at the top of the profession, as he was in Abilene, was in constant danger of being contested. He knew that every upstart gunman of reputation was itching to come face to face with the big boys in the business. If Wes bluffed or killed Bill, it would add vastly to his reputation, but if Bill bluffed or killed Wes it would add little to the older gunman's standing, and it could mean his downfall; the marshal's biggest job in keeping Abilene under control was the handling of Texans and forcing or persuading them to stay in line. Since Wes was a hero among the Texans, Bill could see only trouble if he shot him or clapped him into jail; the Texans might not stand for it.

Another thing—Bill knew full well what the slimmest fraction of a second could mean in a showdown fight, and he had reason to believe that the Texas boy had the speed that counted. So it was comparatively easy for Columbus Carol to "square" Wes with Wild Bill. It was Bill's way of trying to save face in advance.

Carol met Wes and the other boys at the American House and paid them for the long weeks on the trail. Jim Clements was ready to go home; he decided to take the next train to Texas. But Wes said: "I want to get cleaned up, get me some clothes, and take in the town good and proper."

Every Texan knew Wild Bill's rule—no pistol toting in town. But Wes examined his two big pistols to make sure they were in condition and strapped them on over his new clothes, for he figured that being "squared" in Abilene meant he would be an exception to the regulation.

That first night he went out with Columbus Carol to gaming, drinking, and sporting places. In one of the saloons, where a brass band was pouring out strident music, Carol got into an argument with Tom Carson, one of Wild Bill's deputies and a nephew of the noted Kit Carson.

Peace officers in Abilene had little patience with Texans and took no chances. Carson pulled his pistol on Carol. Wes saw this move and, within less time than the twinkling of an eye, both his guns were in Carson's face. Wes backed him out of the place and then shouted: "Don't turn your head 'til you get to the corner; then go get Wild Bill and we'll do him the same way."

Carson knew Hardin. He was aware that the young man was supposed to have been "square" with Hickok, and that was no doubt the reason Carson didn't shoot when he had his gun out. The next morning, Wes and Carol met Carson and Wild Bill on the street. None of them displayed a sign of recognition. However, Wes was certain Wild Bill had received the message he had told Carson to deliver.

Wes headed for the Bull's Head Saloon, which was also a gambling hall and brothel, and there he met Phil Coe, who was as elegant as ever, and Ben Thompson, who was in a very ugly mood. The sight of Wes Hardin gave Thompson an idea on how to get rid of his most bitter enemy—Wild Bill. Thompson told Wes that Wild Bill was a Yankee from away back, that he liked to kill Southern men, particularly Texans, and that someone certainly ought to get rid of Wild Bill. Wes got the drift.

"Look," he said, "if Bill needs killing, why don't you kill him yourself? I'm not doing anybody's fighting except my own. See?"

That was pretty plain talk for a boy to spit out to a man of Ben Thompson's reputation, speed, and marksmanship, but Thompson respected the lad. He made no more suggestions that Wes do a little big-time killing for hire, but he did continue his efforts to stir up trouble between Wes and Wild Bill.

If ever a man was on the spot in Abilene it was Marshal Hickok. This was his first season in the rip-roaring cow town. His reputation as a brave man and as a quick killer was at stake every minute; if he showed the least sign of weakening, the rough crowd in Abilene would take over and either kill him or chase him out. If he showed favoritism—for example, permitting one cowboy to carry pistols and forbidding others to do likewise—the same thing might happen. If he got the drop on Wes Hardin and eliminated him, he would invite the enmity of all the thousands of Texans in Abilene and on their way to the town; on the other hand, if he didn't get the drop on Wes, he himself might be the one eliminated. But could he let Wes Hardin go strutting about town with two six-shooters displayed conveniently while all other men had to leave their shooting irons at camp? One thing was pretty well fixed in everyone's mind—the only way to separate Wes and his guns was to kill him.

Through cronies who were also friends of Wes, Wild Bill arranged a meeting, making it look as if the whole thing were accidental. They first came face to face in a saloon. George Johnson, a Texan, introduced them. They had a few drinks together and a long talk. It turned out that Wild Bill knew all about the bloody fight with the Mexicans on the Newton Prairie. He showed Wes an official paper from the State of Texas offering a reward for the arrest of John Wesley Hardin. However, he assured Wes that he intended no such arrest.

"But let me give you some advice, Little Arkansaw," Wild Bill said, and never explained why he used the nickname. "I'd advise you not to pay attention to Ben Thompson. Don't let him influence you. Let me assure you that if I can do you a favor while you're in Abilene, I'll be glad to do it."

The meeting was warm and friendly, and Wes showed no cockiness. However, Wild Bill said nothing about Wes's guns, and so he continued to wear them. This naturally set off gossip that Bill permitted Hardin to carry pistols because the famed marshal was afraid of the eighteen-year-old boy.

Wild Bill avoided Wes as much as possible so that he wouldn't see the guns and be put on a still hotter spot. But a couple of evenings later the showdown came unexpectedly. Marshal Hickok ducked into a saloon where a crowd of noisy Texans were rolling tenpins. He ordered the men to cut down on the noise; then he saw that the well-armed boy from Texas was in the crowd. Wild Bill had to put up or shut up right then. He walked up to Wes and said:

"Young man, you'd better get rid of your guns 'til you're ready to leave town."

This was Hardin's chance and he tried to pick a fight. "I'm not ready to get out of town," he said flatly, "and I don't put up my pistols, go or no go."

Wild Bill laughed and in a friendly way reminded Wes of the no-gun rule; then he stepped out of the saloon onto the street.

Wes walked away in the opposite direction. He heard some-one yell at the saloon door and he whirled. He found himself face to face with Hickok.

"What you doing with those pistols on?" Wild Bill asked.

"Taking in the town."

In a flash, Wild Bill's pistol was in his hand. "Well, take 'em off," he ordered. "You're under arrest."

Wild Bill had his chance; he could fire before even Wes Hardin could draw, and this certainly proved inaccurate the claim of many that the marshal had intended to shoot Wes in the back.

Wes meekly pulled his guns from the holsters, turned the muzzles toward himself and offered them to the marshal. Wild Bill reached for them. Wes reversed with such great speed that few men saw what was happening. He leaped back and thrust the muzzles of the guns in Wild Bill's face.

"Now put up *your* gun!" Wes ordered calmly, and a peculiar little laugh escaped his lips.

Wild Bill had no choice but to slip his gun into the holster with some two hundred men, most of them Texans, as an audience.

This bit of swift, exciting action was to become the most

controversial moment in Abilene's violent history as a cattle market, with Hickok partisans screaming through the years that it simply couldn't have happened, and Hardin friends shouting as loudly that it certainly did. Few times had an incident become a controversy so instantly when there were so many eyewitnesses.

Men who were standing there and saw it—men like Fred Duderstadt and at least a dozen other reputable cowmen—could scarcely believe their eyes. Men who were no farther than half a block away and arrived and saw Wes Hardin with the drop on Wild Bill simply would not believe that anyone could have pulled the old trick known as the road agent's roll on Bill Hickok.

It might have happened because Wild Bill was positive that no one of Wes Hardin's experience would try to pull such a trick on him or any other gunman of his reputation.

Things were even now: Wild Bill had passed up a chance to kill Wes Hardin and Wes had likewise held his fire when he had the drop on the marshal.

Wild Bill Hickok was no glittering hero or humanitarian and he was never suspected by those who knew him of being willing to spill his blood for the sake of law and order, but he was superb under the threatening guns of the one-boy army from Texas. He saw Carson and another deputy rushing on the double to his assistance, but with his uplifted hands he waved them away, indicating that this was his fight and he would see it through alone.

And now, with the marshal under the guns of the Texas kid, there were suddenly many brave men in Abilene. Several of them—cowboys, gamblers, touts—who would never have thought of facing Wild Bill in a fair fight, now cursed him. Some of them began to ease hands toward concealed weapons. Others urged Wes to shoot him down.

Seeing the motions toward guns, Wes whirled so that he covered the marshal and also the crowd. "Don't touch a gun!" he ordered. "I'll kill the first man that goes for a gun. This is my fight."

Wild Bill was sufficiently crafty to see his chance to close the incident without losing face, or control of Abilene.

"Little Arkansaw," he said, "You've been wrongly informed. You know I'd never shoot you in the back, or let anyone else."

A shy grin flitted across Wes's face when Bill came out with "Little Arkansaw." Bill invited Wes to put up his guns and go have a drink with him. Wes finally decided that Bill was not fishing for the drop but intended to be friendly, and the two walked away together. They had a long talk in a private room. Wild Bill promised all the protection he could give Wes, but he pointed out that this could work only if Wes co-operated and didn't force the marshal into an embarrassing position. They came out friends. Hickok's supporters saw the whole thing as a victory for the bravery and clearheadedness of Wild Bill; on the other hand, the Texans saw it as a feather in Wes Hardin's black Stetson.

That night, late, Wes and a one-armed Texan, Tom Pain, whom he had met on the trail soon after the Newton Prairie fight, went into a restaurant and ordered supper.

Three men staggered in and took seats near the Texans. In loud voices, these men cursed Texas and Texans and expressed the wish that Abilene and Kansas could be forever rid of Texas men. Apparently positive that Wes and Pain were Texans, the men skewed their eyes to see whether their big talk was soaking in. Wes walked over to the men and said:

"I'm a Texan!"

The men leaped up. So did Pain. One of the men threatened to knock out Wes's teeth. Wes pulled a pistol and so did the man. They exchanged shots. The loud-mouthed man's bullet missed Wes but hit Pain in his only arm. Wes's shot blasted the man in the mouth and he fell in the doorway. With his smoking gun in his hand, Wes leaped over the dying man and landed on the sidewalk directly in front of one of Wild Bill's deputies.

Wes dropped the pistol on him and ordered his hands up, and the officer obeyed. Wes backed to a corner and then dashed away into the darkness. Staying with the shadows, he made his way to his horse and then high-tailed it out of town, riding to the Carol-Johnson camp on the North Cottonwood. This was some thirty-five miles away. Wes wanted to be where there were trusted friends and also where there was plenty of room for fighting or making a getaway, while he awaited developments. He didn't know whether he would still be "Little Arkansaw" to Wild Bill Hickok. However, he was determined to go back to Abilene, regardless of what happened.

In this quick sprint from Abilene, Wes rode straight into another adventure.

9

Revenge

The big area on the North Cottonwood, where some forty Texas trail outfits were camped, was in an uproar. At the moment Wes pulled his panting horse to a halt, two men were saddling fast mounts to ride into Abilene to find him so that he could be pressed into duty on a special job.

Bill Coran, who had become Wes's friend on the trail, had been shot to death by a Mexican cowboy who was known only as Bideno. Scores of men had attempted to round up the killer, but they had failed, and Bideno had escaped from the area and headed toward Texas on a fast horse. Coran's cowmen friends, several of them major cattle kings, claimed that Coran had been shot down in cold blood. They wanted the man who had committed the crime. There was only one man in Kansas or anywhere else, they decided, who could be depended upon successfully to track down Bideno, and that man was John Wesley Hardin.

Some of these men had witnessed the fight on the Newton

Prairie; they had all heard of Wes's encounter with Marshal Hickok. The cowmen gathered around Wes and urged him to take Bideno's trail. They offered him their friendship and told him not to worry about expenses. They would give him a letter to bosses along the trail, requesting that Wes be given a change of horses by any outfit he might call on. Wes agreed to attempt the job, provided the cowmen would obtain a warrant for Bideno's arrest.

Men were hurried off to Abilene for the warrant. Wes and a cowboy named Jim Rodgers readied their gear and guns. They left from the North Cottonwood camp at sunup on June 27, 1871, for a mad dash across the plains of Kansas. So many times, Wes had been the pursued; now he was the pursuer and with plenty of sanction.

Near Newton, some fifty miles from the North Cottonwood, Wes found John Coran, a brother of the slain cowman, and he and a trail driver named Hugh Anderson joined in the Bideno chase. Down the trail they rode as fast as their horses could take them. They changed mounts whenever their animals became the least fagged. One trail outfit from which they borrowed fresh horses was bossed by Ben McCulloch, a man who would one day play an important part in the life of Wes Hardin.

Before midnight, Wes and Rodgers had covered a little more than a hundred miles, and they stopped and rested until the crack of dawn and then were in the saddle again. At each Texas outfit they met they asked whether a Mexican of Bideno's description had been seen. Not until they were south of Wichita did they detect a trace of the wanted man; they then learned that Bideno was also riding fast and that he was managing changes of horses by swapping with cowboys on the trail. All morning they received reports that Bideno had been observed streaking southward. They finally found the Mexican in a saloon in a small town on Bluff Creek; he was eating in a back room of the place. Hardin was in charge of his party of four and he elected himself to go in after Bideno. He walked into the back room with his pistols in his holsters, but with his right hand ready for a quick draw.

Bideno was sitting at a rough board table with a plate of food before him, knife and fork in his hands.

"Bideno," Wes said, "I'm after you. If you surrender you won't be hurt while you're in my hands."

The Mexican frowned and shook his head in a sort of shudder. His knife and fork clattered to his plate, and he grabbed for his pistol.

"Throw up your hands or I'll kill you," Wes ordered.

Bideno pulled his gun.

Wes drew and fired across the table. The man tumbled backward with a hole squarely in the center of his forehead.

Wes's companions heard the shot and rushed in. Coran yanked out his gun and said he wanted to shoot his brother's murderer just one time. Wes, who had always despised the practice of shooting into the bodies of dead men, asked Coran not to shoot. Wes pointed out that such action might set off a mob, for it wasn't too safe for Texans to ride into a small Kansas town and shoot a man down. As he expected, a crowd gathered quickly and several men demanded to know what the shooting was about.

Wes stepped outside the saloon, within easy dashing distance of his horse, and explained the situation; then he introduced John Coran, who told of the killing of his brother. The crowd heard his story out, and then started dispersing. Wes gave two of the group twenty dollars to take care of Bideno's burial.

The four men headed north. They stopped at Newton, where Coran arranged for his herd to be driven on up the trail; then he, Anderson, and Rodgers rode with Wes back toward the North Cottonwood. On the way, Wes heard that Marshal Hickok had passed around the word that if Wes Hardin returned to Abilene Wild Bill would kill him. Thereupon, Wes and his friends rode directly to Abilene. The new companions promised to stick to Wes, regardless of what might happen.

The cowmen had their revenge for the killing of their friend, and Coran had a measure of revenge. If Wild Bill desired revenge for humiliation, then Wes would give him his chance.

News of Hardin's success with Bideno preceded Wes and his friends to Abilene, and upon arrival Wes found that he had many new admirers. Cowmen and cowboys chipped in a pile of close to a thousand dollars and handed it over to Wes. Before accepting it, he made it plain that nothing was said about payment before he started on the trail of Bideno. He wanted it understood that he did not kill for money. Besides, he said, Billy Coran had been his friend, too.

So the killing of Bideno added to Wes's prestige in Abilene. In keeping with the violent times, the shooting of the anti-Texan in the saloon just before Wes's speedy departure from Abilene had been forgotten. And since Wild Bill had heard all about Wes's conduct on the trail of the Mexican, he was sufficiently foxy to realize that now many of the leading cowmen trailing to Abilene were on Wes's side; therefore he decided to forget about the threat he had made—that is, to shoot Wes Hardin if he returned. Wild Bill found Wes as soon as possible and made it clear what being "squared" with Wild Bill meant—Wes could wear his guns but he must see that his friends kept their pistols out of sight. If Wes wished protection from the marshal he would have to co-operate; he would have to try not to embarrass Wild Bill. Wes understood, and he gave his promise. He knew that the marshal could give him protection.

Wes told his friends of his deal with Wild Bill—that they would have to put up their guns. They bristled a little and asked why he didn't have to pull off his own pistols.

"The marshal didn't demand that of me," he said, "but I know he is our friend."

Coran, Rodgers, and Anderson agreed to the terms, and for two days they and Wes stayed in town and were not molested. Then the other men left, going to their herds or heading back to Texas, but Wes remained in Abilene.

Shortly thereafter Manning and Gip Clements showed up in town. Manning was highly nervous. He called Wes aside and told him that he had killed two of his cowboys, Dolph and Joe Shadden, brothers from Gonzales County, the night before. The Shaddens, he said, had given trouble most of the way up the trail and had finally grown sullen and wouldn't work but refused to leave the outfit. Manning said they had threatened his life and that he had shot them down when they attacked him.

When Wes had heard the essential facts he broke in and said: "Manning, I'm glad you're satisfied you had to kill them, but even if you weren't, I'd stick to you all the same."

Manning and Wes knew that word of the Shadden killings would crackle back to Texas over telegraph wires and also reach the ears of Marshal Hickok, who would doubtless receive a hurried pickup order for Clements. So Wes told Manning of his deal with Wild Bill. He ordered Manning and Gip to take off their guns; then he hurried to see Columbus Carol and asked him to "square" Manning with the marshal and thereby prevent his arrest on a charge of double murder. However, Carol became involved in other activities and forgot to post Bill on Clements.

That evening Wes and the Clements boys were eating supper in the American House when Wild Bill sauntered in. He greeted them jovially and called Wes "Little Arkansaw." They discussed their recent luck at the gaming table. When Wes and the Clements boys had finished eating, Bill looked at Manning and said:

"I suppose your name is Clements? Well, I've got a telegram about you: You're under arrest."

Wes Hardin hit the boil in nothing flat. No one, not even Wild Bill Hickok, could take advantage of Manning when he was unarmed—not while Wes was around.

Wes asked Bill to step into another room. "Did Columbus Carol square Manning with you?" Wes asked.

"No," Bill replied. "I think he's drinking."

This explained the situation to Wes, but he was not ready to give up on Manning. He reminded the marshal of his promise to do Wes any favor he asked and now he wanted that favor, the release of Manning.

The marshal explained that there were men in Abilene who knew he had orders to arrest Clements; therefore, he had to arrest him, take him to the Bull's Head Saloon so that Clements could be seen in his custody, and then across the street to jail. However, the marshal pointed out quickly that Manning could be freed at midnight. He promised to see that this was done.

"That's the only way you'll avoid trouble," Wes said.

Acting as if he had not noticed the cold threat in Wes's words, Wild Bill specified that as soon as Manning was out of jail he must leave town in a hurry. The marshal would see that Wes was given a key to the jail, and then it would be up to Wes or his friends to release Manning. This sounded like a fair proposition to Wes, but he was a little dubious.

"What time exactly to the minute will you turn over the key?" Wes asked.

"Twelve o'clock tonight," Wild Bill promised.

Wes demanded that they set their watches precisely together and this was done. Wes explained the proposition to Manning, and he agreed, having absolute confidence in his cousin. The marshal took Manning to the Bull's Head, as a sort of public parade of Wild Bill's authority and his ability to get his man, and then across the street to the clinker.

Since Manning would have to get out of town in a hurry, once he was released from jail, Wes went out and bought him a good horse and tied it at a convenient place. When Wes arrived at the Bull's Head, the Texans in Abilene were seething. Two dozen men had formed themselves into a mob and were ready to march on the jail and release Manning Clements by whatever means were necessary. Phil Coe was angry and Ben Thompson was raging.

Manning Clements wasn't this important; aside from men from Gonzales and DeWitt counties, he was virtually unknown. The point was this: it looked as if Wild Bill had double-crossed Texans in general and Wes Hardin in particular. Nearly all the Texans knew that things had been fixed for Wes, and they figured that if Marshal Hickok was keeping his promise, Wes certainly should have been able to keep his cousin out of jail. Cowmen who had sent Wes on the trail of Bideno were determined to see that "Little Arkansaw" got a square deal.

Wes was startled when he sensed the ominous tension at the Bull's Head. He quickly called the leaders aside and told them of Carol's failure to "square" things and of his later deal with Wild Bill. When this news buzzed through the crowd, many of the Texans expressed doubt that Wild Bill would keep his promise and turn over the key; thereupon, Wes addressed the men and pledged himself personally to break into the jail if Manning were not released at the agreed time.

Then he said to Phil Coe: "I'll be with Wild Bill tonight —that's our agreement. I'm asking him to see that you get the jail key. If you don't get it by ten minutes to twelve, send me word. If I don't hear from you by five minutes to twelve, I'll kill Wild Bill. But whether you hear shooting or not, I want you to promise to break open the jail if you don't get the key by twelve o'clock."

Coe promised. Wes told Coe exactly where he would be at ten minutes before midnight. The plan looked good, but anything could happen in a place like Abilene, and Coe was still doubtful. To make sure that Clements would be released, whatever else might happen, Wes and Coe recruited fifty Texans, rounded up guns for them (Phil Coe was a gun collector) and stationed them in the back rooms of the Bull's Head. In addition to the guns, these men were provided with heavy timbers and iron bars to be used as battering rams. Unless otherwise informed, they were to storm the jail at midnight.

In its short violent history as a cattle market, Abilene never had another night so electrically tense. Nearly all the cowmen, cowboys, gamblers, and girls knew of the setup and the midnight deadline.

And young Wes Hardin knew that "Little Arkansaw" was the star of Abilene that night. He went to his room at the American House, which he now shared with Gip Clements, shaved, and polished his boots. He examined his pistols very carefully and placed them in the holsters. At the appointed time of eight o'clock he met Marshal Hickok to "make the town."

They walked the streets and visited the leading gaming

houses to try their luck at monte and faro. At times the marshal gambled with house money and usually lost, proof that the houses were so free of corruption that even the marshal was treated as every other customer. At times, Bill played with his own money, which Wes called a bluff game, and usually won. The marshal was using his own money that night and had a winning streak. Discerning this, Wes simply bet with Bill and shared in the great luck. They picked up about a thousand dollars each.

The marshal, with his long curls shining, dressed in his very best, was glittering and jovial. As the two men walked in the vicinity of the Bull's Head Wes saw the marshal's deputies herding three dancehall girls to the jail. Wes suggested that Bill intercede, release the girls, and tell them to go to their living quarters. Bill thought it a good idea and the surprised girls were released.

In every place the marshal and the Texas cowboy visited, Wild Bill introduced Wes as "my friend, Little Arkansaw." And also every place they went they were followed by an unobtrusive Texan who had been assigned the chore of taking the jail key to Phil Coe, provided Marshal Hickok handed over the key.

When they entered the Applejack, the saloon where Wes had told Phil Coe he would be at ten minutes before midnight, Wes said: "Bill, what time is it getting to be?"

Bill looked at his watch. "Fifteen to twelve."

They ordered wine. While it was being served, at about thirteen minutes before midnight, the marshal reached casually into his shirt pocket, removed a fold of paper and handed it to Wes.

Wes felt of the paper. It contained the key. Wes stepped to the door, gave the key to the Texan who had been following, and told him to direct Manning Clements to the Applejack as soon as he was out of jail. Not a word about the key passed between the marshal and the Texas kid. They sipped their wine and talked of the luck they had enjoyed that evening.

Within a few minutes, Manning Clements, grinning sheepishly, arrived at the Applejack. At the same instant, Wild Bill stepped outside and strolled unconcernedly along the street. Wes and Manning made for their horses and rode to a grove of trees on the bank of a creek a few miles out of town. There they dismounted, squatted on their heels, and made plans.

Manning had to leave, that was settled. Wes felt he had to remain at least a few days so that the Texans who had backed him up would not think he had let them down or had run from Wild Bill. So he would stay in Abilene and keep young Gip Clements with him, and Manning would return home alone. They would meet back in Texas. Having sent his pistol to camp, Manning was unarmed, and he had not received his pay for bossing the herd up the trail. Wes gave him money and one of his guns, leaving "Little Arkansaw" a one-gun man. This was a situation that thrust Wes into one of the most embarrassing predicaments of his life.

The next day and evening, Wes showed Gip the town and at the same time demonstrated to the marshal and the Texans that he was still on hand. When Wes and Gip went to their room about midnight the moon was shining so brightly they didn't need to light a lamp.

An hour later Wes was awakened by a noise at the door. It opened slowly and a man with a gleaming knife walked in. Wes jerked his pistol from under his pillow and fired at the intruder just as he reached the foot of the bed. The man dashed into the hall with Wes behind him. Wes emptied his pistol into the man and felled him near the end of the hall. Realizing that his cap-and-ball pistol was empty and that he had no other weapon, Wes leaped back into the room, slammed the door and shouted a bluff—that he'd kill any man who rattled the door. Gip Glements had no gun, having left his pistols at camp. So the bluff had to be continued.

Wes lived by suspicion. He was doubtful of the sincerity of Wild Bill, knowing that the marshal had been friendly with him and had released Manning only because he had sought to avoid a showdown which could have cost him his control of Abilene, his reputation, and perhaps his life. Wes didn't know whether the visit of the long-knifed man had been a trick planned to lead him into ambush; he didn't know whether there were men waiting in the hall for him to come out. Was Wild Bill at the bottom of this? Had he sent a hired assassin to kill Wes, thereby relieving Bill of the problem his presence in Abilene had created? Wes was convinced that if Wild Bill or any of his men caught him at the disadvantage of being unarmed he wouldn't last two minutes.

Wes looked out the second-floor window, and his suspicion was confirmed in his own mind. He saw Bill and some of his deputies entering the hotel. Had they heard the shots and been attracted to the place? If so, they had arrived very quickly. Wes guessed that they had been waiting close by.

With the officers entering the hotel, there was no time for the tricky job of loading a cap-and-ball pistol, and in this situation one loaded pistol might not be enough, anyhow. Wes told Gip they would have to shuck on their clothes and climb off the mock balcony under their window. Then Wes discovered that the intruder in fleeing had taken his only pair of pants. The pants would be in the hall, but Wes couldn't risk going out there unarmed to search, for he might walk directly into an ambush, and that would be Katy-bar-the-door, the end of Wes and, in effect, victory for Wild Bill.

It would be about the same if Wes stuck to the room and tried to throw a bluff until he could get the pistol loaded. He

decided that he and Gip should get out of there. He told Gip
how to find the home of a friend where he could hide out. Wes
couldn't seek such refuge, for his white drawers would make
him an almost perfect signal flag; he would have to move cautiously and hide until he could find a horse or get his hands on
a gun.

Wes and Gip clambered out on the balcony and leaped to
the alley. Gip dodged around a building on the double as Wes
had instructed him to.

Sticking to the shadows, Wes made his way to the edge of
town and hid in a haystack close to a store. Soon he knew that
a general alarm had been sounded. The hoofs of galloping
horses clattered all over town. Some men rode around the haystack and one of them suggested that they set fire to it. Wes
felt reasonably sure they wouldn't do that since the hay was
so close to the store building, and he kept under cover.

A few minutes later he crept out of the stack and, keeping it
between him and the main view of town, crawled into a small
field of corn and eased row by row out to the edge, where
there was a road. Thirty minutes afterward a cowboy going to
camp came riding along. Using his empty revolver, Wes took
the horse from the man, mounted and rode off.

Tom Carson and two other possemen, seeing Wes ride
away, gave chase, showering bullets all around him. Wes's
white drawers made a fine target, but he soon outdistanced
the pursuers. They kept coming, however. Wes headed for the
Columbus Carol camp. If Wild Bill could have seen him fleeing in shirt, white drawers, and black boots (he had lost his
hat in the haystack) the big marshal would have enjoyed an
uproarious revenge for the embarrassment "Little Arkansaw"
had caused him.

When Wes reached camp late in the morning, he estimated
he was an hour ahead of Carson and his men. He got some

pants, two pistols, and a Winchester. The cook rushed lunch, for Wes was almost famished. He had scarcely finished giving the boys an account of how he happened to dash into camp minus his pants when he saw the three-man posse coming. He ordered the cook to tell the men he had gone to the herd and ask them to dismount and eat. Then he hunkered down behind a mound of earth and stone.

When the officers rode up, the cook carried out orders and the possemen couldn't resist a good chuck wagon meal. The first thing they knew, they were gazing into the glinting muzzle of Wes's rifle.

"Every hand up," he barked.

He had the cook disarm the men; then at gun's point he forced them to take off their boots and pants and mount their horses.

"Now hike out for Abilene," he ordered, "just like I came from there. Give my regards to Wild Bill."

If Abilene had embarrassed Wes Hardin, he now had his revenge.

10

Wes versus Wes

Since the deputies had chased him all the way to camp, Wes was more convinced than ever that Wild Bill had at least known of the attempted assassination in the hotel and that the marshal had at last made a bold attempt to rid Abilene of Hardin by ordering his men to try their best to kill or capture him. The best time for such action had been when Bill and his force knew that Wes was unarmed. Twice Wes had actually bullied Bill in Abilene; he had lived up to his reputation and had pleased his Texas friends. Since the struggle with Wild Bill had now broken into the open, Wes knew that if he returned to Abilene he could do nothing short of killing the marshal. And already, as Wes also knew well, the list of men who had died at his hands was long.

On this trail drive he had observed his eighteenth birthday and had killed ten men: the two Indians; the five *vaqueros* on the Newton Prairie; Bideno, who had aroused the ire of the

big cowmen; the anti-Texan in the Abilene restaurant; and
the unknown man who had stolen his pants.

These deaths brought his certain total to twenty-three. He
could remember them in order, the first thirteen being:

Mage, the Moscow Negro,

The three soldiers in the creek at the edge of Logallis
Prairie,

The soldier in Navarro County when Wes was riding with
Simp Dixon,

The gunman at Boles Race Track at Towash the Christmas
Wes's father had tried so hard to get him home,

The circus hand at Horn Hill,

The resentful lover at Kosse,

The officer who had made the mistake of letting Wes get
the drop while on a cold trip from Longview to Waco,

Three state policemen near Belton,

At least one Mexican at the monte bank in Gonzales
County.

Now, as he thought of this violent past, a feeling of home-
sickness seized him, against which all the fun he had had in
Abilene—painting the town red, as the cowboys said—counted
for little. Now he yearned only to return to Texas and once
again hold little Jane Bowen in his arms. One of his frequent
spells of fighting with himself—the good in him battling with
the outlaw instincts, as had happened when he had agreed
with his father to go to school and study with his brother—was
upon him. His exploits in Abilene had brought him only mo-
mentary excitement and perhaps a bit of glory, but now all
this seemed strangely valueless and unsatisfying. Wes was
homesick for Jane; he wanted to head for Texas.

On the day after the disrobing of Wild Bill's posse he hired
a cowboy to return to Abilene the horse he had taken for his
flight. He also sent along money to pay his hotel bill. Then

Gip Clements rode up to the North Cottonwood Camp, and he and Wes turned their horses south toward Texas.

Wes and Gip were the same age; except for the fact that Wes was handsomer and dressed better and more neatly, they looked a good deal alike. But what a difference in the lives they had lived and the future they faced!

As far as they could see in every direction on the now browning and dusty prairie were camps, cows, and men on horses. And, even this late in the season, more outfits were coming in off the trail, their weathered chuck wagons rattling and their saddle-worn men and boys anxiously anticipating the ride into Abilene to wet whistles, flip pasteboards, and otherwise celebrate the end of the long journey.

But Abilene could never be quite the same again; it had had its big day.

The boys had nothing to do except ride and talk, and they discussed their plans. Gip was going back to Texas and within a few months marry Annie Tenelle; he intended to go into the cattle business on his own, settle down, and raise a family. He could hardly wait to get back to Annie.

Wes felt about Jane Bowen just as Gip did about his girl, but could he hope to marry and settle down? Back in Texas the state police and his enemies waited, thirsty for his blood. No doubt his tumultuous experience on the trail and in Abilene, particularly his standing up so successfully to Wild Bill, would have added to his reputation at home and make him much richer game for the men who would kill for fame or notoriety.

During these conversations with Gip, who grew more lovesick by the hour as they rode across the dry, hot prairie, Wes began to size up his own situation and his prospects for the future. As had happened so many times before, he was engaging in an inner fight with himself. He envied the colorless Gip his freedom to plan and his privilege of going home and marrying the girl he loved.

Wes decided that the peaceful life might hold charms; he determined that from that hour on he would avoid trouble and do his best to live down his past.

That night at their campfire in a grove of cottonwoods on the shore of a small creek, Wes told Gip of his resolution.

The next day at about noon when the boys were riding somewhere near the border of Kansas and the Indian Territory they saw a camp and figured they might be able to get a good meal.

The camp was that of a trader with the Indians, a large, rough-looking man with a short, iron-gray beard and fierce black eyes. His clothing was disheveled and dirty and he wore a black derby. He had a large covered wagon loaded with articles to sell to the Indians. His motley team, a black horse and a gray mule, grazed nearby. A Winchester leaned against the back of the wagon.

The trader invited Wes and Gip to eat with him. They unsaddled their hot horses and staked them out to graze. During the course of the meal, the man noticed the cowboys' guns. He told them how he had been, and still was, a crack shot with a pistol, and he challenged them to a shooting match. Wes accepted. They walked about fifty feet from the wagon for the contest.

They would shoot for twenty dollars. Each one would toss his hat into the air at least twenty feet and the other would see how many times he could hit it before it touched the ground. It was understood that if the hat toss didn't satisfy the shooter he could refuse to shoot and ask for another toss.

Wes tossed his dusty black hat first. The trader opened up on it. He shot four times and hit the hat only once—in the brim—before it landed.

Then the trader tossed his derby and Wes opened up. He emptied his right-hand gun and hit the hat every time, cutting it all to pieces. When the trader picked up his perforated sky-piece the severed sweatband was hanging out four inches.

He turned a glowering face on Wes. "You dirty little crook!" he hissed. "You didn't play fair."

He reached for his pistol. As quickly as any steel trap ever snapped, Wes swept out his left-hand revolver and cocked it in the man's face. Gip sprang forward and grabbed the trader's gun and managed to get between Wes and the man.

"Don't shoot, Wes," Gip said in a pleading voice. "We can handle him without it."

Gip took the gun away from the trader. Wes guarded the man with pointed pistol while Gip saddled the horses and led them up. The man kept trying to edge toward his wagon and the Winchester, and Wes finally told him:

"If you move another inch I'll blow your head off."

Gip tossed down the man's pistol some thirty feet from the trader. He guarded the man while Wes rode out of effective rifle range; then Gip mounted his horse and caught up with Wes.

The trader was not angered at Gip, but he had wanted to kill Wes. The shooting match was fair and according to the rules the two had made. Perhaps it was Wes's mild, boyish appearance and his unexpected ability with a gun that had fooled the man and, therefore, angered him.

But if Wes could strike up with a solitary old trader a hundred miles from nowhere and within thirty minutes be on the verge of killing him, could he keep the good resolution to avoid trouble?

On the way from Abilene Wes passed within half a day's ride of the home of his parents; he had not seen them since their sorrowful parting eight months before, but he did not take the time to stop. Instead, he hurried on to the Sandies country to see Jane.

Wes was as overjoyed as Gip to be home; he was glad to be back on Elm Creek so close to Coon Hollow.

But there was news for Wes. During the time he had been away the state police force had almost doubled. Governor Davis had increased the number of privates from one hundred twenty-five to two hundred ten men, and the force, although it had pillaged several towns over the state in 1871, was centering its main efforts in DeWitt and Gonzales Counties. Wes Hardin was still at the top of the "dead or alive" list. In less than a month after he returned to the Sandies the resolution made on the Kansas prairie received a jolt.

One morning in September, Wes rode into Smiley, the little town beside the lake. He hadn't been in the village two minutes when he learned that two Negro state policemen were there looking for him. They had gone from house to house inquiring about him and, simply by their presence, had terrified nearly all the women and children in town. Wes rode down the village street searching for the police. At about noon he tied his horse at the back of the general store and sauntered in. The policemen, Green Parramore and John Lackey, were at a counter eating cheese and crackers.

Wes walked up to them and asked: "Who you looking for?"

"Looking for Mister Wes Hardin," Parramore answered, "and if we find him we're going to put him in jail."

Wes grinned. "Would you know Hardin if you saw him?"

They told him they had never seen Hardin but that they intended to find and arrest him.

"Well," Wes said, "you see him right now!"

His right-hand pistol was out belching lead. A bullet hit

Parramore in the head and he crumpled to the floor a dead man. A ball ripped through Lackey's mouth, knocking out several teeth. He dived for the door and in doing so maneuvered himself between Wes and some onlookers. Wes held his fire. Lackey dashed out of the store with blood gushing from his mouth, raced to the nearby lake and dived in.

Not knowing whether there might be other policemen waiting for him in the street, Wes ran out the back way to his horse. By this time, Lackey was out of sight in the lake, holding himself under water with only his nose above the surface. Wes rode around the lake several times and crashed through the brush, but he finally gave up the search. Lackey escaped that night and lived to see Wes another day.

News of this attack on the police soon spread. Smiley was mentioned as the scene and as Hardin's address. Quite a few persons in many parts of the state wrote him there, congratulating him on "being brave enough to carry on a lone fight against the state police." Wes was fast becoming a legendary character. The term "the notorious John Wesley Hardin" came into wide use.

F. M. Fly, a boy in Gonzales, had often been told by his mother that if he weren't a good boy "Wes Hardin'll get you," and of course young Fly thought that Hardin had horns and a fiery tail. One day on a street corner in Gonzales he heard some men talking of the fight at Smiley and one said: "Wes has got the guts to stand up and do what a lot of us men really want to do and ought to do."

In another quarter the attitude was different.

Governor Davis and Adjutant General Davidson were incensed; they declared that the state police would never rest until it rid Texas of Wes Hardin. Moreover, many Negro citizens in Gonzales and Austin were up in arms. Only a few days after the fight in Smiley fifty of them congregated in Gonzales and hatched a plan for reprisal; they would ride into the Sandies, shoot down Wes Hardin and his friends and burn every house.

When news of this plan reached Wes by word of mouth he and Manning Clements got together twenty men. They sent word to Gonzales inviting the posse to come on, "as a warm reception has been arranged." Hearing of the impending clash, some of the levelheaded white men in Gonzales, who could see that each new conflict prolonged the duration of the terrifying rule, went to the possemen and talked them out of their raid.

However, some of the men, especially those from Austin, were not satisfied; they organized their own posse for the express purpose of catching or killing Wes Hardin.

This was the posse that Wes rode out alone to meet and in his surprise charge, on a prairie strip north of Salty Creek, killed three men and sent the others scurrying for cover.

It was the continual threat of police and posse that made Wes realize that he, with his reputation as the champion killer of the nation, could not suddenly cease being a hunted man and keep his good resolution to avoid trouble and settle down to a peaceful life with Jane Bowen. This led him to his big decision while on a long, lonely ride over Texas in September of 1871, the decision to postpone his marriage to Jane and go to the mountains of the Big Bend Country and try to make a new start.

Then on that long-remembered March evening he had ridden into Coon Hollow to break this news to Jane, and she, declaring her love and her eagerness to share his troubles, had changed his mind before midnight.

11

When a Man Marries

Two days after their big decision under the moon-shadowed oak in Coon Hollow Wes and Jane went to the little town of Riddleville and were married by a Methodist preacher. Come what may, Wes would live in Gonzales County with Jane beside him. They moved into a small three-room house at the edge of a wood on the Fred Duderstadt ranch in the Sandies. Duderstadt, who had been impressed by Wes on the trail, was happy to have the honeymooning couple on his place. Wes still had money from his Abilene adventure, and he and Jane had no worries except the keeping of a constant vigil for the state police and other enemies, known and unknown.

In the previous summer Wes had seen the cattle market collapse and he figured that the trail business might not be good in 1872. Therefore, he decided to buy horses and try driving them to market in Louisiana. Jane was happy about this because the trip to Louisiana wouldn't take a long time.

Jane's first lonely days and nights came two months after

the wedding when Wes rode away to see about the availability of horses, but he promised he would be gone only twelve days. This trip took him across the coastal country to the vicinity of Corpus Christi on the Gulf of Mexico.

Eleven days after he had kissed Jane good-bye, Wes was in the small, Spanish-style village of Banquette a short way inland from Corpus Christi and about one hundred miles from his home in the Sandies. The moon was full that May evening and a soft sea breeze cooled the countryside. Sweet-scented flowers were in full bloom and the trills of mating mockingbirds came from the tops of tall trees. At about nine o'clock Wes heard the strains of soft music, peals of laughter, and the occasional shout of an exuberant *vaquero*. A fandango had started nearby, and Wes walked over to watch.

The guitars were playing a lively serenade. Wes saw the dark-eyed girls sway and swirl in their full skirts of flaming colors and he heard the occasional click of their castanets. Wes swayed to the sound and swirl, whistling through his teeth.

Suddenly he wanted to be with Jane—not the next day or the next night, but that night. He hurried to the stable and saddled Old Bob. Back at the fandango, he clamped the spurs to his horse and thundered once around the dance, shouting at the top of his voice and firing a pistol into the air. The dancers and spectators scattered in every direction. This was Wes's way of telling the world that he was heading for home.

When he was out of the town, Wes slowed Old Bob to a long lope. It was now almost ten o'clock. Wes knew that no horse could stand a one-hundred-mile ride before morning without being foundered and ruined, but he intended to be with Jane before sunrise. Old Bob, a horse that had been with Wes on many an escapade, was easily worth two hundred fifty dollars. Wes was a lover of good horseflesh, but yet to him a horse was something for his use. Bob was his horse and he wanted to go home. The old bullheadedness which had caused him to climb after the coons long ago was still within him; he wanted his own way in his own time.

Wes flashed across the unfenced, thinly settled prairies, hills, and hollows. Occasionally he slowed down and let the horse "blow" or paused briefly for Old Bob to drink. Hour upon hour the horse's hoofs pounded the turf.

Shortly after four o'clock Wes stopped in front of his house and yanked off the sweat-soaked saddle, knowing full well that Old Bob was forever ruined.

He went into the house to his wife.

Wes soon started the work of assembling his horse herd, but before he was ready for the trip to Louisiana, Jane talked to him about the future. They were going to have a baby. Wes was overjoyed and couldn't wait to tell Manning Clements.

Wes hired cowboys to drive his horse herd to Hemphill near the Louisiana border while he rode on ahead to look for buyers. Spending a little time at Hemphill, he observed what he considered the usurpation of a Texan's legal right, and characteristically stepped in to see that justice was done. A Texan on his way from Louisiana to his home in Austin had been picked up at Hemphill by a state policeman named Spites and charged with carrying a pistol. The traveler was taken before the judge, fined, and relieved of his gun.

Ignoring possible consequences to himself, Wes stalked into the courthouse and informed the judge that in Texas a man was permitted to carry a pistol when traveling. At the moment, Wes had a derringer and a big-caliber pistol. His interference in the case drew a crowd, which policeman Spites joined. Wes berated Spites for arresting the man. Thereupon the policeman warned Wes that if he didn't keep his mouth shut he would be arrested. Spites reached for his pistol.

Wes whipped out the derringer with his left hand and shot

the policeman in the shoulder. Spites dashed into the court-house. Wes leaped on the nearest horse and rode it a few blocks to where his own mount was tied. He headed out of town with a quickly formed, but not very determined, posse behind him. He found safety at the home of an acquaintance about two miles out in the country.

Within a few days Wes sold his horse herd profitably at Hemphill instead of going on to Louisiana, and he started to-ward home over a route which led through Polk and Trinity Counties, where there were many Hardin kinfolks. His round of visiting finally brought him to the Barnett Hardin home, where his troubles had started so long before. There he again met Barnett Jones, the cousin who had been his partner in the ill-fated wrestling match with Mage. Wes and Barnett tramped the old haunts of boyhood, wandering through the woods, hunting and fishing. Then they rode up to Trinity County to see still more relatives. On this trip Wes confided in Barnett that he didn't mind having a little fun, but that, being a married man with the promise of a family, he didn't want to get into any real trouble.

But trouble, never far from Wes, was lurking in a tenpin alley at Trinity City.

The two cousins stepped into a saloon to while away an hour and Wes, who was almost magical at tenpins, began to roll. He intentionally lost and bought drinks for the crowd. Seeing what looked like an easy mark in an arrogant young-ster, a man named Sublett matched a game with Wes for fifty dollars—ten balls at five dollars per ball.

Wes shifted into his best form and won the first six in a row. Seeing his money slipping away in a hurry, Sublett said he was quitting. Wes reminded him that he had agreed to go all the way. A fit of anger seized Sublett. Calling Wes an impu-dent pup, he dropped his hand to his revolver.

Wes shoved his pistol into Sublett's face and told him to keep quiet.

Others in the saloon interceded and Wes put up his gun. Sublett agreed to go ahead with the game. Wes won the next roll, bringing his winnings to thirty-five dollars; then he suggested that Sublett draw down the rest of his stake and lose no more.

Wes bought the drinks and Sublett, apparently satisfied, left the place. He returned shortly with a shotgun. Getting Wes framed in a doorway, he fired point-blank. The charge of buckshot hit Wes in the left side, just below the waist.

Sublett dropped his shotgun and ran. Wes pulled a pistol and took out after him, trying for a shot. Sublett dashed into a dry goods store, startling the clerk and three or four customers. Wes, bleeding and in great pain, came crashing in, a few yards behind, and fired at Sublett as he dashed out the back door; the bullet hit between the shoulders but it wasn't fatal. Wes staggered to the back door, seeking one more shot; then he reeled against a counter and said to the clerk: "I think I'm killed."

Barnett Jones ran in and caught Wes as he started to fall. "I reckon I'm done for," Wes said to Barnett.

Then he told his cousin he had two thousand dollars in gold in his belt and two hundred fifty dollars in silver in his saddlebags; he asked Barnett to take the money to Jane.

"Tell her I honestly tried to keep out of this trouble," he said. "Tell her—when I was shot I ran my foe—made him pull his freight for his life."

Wes was taken to a physician's office where two doctors examined him. The charge had made a great wound in his side, a kidney had been punctured, and buckshot were lodged against the backbone. An operation was necessary, since the buckshot had to be removed. The doctors asked him if he could stand an operation without opiates.

"Yes," he said. "That's the way I want it. If it's fatal I want to die with my head clear."

They placed him on the table on his face. His fingers clawed into the table until his knuckles turned white; the cords in his neck and the muscles in his legs stood out like tight cables and quivered, but Wes uttered no sound. The doctors probed until they found and removed the shots; they cleaned and stitched and finally swathed Wes's middle with bandages.

They told him frankly that he had only a slim chance to recover if he remained quiet, and none if he didn't follow their orders strictly. Wes agreed to obey as long as circumstances would permit, and he was placed in a hotel room. He called Barnett Jones to his bed and whispered that he was not to notify Jane or his family anywhere for fear that enemies might hear of his whereabouts and condition, and strike quickly. He asked Barnett also to cut the telegraph wire leading into town so that news of his shooting could not be sent out and any telegraphic warrants for his arrest could not be received. Then he lapsed into a fevered delirium.

Barnett cut the telegraph wire, isolating the town for a time, but it did no good; word of Wes Hardin's helpless condition seeped out, and the state police saw their chance. Before Wes was well enough to sit up in bed, Barnett and four other men hurried into the room and told him he had to be moved, that the state police were on their way to Trinity City. The men carried him to a hack and raced him to a country village several miles away. The police soon found that hide-out and friends had to flee with Wes at midnight; they hauled him twenty miles over rough roads to Sumpter, his old home town, where he had the services of the physician who had served the

Hardin family when all the children were small. He was put to bed in the doctor's home.

When the police showed up in Sumpter on the wounded man's trail, Wes suggested strategy—that he be moved to the country for a day or two and then boldly back to the doctor's home and in this way throw the police off the trail. This was done, but it worked for only a short time.

Late one day the doctor told Wes that a posse of police was in Sumpter and at that moment on their way to the house. Wes would have to ride his horse this time, for there was no other way to escape. He had not yet walked and he was drawn almost double, but he managed to stumble to the back door. Two friends were there with his horse. Slowly and painfully he mounted. At that moment the posse came thundering up to the house. Wes and his helpers went into a dead run. They dodged the posse and escaped into the dense timber. They rode all night and stopped in Angelina County at the home of a farm couple Wes had known in other years.

The deep wound was bleeding and Wes burned with fever, but there was only one day of rest. Then the farmer saw two state policemen approaching his house. He placed a double-barreled shotgun on the pallet where Wes lay in the front room and ran to the corral to saddle horses for a getaway.

The Winchester-armed policemen galloped up, dismounted, and started into the house. The farmer's wife met them in the yard and ordered them away. They opened fire on the house. One of the bullets crashed through a window and hit Wes in the thigh. He picked up the shotgun, crawled to the door and fired on the officers. One of them fell fatally wounded. The other fled.

Wes was white as a sheet. The new wound, an ugly and painful hole, was bleeding badly and needed quick attention. But there was no doubt that the police would be back in force, and Wes couldn't stay there. The farm couple helped him on his horse and rode with him ten miles through the woods to the home of friends. Upon arrival there, Wes realized that he couldn't keep moving and dodging the hounding police every day, and he asked the men to go to Rusk and make arrangements for Dick Reagan, the Cherokee County sheriff, to arrest him. Wes had known the sheriff in the past, and he was no friend of the state police. However, Wes laid down some provisions: he would not be taken to jail, but to a private home; the sheriff would see that he received medical aid, protect him from any mob, and take him to Austin for transfer to Gonzales as soon as he was able to travel.

The sheriff showed up with four deputies to arrest Wes. Leaving his men on the front porch in sight of the room where Wes lay, the sheriff walked in, introduced himself, and said:

"I'm here to arrest you. I've been told you want to surrender."

Wes went over the proposition he had made, to be sure of no misunderstanding, and the sheriff agreed to it.

"Where are your guns?" the sheriff asked.

"One's in the holster there on my belt," Wes explained, "and the other's here under the pillow."

He reached under the pillow and pulled out the pistol.

One of the deputies, a highly excited young man, saw the movement and thought Wes was going for his gun to shoot the sheriff. He dashed into the room and fired. The bullet hit Wes in the knee.

For a split second the unfathomable gray shone in Wes's eyes; it looked as if he would open up on the sheriff and all his deputies, but instead he accepted the sheriff's quick apology.

Wes recovered rapidly in custody, and within about three weeks, toward the last of September, 1872, he was able to make the trip to Austin, the state capital. Reagan and a deputy turned him over to the sheriff there.

At once Wes hired a lawyer who arranged for him to be transferred to Gonzales to stand trial for killing the state policeman in Smiley. This was exactly what Wes wanted, for he had many more admiring friends than enemies in that county. But there was one fly in the ointment: four state policemen were assigned the job of taking him to Gonzales. At last he would fall into the hands of the police force that he hated with all his being.

There was one consoling aspect: the state police were so unpopular over the state that by comparison Wes Hardin was truly a hero. In fact, the organization was growing shaky. Governor Davis was up for re-election, and his police force was a big issue. If a man as famous as Wes Hardin left Austin in shackles, chained to a horse—when he was barely able to ride —and was "killed while attempting to escape," the state police would have a difficult time making the story ring true.

The four policemen put Wes in irons and chained him to his mount. At a small town on the way the horse became lame, and the police recognized an opportunity to humiliate their prisoner. They obtained a gray mule for him, chuckling over the thought of the great Wes Hardin riding back into Gonzales in so lowly a fashion.

Wes, still retaining his boyhood dislike of mules, flatly refused to mount the animal, which was a skittish one. The police harangued and threatened him, but he told them to do as they pleased; he would not ride the mule. When a crowd began to gather, one of the policemen capitulated. "Hell, I'll ride it," he said.

He mounted, and the gray mule put on one of the most fantastic exhibitions of bucking ever seen on a Texas prairie. What happened to the policeman was described by an onlooker: ". . . and that gray mule throwed him so high the birds had time to build a nest in his shirttail before he hit the ground."

The squad commander then arranged for a horse for Wes to ride. Again he was chained to his mount, and thus he rode into Gonzales.

Remarking that he might as well release Wes to his friends in Gonzales as to put him in jail there, the policeman in charge turned Wes over to Sheriff W. E. Jones. The latter was an appointee of Governor Davis, but he was an adroit man of personality and, despite the Davis stigma, was popular in the county. A crowd, including some of Wes's close friends who had gathered to see him arrive, stood watchful in the background, and there were loud mutterings because he was loaded with so much iron that he could scarcely walk.

Manning Clements and quite a force of other friends soon began to cast their eyes on the second floor of the county jail. They went to a prominent blacksmith and asked him bluntly whether he would make a file to cut through the bars of the building.

"Who you trying to get out?" he asked.

"Wes Hardin," Manning told him.

"I might be able to," he replied. "We'll see."

When Manning returned, the blacksmith handed him a beauty of a hacksawlike file which he had given special tempering until it was almost sky blue.

"How much do we owe you?" Manning asked.

"No charge at all if you get 'im out," the blacksmith remarked, resuming his work.

Manning managed to get the file to Wes, and the latter started the work of cutting the bars in his narrow window. When this job was completed so that he could lift out the bars when he desired, Wes signaled a man who rode by on a horse. Shortly after dark that night, October 10, 1872, Manning and friends were on hand. They tossed a lariat to Wes, who tied it securely so he could climb down it. But when he tried to squeeze through the window, which was studded with the stubs of the bars he had cut, he found that his chest was too thick for the opening. He told Manning to throw up another rope, that he'd have to be pulled through.

Wes looped this rope under his arms and pushed as hard as he could.

"Pull me through," he called out to Manning, "even if it takes off all the hide."

Manning put the weight of his horse against the lasso and Wes came through the window with the steel stubs ripping off his shirt and cutting deeply into his back, chest, and hips. He took the pistol his friends had for him, mounted the iron-gray horse they had brought him, and headed straight for the little house on the Sandies.

12

Troubles to Share

The trouble-sharing which Jane had mentioned tenderly seven months before now came to the Hardin household. Jane welcomed Wes home with open arms and unrestrained joy. She cleansed and dressed the bar-stub wounds and the inflamed scars from the shotgun blast, the rifle shot in the thigh, and the pistol ball in the knee.

Manning Clements, looking peculiarly grave, stopped by to bring Wes up to date on the more threatening events that had taken place while he was away. The Taylor-Sutton feud was as bad as could be, Manning reported. The old conflict was rumbling to a showdown and anything might happen. The main reason for the present tension was the ambushing of Pitkin Taylor, who now lay at the point of death.

Pitkin was the patriarch of the Taylor clan. Although he had lived a life of feuding and violence, he nevertheless had walked into a trap cunningly set by members of the Sutton forces. Having stolen a bell from an ox belonging to him, one night they sneaked into a corn patch near his bedroom and sounded the bell in the cadence of a grazing steer. Thinking the animal had broken into the growing corn, Taylor crawled out of bed and trotted in his drawers into the field, there to meet head on the burst of bullets that cut him down. He had been hovering between life and death for three months.

The likelihood that the feud would eventually involve nearly everyone in Gonzales and DeWitt Counties terrified Jane, and she insisted that Wes do everything within his power to stay out of it. During those fall days of morning mists and evening hazes in the Sandies, Jane talked of the future as she lovingly nursed Wes back to health. And then it came time for him to share a burden that had come unexpectedly to her.

Shortly before Christmas in 1872, several men and boys happened to congregate at Billings', a general store at a crossroad. Among them were Wes, Tom Halderman, and Jane's brother, Brown Bowen. The rickety store with its jumble of barrels and its cluttered counters was dark and aromatic. The strong, seasonal smell of Christmas apples and oranges mingled with the everyday odors of coffee, side bacon, saddles, and new gingham. The big iron stove at the back of the store glowed red.

Thirteen-year-old Mac Billings, proud to be among the men, carried in an armload of oak wood and laid a couple of sticks in the stove.

Brown Bowen, observing that this was the first time Wes had been able to be away from home after his ordeal of the past summer, suggested that they undertake a suitable celebration of his recovery. A lean, wiry youth with light-streaked brown hair and a sallow complexion, Brown was about Wes's age. He tried hard to be one of the boys but never quite made it. Privately he resented the fact that he was best known as Wes Hardin's brother-in-law.

Wes tolerated Brown and went along good-naturedly with the celebration. A few bottles were uncorked. It was purely by accident that Tom Halderman was at the store that day, but he was glad enough of the opportunity to display his capacity for good, red whiskey. Within a little while, Halderman was drunk, but not gloriously; instead of being bold or belligerent, he was sleepy. Accordingly, he crept under a bin near the stove and passed out in a drunken stupor.

The other men sauntered outside, where they looked at horses and saddles and squatted in the warming sunshine to talk. Suddenly the echoing thud of a shot sounded in the store, and all the men rushed back in. Tom Halderman lay dead under the bin, a gaping wound in his back.

Young Mac Billings, now big-eyed with excitement, said he had been doing chores at the rear of the store and had seen Brown Bowen slip in and shoot Halderman in the back.

Brown was arrested the next day and jailed in Gonzales on a murder charge. Sheriff W. E. Jones kept him handcuffed in his cell to lessen the chance of his breaking out. There was threatening talk of stringing Brown up, for the shooting of a peaceful man in the back set off intense feeling even in this feuding country.

Jane, heart-sick over her brother, had terrifying nightmares. She feared he would be mobbed and that Brown could not take care of himself. Wes stepped in immediately. He and a few friends smuggled a file to Brown and were on hand to grab him and run when he had cut through the bars. They took him to the country and pried off the cuffs, and Brown fled from Texas to live in Florida and Alabama, where the Bowens had kinsmen.

Wes soon took Jane to Gonzales; and there on February 6, 1873, their baby, a girl, was born. They named her Mary Elizabeth for his mother and grandmother, but from the first they called her Molly.

No bright-eyed little girl was ever born in a time and place of greater mob hatred. A few days after her birth, Pitkin Taylor gave up the ghost, and sorrowing relatives and friends gathered in a small cemetery near the Guadalupe River just outside Cuero for the funeral. As the coffin was lowered into the ground, Bill Sutton and several of his cohorts rode up on the other side of the river and jeered, cursed, laughed, and fired their pistols.

Pitkin Taylor's widow sank to the ground. Jim Taylor, her oldest son, helped her up. Holding her close, he promised:

"Don't cry, Ma. I'll wash my hands in Bill Sutton's blood."

A few days after the funeral, Jim spotted Sutton in a billiard room at Cuero and opened fire. Perhaps because he was too anxious, his aim was off and the bullet only shattered Sutton's arm. However, that shot incited the Suttons and Helm to new pledges to rid the country of the Taylors and their friends. The feud raged anew. Each side longed for the fastest and most effective guns in Texas: Jim Taylor felt out friends of Wes on his attitude toward joining the Taylors, and Jack Helm sent emissaries to Wes to try to arrange a meeting.

Wes, a new father with increasing family responsibilities, remained aloof. He was in the cattle business again, buying herds for shipment by rail to Indianola on the coast and thence by boat to New Orleans. This work took him frequently to Cuero, the nearest railhead, but the town was only twenty-five miles away and Wes was usually home at night.

On one of these trips to Cuero he spied ahead a horseman who was obviously waiting for him. Wes rode on cautiously, eying the stranger. The man was Jack Helm, who knew Wes made these trips. In addition to being a leader in the Sutton party, Helm was the new sheriff of DeWitt County, an appointee of Governor Davis.

Wes and Helm had never come together before, but Wes recognized him.

"Live around here?" Helm asked, pretending that the meeting was quite by accident.

"On my way from San Antonio to Cuero," Wes parried. "How far is it to Cuero?"

"About seven miles. Well, I just been over to old Jim Cox's. Had to serve some papers on him. I'm sheriff of this county. Have I met you?"

By this direct question, Wes knew Helm was getting down to brass tacks, and he also discarded evasive tactics.

"I'm John Wesley Hardin."

Helm didn't bat an eye. "Oh," he said, "are you Wesley?"

He offered his hand. Wes declined it and dared the sheriff to try to arrest him. "You're armed and you can defend yourself," Wes said, pulling out his pistol. "You've been going around killing men long enough."

Helm didn't make a move toward a gun, and Wes could have blown him out of his saddle. Helm said he didn't wish to fight, but to be friends. He added that he had in his pocket a governor's proclamation offering a reward for the arrest of John Wesley Hardin, but that he would never try to serve it.

Gradually the talk grew less bristling, but the men were no less watchful. They rode together toward Cuero, two men who yearned to kill each other. Helm invited Wes to join what he called his vigilante band, the Sutton party. Wes declined, saying that he and all his close friends, including Manning Clements, desired to be neutral.

But Helm had still another proposition: he invited Wes to meet with him and his friends at the home of Jim Cox a few nights later. Helm hinted that he would be in a position to help Wes out of all his past troubles and clear his name so that he could live at peace, free of the burden of watching constantly for the state police.

Wes was curious, but he asked no questions. He agreed to the meeting, provided he could bring along Manning Clements and another friend. Helm approved this stipulation and the two men parted near the edge of Cuero.

Later in the day, after checking on a shipment of cattle, Wes met some friends in a saloon and had a round of drinks with them; they spent an hour at poker in a back room and then returned to the bar. J. B. Morgan, a man Wes had never seen before, slapped him on the back and suggested that Wes set him up to a bottle of champagne. Morgan was tipsy enough to buddy-pal Wes in the presence of the bartender and the others. He was one of many who knew they could attain some notoriety by rubbing shoulders with this man of repute.

Wes was in a hurry and didn't want to be bothered. He waved Morgan away. This angered Morgan and he clenched his fists. Wes laughed and moved away. Morgan reached for his pistol, which under normal circumstances would have been about the same as instantaneous suicide, but Wes, not wanting trouble, did not draw a gun. Some of Wes's friends grabbed Morgan and made him put his gun in the holster.

"Look," Wes said, "I don't want a row." And he turned and walked out.

Within a minute Morgan came striding out of the saloon. He stuck out his chin and accused Wes of ignoring and insulting him.

"You got a gun?" Morgan asked.

"Yes."

"Well, it's time you was defending yourself," Morgan said, reaching for his pistol.

Wes shot him in the head, and the man was dead when he hit the street.

Wes walked to the nearby stable where he had left his horse, mounted, and rode home. He told Jane he had been forced to kill a man in Cuero; then he related the circumstances and insisted that he had honestly tried to avoid trouble. He convinced her that the shooting was altogether in self-defense and she never forgot this.

Nevertheless this was new trouble, a killing in the county in which Jack Helm was sheriff. Naturally, Wes couldn't forget the promises and half-promises Helm had made, and he kept his date with the man on the dark night of April 16. He, Manning Clements, and George Tenelle rode across the prairie and into the woods to the Jim Cox home. Several saddled horses stood in front of it.

Could this be an ambush similar to the one that had fooled shrewd old Pitkin Taylor?

Meeting the men outside, Jack Helm told them that Wes was to be their spokesman and that Clements and Tenelle must remain where they were while Wes went in to talk. Wes nodded his head to his friends and they waited on their horses.

Wes followed Helm to the door and insisted that Helm go in first. Framing a man in a door was a good way to get rid of him, as Wes had learned to his great cost the year before at Trinity City. He therefore stood to one side, his eyes quickly surveying the room. Eight men, all with their hats on, sat there with Cox and Helm. Wes stepped inside. Cox motioned to a chair across the room.

"I'll stand here," Wes said. His guns were outnumbered ten to one.

It didn't take Helm long to outline his plan. He read a long list of the names of men who were marked to be killed. Among them were Manning Clements and George Tenelle. But by joining Helm and the Sutton party and taking Clements and Tenelle in with him, Wes could immediately cross their names off the death list.

Helm said he had powerful influence with the Davis administration in Austin. Therefore, he was in a position to help Wes clear up all the state's charges against him. The rewards would be cancelled. The state police would leave him alone; they would be for instead of against him. Wes could go about his business a free and unhunted man and enjoy life with his wife and baby. All he had to do was join the Sutton force and, of course, shoot with them.

This was enticing to a young father of Wes Hardin's troubled situation.

"But if all the old charges are cleared up," he said, "and I get into a lot of shooting scrapes with you, there'll be new charges."

"No," Helm corrected. "No new charges."

He then pointed out that the state police would not interfere with his vigilante band and that sheriffs in the region were powerless to buck him and the state police. He mentioned the Morgan shooting in Cuero as an example. He could see that nothing came of that.

Wes stood there tense and alert, his gray eyes studying the stern men waiting for his answer. Even with Manning and George waiting outside, he was vastly outnumbered. These men obviously desired either of two situations—the elimination of Wes Hardin and his guns as a potential threat to them or else to have those guns on their side. The respect for the guns was the only reason Wes had been invited to such a conference and also the only reason the men did not open up on him once he was there.

Wes knew what they wanted. He knew there could be honor among killers, assassins, and feudists, as well as among thieves.

And they were offering him a chance to walk away from many of his old troubles. Ever since he was fifteen years old, he and his family had hopefully talked of the day when he could clear up the charges against him and start life anew. Jack Helm was politically powerful enough to have all the state's charges against him dropped. Then Wes could ride anywhere in Texas without being hounded by the state police; these officers would be his friends because Helm could influence the governor to pass along that word.

Wes had avoided involvement in the feud, for he didn't like it. However, he felt that he would eventually be forced into it if he remained in that part of the country. By joining Helm and Sutton he could tilt the balance against the Taylors and eliminate them quickly; then he would be sure of being on the winning side and also of having the criminal charges against him voided. By throwing in with these men he had a chance to save his own skin. To a great extent, whatever future he could hope for was at stake in this tense, gun-bristling room.

This was the first time in his career outside the law that Wes had been presented a chance to leave his old troubles behind him—as far as the laws of Texas were concerned. But if he joined Helm, he would have to turn his back on men who had been his friends; moreover, he would have to turn his deadly guns on them. He had fought and killed, using his advantage of quickness and deadly shooting to eliminate men who had sought his life. But he had never once double-crossed a man. He had never turned his back on a friend and had never tried to appear to be one thing while actually being something else. Ingrained in him were his father's teachings of honor and integrity. He had never been bought and had never deserted a cause.

The fact that these men had offered him a proposition that would help him personally but at the same time reflect on his honor and make of him a turncoat for possible gain enraged him in every fiber. A mild little smile came to his face and there was a tenseness about his hands, which were close to his guns. He had an impulse to jerk them out and rid the earth of men who would stoop so low as to offer to trade human blood for gain or honor for victory. But he held himself in check.

"I can't join you," he said calmly. "Manning Clements and George Tenelle can't either."

The men exchanged glances as if looking for a signal.

Helm was as calm as Wes. "Wesley," he said, "won't you think it over a few days? We'll let the offer stand."

"I've thought it over," Wes replied. "I've not been in this fight. There is no difference between us. I have a proposition of my own: if you'll stay out of our part of the country and leave us alone, we won't bother you."

Helm felt that he could eventually trick Wes into his proposition and he played for time. He agreed to the idea of peace with Wes and his friends, but, as a warning to Wes that there was still deadly trouble, he made it clear that the war on the Taylors and their cohorts would never cease as long as there was a Taylor or a cohort.

Knowing that one day this gang probably would be gunning for him, regardless of whether he lined up with the side against Helm and Sutton or remained impartial, Wes walked slowly to his horse. As soon as he was outside the house he saw that Clements and Tenelle had their guns drawn and were ready to open up on any man who might slip out and try to shoot Wes in the back.

The three men rode into the woods as quickly as possible for the advantage of cover. Wes gave them details of what had been said in the strange conference. When he mentioned the pledge of peace on the part of Helm, Manning snorted. "Hell," he said, "they'll break that promise in less than a week. You just watch and see."

Helm's promise to Wes of state police forgiveness and protection would have been empty indeed, for the long-hated force was now in serious trouble, of which Helm was well aware. A few months before, Adjutant General Davidson, who had headed the state police for Governor Davis and had put Hillsboro and other towns under martial law, had absconded with $37,434.67 in state money. He had boarded a ship at Indianola and sailed away to Belgium. This had shown what many Texans considered the true colors of the police.

A few days after Hardin's visit to the Cox home, the legislature at Austin passed a measure doing away with the state police. Governor Davis promptly vetoed it. Then on April 22, 1873, both houses of the legislature overrode the veto and the police force was no more. As the good news spread across the state, nearly every community had a spontaneous celebration.

John Henry Brown, a member of the legislature, wrote a story which was published in *The Dallas Herald*. It began:

"The police law is abolished over the governor's veto.

"Glory to God in the Highest; on earth peace, good will toward man.

"The people of the State of Texas are today delivered of as infernal an engine of oppression as ever crushed any people. . . . The damnable police bill has been ground beneath the heel of an indignant legislature. . . ."

Lieutenant Redmond of the state police was in Denton, the Texas home of young Sam Bass, on the day the news came. He wrote headquarters a few notes on his impression of what happened there:

"I found great rejoicing over repeal of the police law by the Ku Kluxers, murderers, and thieves. When the news was received here, the people of this place fired anvils for hours. I believe there are in this county men, if they had the power and it would not be found out on them, who would murder every Republican in it. . . ."

Wes Hardin had fought the state police more stubbornly and violently and more openly than any other man. He could now have the satisfaction of knowing that the vast majority of Texans shared his attitude. Indeed, many persons, overlooking Hardin's other activities, openly admired him for the fight he had carried on against an organization they abhorred. And this won Hardin a sort of legendary status summed up in one statement, which, like all legends, was somewhat of an exaggeration: "Before he was twenty-one, Wes Hardin vanquished the state police from the Rio Grande to Red River and from Matamoros to Sabine Pass."

But the good news of the demise of the state police came too late for Wes.

13

The Men of Mustang Mot

On the day after the police bill was killed, but before the word had penetrated into the Sandies country, Wes, Manning Clements, George Tenelle, and several other men were out hunting cattle. Upon his return home, Wes found Jane in tears. She was clutching Molly as if she feared the baby would be snatched from her arms.

That afternoon had been the most frightening of her life, she told Wes. Jack Helm and about fifty other men had surrounded the house and called for Wes. They had talked roughly to her, threatening her because she had refused to tell them where he had gone. Then they had asked her questions about the Taylors and Wes's attitude toward them. They had taunted and insulted her when she refused to answer.

Hardin's eyes flashed a deadly gray, and his sunburned face flushed slightly. Never before had he been called on to defend the honor of his wife; never before had he felt concern for the safety of his little daughter. If Jack Helm, who had schemed so craftily to get Wes into the feud on his side, had planned carefully a full year he couldn't have contrived a surer way to make a deadly enemy of Wes. Shooting down armed men was one thing; riding through the community and threatening women was another. Wes had strayed from his early teachings in many ways, but he had never abandoned the ideas of honor, chivalry, and the protection of the home. Wes had never spoken a profane or indecent word to a woman. Always he had respected women regardless of their character or behavior. In Abilene he had persuaded Wild Bill Hickok to release three dancehall girls who had been picked up and led off to jail.

Like other men on the frontier, Wes had often ridden away and left Jane alone in the little house, there to shift for herself until his return, but that was accepted custom; a man had to make the living and on the frontier he had to be away from home often in order to do it.

But to take advantage of any woman, and especially a defenseless young mother—that was a violation of the code. It was an outrage, a reason for killing on sight. The thought that Helm or any other man—let alone fifty of them—would threaten and insult Jane enraged Wes and his hands automatically encircled the handles of his pistols.

Taking Molly from Jane, he said: "I'll have to make a little ride tonight."

But he didn't have to ride alone. Within a short time, Manning Clements and George Tenelle showed up at his house. They were in a rage. The mob of riders had stopped at their homes and threatened and frightened their families also.

Seeing the handwriting on the wall, the three men decided then and there to join the Taylors and make unrelenting war on Helm and the Sutton party. Manning was given the task of sending word to Jim Taylor to get several of his key men together for a night meeting in Mustang Mot. This large clump of trees was one of the best known landmarks in the region; in years past, wild mustangs had watered at a small lake nearby and then shaded in the grove, giving the mot its name.

A few nights later, a lone horseman rode into the mot; then another and another. Each man came singly to the secret conference—Wes Hardin, Jim, John and Scrap Taylor, Manning Clements, George Tenelle, and thirty others. They tied their horses and formed in a circle in the center of the mot. Six sentries stood behind trees at the edge of the grove to make sure there were no spies and to warn of a possible attack.

This was as angry and as tough a group of men as ever assembled on the Western frontier.

Hardin announced that he and his friends were ready to join the Taylors in an unending war on the Sutton men because "they have stooped to abuse innocent women and children."

Jim Taylor, the head of his clan since the death of old Pitkin, stepped out of the circle and suggested that Wes Hardin be made head of the Taylor party and that all men in it follow his leadership. Yells of approval made this selection unanimous.

Wes, who was by far the youngest man in the group, had some immediate plans—to kill the leaders, Jack Helm, Jim Cox, Bill Sutton; to shoot any or all of them down on sight. Moreover, Wes advised the men to go on the offensive, to gang up and hunt down their enemies, "and put an end to mob law."

His trip to Mustang Mot that night marked the beginning of a new era for Wes Hardin as irrevocably as his journey on Old Paint to the sugar-cane harvest had catapulted him into serious trouble when he was fifteen years old. Before the night in the mot he had been a lone wolf, often feeling himself a man with a mission; but that night he became a member of a group —more than that, he became the general. His enthusiasm flamed. He was a commanding officer with his army in the field and a battle in view. He was in the feud, and he was in there to win; the ends justified the means, he felt. He was impatient with those who were wishy-washy or suffered pricks of doubt as to the rightness of their proposed deeds. Wes had studied law at Round Rock—but in the Sandies he was the law.

The change of leadership in the Taylor party brought quick results. Within a month after the Mustang Mot meeting, Jim Cox and a man named Christman were ambushed and killed by Taylor men. Wes was generally credited with engineering this ambush, but he was not present when the shooting took place.

Armed with shotguns loaded with buckshot and with pistols, Wes and Jim Taylor took out after Jack Helm, who was now more difficult to find. This hunt took them to the village of Albuquerque in neighboring Wilson County on a day in May. They had taken a look at the town without finding their quarry and were leaving when Wes's horse broke a shoe. They stopped at a blacksmith's to have the horse shod and struck up conversation with three or four men who were hanging around the shop.

When the shoeing was finished, Jim was squatting on his heels talking to the men. Wes had removed his shotgun from the saddle and was replacing it.

Someone yelled, and Wes looked around—to see Jack Helm lunging at Jim Taylor with a long knife. Helm and half a dozen others had appeared suddenly and without warning. Whirling, Wes fired a charge of buckshot into Helm's chest. He then dropped his gun on Helm's surprised men and drove them away. Helm, who turned out to be a fighter to the last, sprang up and made another thrust at Taylor. Jim poured several bullets into his head.

Wes and Jim jumped on their horses and galloped away.

They now turned their efforts to Bill Sutton. He had moved some fifty miles to Victoria and was keeping out of sight. Wes and Jim went to Victoria and searched for Sutton several days, but failed to find him.

Hardin's Mustang Mot call to the offensive began to take shape. But most of the Sutton forces were not scared, running, or hiding; they were going on the offensive, too.

And now there was a prospect of pitched battles involving as many as two hundred men to the side; the struggle was no longer a feud but a war. Men of leadership in the region, who because of their standing as citizens or their determination had remained aloof from the feud, began to get together to discuss means of ending the useless fight. They launched a course of reasoning and persuasion. Twice that summer the warring parties maneuvered into battle position with more than one hundred men to the side; each time peace-loving citizens persuaded the feuding factions to hold their fire. Twice the parties signed peace treaties and had them officially notarized.

Each time, Wes Hardin was a signatory, and each time Jim Taylor signed with one stipulation, that Bill Sutton was excepted as far as he was concerned. If possible, Jim would keep the graveside promise to his mother.

The kind of aggressive citizenship that had led prominent citizens into the Sutton-Taylor feud as peacemakers was spreading over Texas. Change was coming to the sprawling frontier state. For the first time since the end of the Civil War, Texans could vote that November of 1873 without standing under guns. And they resoundingly defeated Governor Davis, who had lost most of his grip on the state with the outlawing of his police force.

Richard Coke, a Democrat, was elected governor. Davis contested the election, and the courts, which he had controlled, upheld him. Therefore, in January of 1874, when it was time to change governors, Davis refused to surrender the office.

Coke moved in with an armed guard and occupied one end of the capitol at Austin, and Davis, also with an armed guard, held the other end. While this stalemate was in effect, several newspapers suggested that if Texans really wished to get rid of Governor Davis they should send John Wesley Hardin to Austin.

But Davis paid no attention to such jibes. He appealed to President Grant to sustain him and oust Coke with federal troops. The President declined and in effect repudiated Davis, who then backed out of the capitol into obscurity.

About this time, Wes, who could now travel about Texas without fear of a state police, took Jane and little Molly to Comanche to visit relatives—lots of them. Preacher and Mrs. Hardin had moved their family to this Central Texas town, where their son Joe was lawyer, real estate agent, and postmaster. A flock of other Hardin kinsmen had also come westward to this community. Alec Barrickman, who had been with Wes at the circus camp at Horn Hill, was there; so were some of the Dixons, relatives of the late Simp Dixon.

The Hardin clan in Comanche was on the natural increase, too. Joe and his wife had a little daughter, Dora Dean, and they were expecting another baby. Ma Hardin was expecting her seventh child.

While going about town with Joe, Wes bought a fine quarter racing horse named Rondo. Joe had a dandy racer he called Shiloa, and the brothers worked out their horses together.

It was a happy family reunion, and a hopeful one for Preacher Hardin and his wife. The conditions and the issues which had made Wes a fugitive and a killer at the age of fifteen were no more. The offers of rewards for Hardin, dead or alive, had been forgotten, and no county was seeking him to bring him to trial on the old charges; there had not even been an indictment in the Morgan killing at Cuero. For the parents, this looked like the day for which they had prayed so often. They didn't know that Wes had gone far beyond the calling of an unreconstructed rebel.

Wes soon took his wife and baby back to the Sandies. He knew that a man—at least one more—had to be killed.

14

Twenty-First Birthday

Only one star protagonist remained on the Sutton side of the feud. As long as he lived it would be a fight to the finish; with him gone, perhaps peace could be made real. All vows would be fulfilled and the last connection with the old Regulators broken. That man was Bill Sutton and it seemed as if he led a life of fantastic luck. On two occasions since the time Jim Taylor had plugged Sutton's arm, two horses had been shot from under him, but Bill had not been hurt.

While rounding up longhorns early in 1874 for the Kansas trail, Wes garnered the very valuable information that Sutton planned to send a herd overland, take a boat at Indianola for New Orleans, and then travel by train to Kansas to receive his cattle. Sutton was not riding himself; he and his wife had a new baby, and Bill was staying out of range of the feuding guns. However, behind the scenes he was still directing the actions of the Sutton party.

Wes's chance to get a line on Sutton came early in March

when Joe Hardin and Alec Barrickman rode down from Comanche for a visit. Joe desired a first-hand look at his brother's situation. Wes told Joe and Alec that Bill Sutton was his deadly enemy and was all that stood between him and a new life—or perhaps any life at all. With his argument that the killing of Sutton could end the feud he was able to talk Joe and Alec into going into Indianola to gather exact facts on how and when Sutton would leave for New Orleans; he didn't try to conceal his plan, but told Joe and Alec frankly that the information they obtained would be given to Jim Taylor and his brother Bill, and that the Taylors would try their best to kill Sutton. Wes explained why Jim felt honor bound to wash his hands in Sutton's blood.

It was almost inconceivable that peaceful Joe Hardin, who had avoided trouble even during the most troublous days, could be talked into an assignment like this. However, Joe and Alec did their work well. They even talked to Sutton and got directly from him the information that he was to sail from Indianola on the *Clinton* bound for New Orleans at a specific hour on March 11.

This word was passed to Wes and then to Jim and Billy Taylor. Wes had several men branding his cattle at Indianola that day so close to the Ides of March. Two swift horses stood saddled at his stock pens. Half-a-dozen friends were stationed at strategic points in the port town. Jim and Billy Taylor kept out of sight, biding their time.

At the appointed hour, Sutton, his wife, and Gabe Slaughter stepped aboard the *Clinton*. Slaughter, a Virginian, had lived in the vicinity only a short while, and he had no interest in the Taylor-Sutton war. No one knew why he happened to be with Sutton that day; it was a happenstance that made his name dreadfully fitting.

Jim and Billy walked to the deck of the *Clinton* so boldly

that Sutton was taken unaware. His charmed life was over. Jim Taylor kept the graveside promise to his mother. Billy killed Slaughter. All this happened so suddenly that everyone who saw and heard it was stunned. The Taylors dashed off the boat, hurried to the stock pens and mounted the horses waiting there; they didn't stop until they reached Wes Hardin's roundup camp far out in the country.

This carefully executed killing rocked Texas and focused state-wide attention on the Taylor-Sutton feud; it caused the speedy reorganization of the Texas Rangers, who had been outlawed during the state police era, and the establishment of the Frontier Battalion, which had its first assignment in De-Witt and Gonzales Counties.

Meanwhile, Wes worried about Jane and Molly, fearing that they were in grave danger of retaliation while he was on the Kansas trip. So he sent them out to Comanche with Joe and Alec.

Wes put his cattle on the trail with Joe Clements in charge. The other Clements—Manning, Gip, and Jim—were also going up the trail with various herds. Billy Taylor had been arrested and quickly taken to Galveston aboard the *Clinton* and jailed there out of reach of Gonzales guns. This left Jim Taylor, and he didn't relish the idea of staying in his home community with all his supporters gone. So he and Wes decided to get together another herd for the trail; Jim could go with Wes to receive the cattle. They hired J. B. (Doc) Bockius as trail boss, and his hands included Jim White, Kute Tuggle, and Scrap Taylor, a cousin of Jim.

Doc Bockius was a small, kindly-faced man of mystery; no one knew the first thing about his background or why he was in Gonzales County. He was not a doctor but he doctored and he delivered babies. He operated a little store and the post office at Sedan south of Smiley in the Sandies country. Once a man on horseback who was delivering several bottles of medicine to Sedan was caught in a hard rain without a slicker, and the labels slipped off the bottles and became mixed. Doc Bockius examined the medicine and tasted each bottle; then he relabeled it, and the people took the medicine with full confidence.

Doc had been friendly with all, bestowing a smile, a nod, and a kind word on everyone. He had never shown any favoritism until he was captivated by the audacious personality of Wes Hardin. Taking a job with Wes and Jim placed him squarely in their camp.

With this second herd started, Wes and Jim went on to Comanche, leading Wes's race horse Rondo behind their double buggy. Wes rejoined Jane and Molly and his parents' family, who took Jim Taylor into their home as "a friend of Johnny's."

Wes and Joe Hardin talked plans for some racing. While they worked out and trained Rondo and Shiloa, Wes made a deal to buy a little bunch of cattle from Joe and put them in the Hardin-Taylor herd when it passed through that part of the country.

Joe's cattle were twenty miles west of town in Brown County. They had been in litigation, but Joe had come legally to own them. However, he was not positive he could take possession of the stock without trouble with the previous owner. So when Joe was ready to go for the cattle he arranged to take along a Comanche County deputy sheriff, Bill Cunningham, who really had no jurisdiction in Brown County. Joe also asked some cousins—Jim and Ham Anderson, Bill and Tom Dixon, and Alec Barrickman—to make the trip with him.

Having nothing else to do, Wes and Jim Taylor decided to

go along "to see the country." The result was that Joe Hardin had no trouble in taking possession of his cattle and driving them home. But this didn't end the incident.

Word spread over Brown County that Joe Hardin had invaded the county with two of Texas' best known gunmen and feudists. Many residents resented this. The sheriff's department was especially disturbed because a Comanche County deputy had made the trip. Immediately reprisals were planned against Comanche County and, if possible, Wes Hardin and Jim Taylor.

Not knowing of the simmering resentment they had caused, Wes and Joe together with Bud Dixon matched some horse races for May 26; they would put Rondo, Shiloa, and Bud's horse, Dock, on the track. The early matching was made so that word of the races could be well circulated, thereby assuring a crowd and money for wagering.

While waiting for the event, which was set for Wes's twenty-first birthday, one more Hardin relative came into the world. Little Joe Hardin, Jr., put in his appearance on May 24.

Comanche was a small place, its stores, saloons, and liveries scattered around a large square, the rock courthouse in the center. It was a comparatively new town very close to the Western frontier of Texas, and it seldom had great excitement except for an occasional shooting or matched quarter horse races.

The town came excitedly alive on May 26. Men rode in from miles around, some on horseback, many in wagons, buggies, and hacks. As in Gonzales, there were large numbers of live oaks around Comanche, and there were horses tied to every one. The doors to the saloons swung constantly.

The biggest event on the schedule was the Rondo race. He was matched against a mare that had once beaten him, but this was before Wes had trained the horse.

Just before the races, something happened that made Wes's eyes turn a suspecting gray.

Three of his cousins called him aside and told him that Charles Webb, a deputy sheriff from Brown County, and a dozen or more other men from that county were in Comanche and that Deputy Webb had been boasting that he intended to kill Wes at the race track.

"I hope he'll put it off," Wes quipped. It was time for the races.

The horses belonging to Wes, Joe, and Bud Dixon won every race. Wes was jubilant. He had won three thousand dollars in cash, fifty head of cattle, two wagons, and fifteen saddle horses.

It was a clean sweep for the Hardins, and no one could say the races were crooked. Yet the losers weren't very content; they didn't like to see a nonresident—especially such a well-known one—come into town and make off with that much loot. Wes attempted to assuage any hurt feelings by being the good winner and setting up the drinks. At one place he threw a handful of gold coins onto the bar and invited everyone to step up and drink on him.

The town square was crowded with men, women, and children, and everywhere in sight there were more horses, buggies, hacks, wagons. Wes and his friends went from saloon to saloon to celebrate. At one of these, Jim Anderson whispered to Wes that the word was out that Charles Webb had "sworn to kill Wes Hardin before sundown or die in the attempt." Wes immediately asked his little brother, Jeff Davis, to go to Joe Hardin's stable and get a horse and buggy to drive him and Jim Taylor to the home of Wes's parents out in the country a couple of miles.

Wes, Jim Taylor, and several others stood around in front of the Polk Wright Saloon on the northwest corner of the square.

Little Jeff Davis Hardin drove up in the buggy, stopped, and called to Wes that he was ready to go.

Wes proposed to buy one more round of drinks. Jim Taylor met him at the door and suggested that he drink no more, that he would like to go with him to his father's home. About then, someone called out:

"Yonder comes that damned Brown County sheriff."

Wes looked around and saw a man with two pistols swinging low walking along the street. The man was Charles Webb. He had one hand behind him and acted as if he were going to pass the saloon, but he stopped suddenly in front of Wes.

"Do you have any papers for my arrest?" Wes asked.

"I don't know you," Webb replied. "Who are you?"

Wes asked him what he had in his hand behind him, and Webb showed a stump of a cigar.

"Who are you, anyhow?" Webb asked.

"I'm the notorious John Wesley Hardin. I understand you've been saying that Sheriff John Carnes of Comanche County is no sheriff at all and has been harboring me, that you've come over here to attend to John Carnes's business and kill Wes Hardin before sundown or die in the attempt."

"Now I know you," Webb said. "I have no papers for your arrest. Besides, I'm not the sheriff of Brown County. I'm only a deputy. My name is Charles Webb. I'm not responsible for what the sheriff of Brown County does or says. Besides, I think Mr. Carnes is a brave officer and a gentleman."

"Then, Mr. Webb," Wes said, "there is no difference between us."

Someone in the crowd introduced the men. Wes invited Webb to have a drink or a cigar, and turned to go into the saloon. As he did so, he heard someone shout: "Look out!"

Wes sprang around. Webb was leveling a pistol on him. Wes

jumped to one side and pulled his pistol in the same movement. Webb fired and the bullet plowed through Wes's side.

Wes shot Webb in the head. A fraction of a second later, Jim Taylor and Bill Dixon shot Webb again as he crumpled. He fired another shot—wild, into the air—and fell. He was dead when he hit the street.

At that moment, thirteen-year-old Jeff Davis Hardin, who had been waiting in the buggy, whacked the rump of his horse with the end of the lines. The horse took off with a burst of speed almost equal to that of Rondo. Jeff Davis had seen his brother Johnny in action for the first time.

Men surged toward the corner. Almost as if by magic, nearly every man had a gun. The men from Brown County and the recruits they had picked up in Comanche—from the ranks of the heavy losers at the races—quickly formed into a mob and moved in toward Wes and his friends and cousins. The sheriff, with his shotgun cocked, stepped between Wes and the crowd. He was instantly disarmed.

For five years Wes Hardin had been deathly afraid of being cornered by a mob. Here at last was one, and it was howling its fury. Wes and Jim dashed across the street to some horses, Wes yanking out his pocket knife to cut the hitching ropes. As he and Jim mounted, the excited horses whirled so that the men were facing the mob. Taylor wanted to charge the surging men.

"No!" Wes shouted. "Don't do that!"

In a quick glance at the crowd, Wes saw Jane and their baby and his sister, Matt; he also got a glimpse of his father and Joe racing across the square toward him. But he and Jim Taylor whirled their horses and dashed out of town with bullets whizzing around their heads.

Within a matter of minutes, at least one hundred and fifty

men—armed with pistols, rifles, shotguns, knives, and clubs—milled in the public square and shouted for the blood of Wes Hardin and Jim Taylor. That was more men than lived in all Comanche, or even in the county. Apparently nearly all of them were from Brown County; they had invaded Comanche County just as the Joe Hardin party had invaded Brown County, and there was no doubt that they meant business. Sheriff Carnes quickly telegraphed for as many Texas Rangers as could be rushed to Comanche. The nearest detachments of Rangers were men on special assignment to this part of Texas and to the north, to protect settlers against Indian raids.

Meanwhile, Wes and Jim rode to the Hardin home and walked in. Wes's mother, who was closely approaching the time to give birth to her last child, was spreading creamy white icing on a layer cake for Wes's coming-of-age birthday. She was large now and looked much older than her years. Her once golden hair had turned to a sandy gray.

The instant she saw Wes, her half-smile faded. From her long years of experience with trouble, she knew that something was wrong. Then she saw the blood on Wes's shirt from the bullet hole in his side.

"You've been shot, Johnny!" she cried.

Within a moment or two she had soapy warm water, salve, and white cloth to clean and dress the wound. It was a flesh wound, not serious, but the kind that could be very painful. While the mother was busy with the dressing, Wes told her briefly what had happened.

"And he shot first?" she said. "You had to do it, Johnny?"

Just then the father with Joe, Alec Barrickman, Ham Anderson, Bud Dixon, and the sheriff arrived. Wes offered to surrender, along with Jim Taylor, provided the sheriff could guarantee protection from the mob.

"Hell," said the sheriff, "I can't do that. You ought to see that mob! And they may be out here any minute. If you don't want a fight right here you'd better get going."

It was quickly decided for Wes, Jim Taylor, Alec Barrickman, and Ham Anderson to ride to Round Mountain, some four miles away, and hide out until things cooled off.

Wes and Jim rode the horses they had so hurriedly appropriated in Comanche. They found water in a small stream that meandered at the foot of Round Mountain, but they had no food. They slept in the brush with their saddles at their heads and their horses tethered nearby.

The next morning Alec and Ham wanted to ride into Comanche to take a look at the situation; they argued that no doubt the excitement had subsided by this time. Jim Taylor was ready to go to Comanche and shoot it out if there were any opposition.

"No, we can't go in," Wes warned. "Always be sure about mobs before you take action. Joe will be out in a little while and we'll know then what to do."

The hours dragged on, and there was no Joe. Alec and Ham grew impatient, and also hungry. "It's my guess it's all over and they've forgotten about us," Ham suggested.

"We'd better wait," Wes said. "You know good and well Joe will be here if he can get here. If he doesn't come, we'll know something is bad wrong, and then we'll go in and see about it."

Shortly before noon the men looked down from their hillside hide-out and saw Joe and the Dixon brothers riding up the valley of the creek. They were leading two saddled horses. Wes ran anxiously to meet Joe and saw that he was haggard and worn.

Joe had brought the horses for Wes and Jim and saddle pockets filled with food and ground coffee.

"You can't go in—not for a good long while," Joe told them.

"The mob is everywhere—all around Pa's house and my house. The State Rangers are coming in. The sheriff can't keep the mob off you. The Rangers can't either, and I'm not sure they want to."

Joe told of a harrowing night, with an armed mob camped all around his father's home, and as big a mob at his own house. His wife, with their two-day-old son in bed with her, was hysterical with fright. Moreover, there were posses around the Barrickman and Dixon homes. Joe told the men that these posses were stationed around the homes to catch the men if they showed up and also to prevent the families from giving any help.

"It took me all morning to dodge around and get these horses and get out here," Joe explained. "We had to come about fifteen miles out of the way to give them the dodge."

Joe advised Wes to remain in hiding. They decided on definite spots where he would go if he were flushed—Joe would find him at one or the other and keep him informed of developments. Now that he and Jim had mounts of their own, Wes sent the "borrowed" horses and the pistols he had found in the saddle pockets back to Comanche by Joe. He also sent Jane a handful of gold.

An hour after Joe had left, Wes spied a posse circling Round Mountain. He and his men kept deep in the brush and later cut in behind the posse and moved to one of the places Joe had designated, a heavily wooded spot near a small lake.

For two days, Joe didn't come. Wes and his friends had no way of knowing what was happening in Comanche except what they could deduce from what they saw—posses of armed horsemen obviously searching for them. Wes was worried about his family, especially Jane and Molly. He knew, too, that it was nearing the time for Doc Bockius to show up in Comanche; he had been instructed to halt the

Hardin-Taylor herd at nearby Hamilton and ride into Comanche to report to West and Jim Taylor.

The wound Deputy Webb had put in Wes's side had swollen and was draining. With both worry and pain pressing on him, Wes decided to find out what was going on in Comanche. That night he and Jim Taylor left Alec and Ham in camp and rode stealthily to the vicinity of the Hardin home.

The night was cloudy and a drizzle was falling. Wes and Jim could see only the light in the house and a campfire in the yard near the well, but they could hear enough activity to convince them that at least thirty men and horses were stationed there. They inched up toward the place. Jim's horse stumbled over a tree stump and made a clattering noise in regaining his footing.

They heard a man yell. Then a roar of guns sounded in the midnight mist. Bullets whizzed close to the hiding men. They turned their horses and dashed away. Returning to camp, they learned that Alec and Ham had decided to go to the home of an acquaintance, a rancher, take him into their confidence, and remain there until the mob spirit died down. Wes advised them not to do it.

"When there's a mob, you have to be careful who you trust. We're leaving the country. You don't have to go with us, but I advise you to leave the country and stay gone for a good while."

But Alec and Ham were growing tired of hiding. Alec, particularly, yearned to get home to his young wife and baby.

"I think you're just scared of a mob, Wes," Alec said. "You know everybody in Comanche likes Joe and your pa. You know Joe and your pa can handle things."

But Alec hadn't heard the whizzing bullets at the Hardin home and he didn't have Wes's experience; he and Ham rode off to the trusted rancher's home.

The next morning the dark clouds hung low. Occasionally there was a jarring rumble of thunder; rain poured down and the whole soggy world seemed to drip. Every little ditch and draw was a raging torrent. Wes took a bloody handkerchief—the one he had used to swab the wound in his side—from his pocket and tied it to his shotgun so that it covered the caps and kept them dry. He and Jim started toward Gonzales County.

The weather had not deterred the posses. This was the first really big job of the newly organized State Rangers, and their orders were to get Wes Hardin and Jim Taylor at all costs. Captain Bill Waller was in charge of the man hunt, and by that time nearly all the men on the force stationed in Northern and Western Texas had been dispatched to assist him. The Rangers had figured that if Wes was cut off from communication with his family he would probably head for Gonzales; therefore, all routes leading toward Gonzales were under heavy guard, day and night.

Wes and Jim dodged several bands of armed and mounted men that morning. Just before noon they rode out of the brush to the edge of a prairie glade. Captain Waller, who was riding far in advance of a posse of about fifty men, saw the fugitives, and he charged them.

"Wait a minute, Jim," Wes said. "I guess he wants to become famous all at once."

Wes raised his shotgun at about the time the captain was within range, and pulled the trigger. At that instant a puff of wind flipped back the handkerchief. The hammer hit the handkerchief and the gun snapped, saving Waller's life. At that instant the captain stopped as if waiting for his men to catch up, and Wes and Jim took to the brush.

Later in the day, Wes and Jim spied a small grassy hill with a gentle slope ahead of them and decided this would be a good place to look around. They were riding more slowly now to give their tiring horses a chance to regain their wind.

As they started up the slope they heard a thunderous clatter behind them. They whirled quickly and saw a dozen horsemen riding directly toward them at a dead run. The men were still out of effective shooting range, but they were coming fast.

Wes and Jim spurred their horses and headed up the hill. They could see the tops of trees over the hill, and they hoped to reach that timber before the posse could overtake them.

When they reached the brow of the ridge they saw a posse of ten or fifteen men riding in a trot toward them. This new posse was between them and the protective timber. They stopped quickly and from this vantage point could see both posses.

"Not much choice here, Wes," Jim remarked. "I reckon this is it."

Remembering how his surprise charge on the posse north of Salty Creek in Gonzales County had demoralized the men, Wes said:

"Stick with me, Jim. We'll charge this bunch coming up from the timber."

They forced their horses and charged down the ridge at a run. Within a few seconds they were in the midst of the surprised men. Several of them had to yank their horses out of the way to avoid collision. The men were so amazed and confused that they didn't fire a shot. For one thing, shooting would have been almost impossible without hitting members of their own party.

As Wes and Jim crashed into the timber, the possemen recovered from their shock. A volley of bullets whistled and whined through the trees. One of them grazed Wes's horse in the rump, but it did not lame him.

Almost every step for nearly fifty miles Wes and Jim fought and dodged their way, at times having to backtrack to keep out of the way of the armed posses. They finally arrived in safer country near Austin on the dark night of June 5. Jim was almost dead of dysentery. Wes's wound, unattended for ten days, was badly festered and throbbing. They went to the home of a relative of Jim's about six miles from Austin, out in the dense cedar brake country, and there they rested and treated their ills.

Two nights later, on June 7, Alf Day (a nephew of Jim Taylor) and two other men who had been with the Hardin-Taylor herd, rode in on spent horses, their clothes in tatters and their faces matted with mud, blood and whiskers. The things Alf Day told Wes Hardin made him cry like a whipped little boy.

15

Hardin Blood

On the day after Wes and Jim had been greeted with bullets when they approached the Hardin house, Wes's father received a letter in an envelope bordered in jet black. The letter, which was also bordered in black, warned that if he turned a hand to assist Wes Hardin or to get information to him, Joe Hardin would be arrested and hanged—next the father, and then "your women folks" would be killed if a member of the family made a single effort to help Wes or refused to aid in his capture.

Hardin, his wife and children, and Jane didn't have long to speculate on this threat. Texas Rangers and sheriff's deputies arrived and arrested the preacher. He was taken to Joe's home, which was under guard. The officers also "quarantined" Alec Barrickman's family in Joe's house. Joe's wife, fearful for the lives of her babies, was violently ill.

On that same day, Doc Bockius, suspecting nothing, rode into Comanche, as he had been instructed to do, to tell Wes and Jim that the herd was at nearby Hamilton. More than one hundred men swarmed around Bockius, arrested him, and put him in jail. He was pumped for hours about the possible location of Wes and Jim. Some fifty armed men hurried to the herd at Hamilton, took it over, and arrested the six cowboys. Alf Day and his two companions—Ples Johnson and Pink Burns —escaped during a rainstorm, but the others—Scrap Taylor, Kute Tuggle, and Jim White—were taken to Comanche and jailed. Alf, Ples, and Pink ventured into the vicinity of Comanche to find out what had happened to Wes Hardin and Jim Taylor.

The next day the Rangers and the sheriff put Joe Hardin and Tom and Bud Dixon under technical arrest and placed them in the courthouse under guard; this was for their own protection and to keep them from communicating with Wes. The mob, and also the officers, knew that Joe had visited Wes the day after the Webb killing, for they had seen him return the horses Wes and Jim had borrowed.

Word of the various skirmishes of the Rangers and posses with Wes and Jim trickled into Comanche for a few days, and then there was no more news and the mob grew sullen and restive. The men milled in the square all day on June 5, the day Wes and Jim arrived in Austin. A minute past twelve o'clock that night a large part of the mob stormed into the courthouse. Dozens of men grabbed Joe, Tom, and Bud and forced them to take off their shoes; then the men looped strong ropes around their necks and led them out of the courthouse. Out on the square the howling mob enfolded the three barefooted men. Joe and the Dixons were led to a large live oak and hanged. Then a dozen men, having been tipped by the rancher as to where Alec Barrickman and Ham Anderson were hiding, rode out and shot Alec and Ham to death on the quilts on which they were sleeping.

The bodies of Joe, Bud, and Tom were left swinging the rest of the night. The next morning Joe's sister Matt slipped out and saw the bodies "cold in death." The families were afraid that if they stepped outside the house or made any attempt to recover the bodies, or even inquired about them, the elder Hardin and perhaps Jeff and the women and children of the families would be killed. The mob cut down the bodies and buried them in a grove out at the edge of town. Joe Hardin's grave was about midway between two live oaks.

The Barrickman family and the elder Hardin were permitted to go home, and the guard was taken off the Joe Hardin home, now that it was occupied only by a grief-stricken young widow and two babies. But they were warned that every action would be watched and that if any effort were made to help Wes Hardin the rest of the family would "be given justice." Preacher Hardin returned home, where his family and Wes's wife were in a state of terror; they had been told by men watching the house that Joe Hardin and the Dixons had been given their "just dues."

The mob made off with the Hardin-Taylor herd, along with the horses and equipment. Joe Hardin's cattle and his horses, including Shiloa, were taken. His widow managed somehow to get in touch with her family at Mt. Calm, and a relative came to Comanche for her. About all she managed to salvage from Joe's possessions were his desk name plate, his brand book, a permit to practice law, a certificate of his appointment as Comanche County Treasurer, a commission of his appointment as postmaster of Comanche in 1872, and a letter which was never mailed.

The letter, written on the letterhead of J. G. Hardin, Attorney at Law and Land Agent, Comanche, Texas, said:

Dear John Dean:

I leave here tonight to save my brother. I do not want fight in mine. Take charge of Shiloa and keep him in trim. Tell all my friends no one will be hurt.

Yours truly,
Joe G. Hardin.

The letter was undated. Apparently it was written hurriedly a few moments before Joe's arrest.

When Alf Day and his companions heard and saw the unbelievable things that had happened, and were happening, they had fled. Like Wes and Jim, they had dodged almost numberless posses.

During the time Alf hesitantly told of the tragedies in Comanche, Wes's face turned an ash gray. He buried his face in his arms; his shoulders shook. Finally he looked up at Day.

"I just don't believe it, Alf," he said. "Nobody would hang a man like Joe Hardin."

"That's what I heard, Wes," Alf replied. "I'm afraid it's so. I don't know what'll happen to Doc Bockius and the other boys."

There was no doubt about what Wes would do. He headed back to Comanche, leaving Alf Day to accompany the ailing Jim Taylor to Gonzales County. Arriving at his father's place at midnight, Wes tied his horse far from the house and crept to the well in the yard. There was no sign of life in or about the house. Wes drew a bucket of water and the rope pulley squeaked slightly.

Presently a man approached. Wes leveled his rifle. When the man was ten steps away, Wes said: "Your life depends on your action."

"Don't shoot, Johnny," the man said. "I'm here to help."

Wes looked the man over and questioned him sharply. He identified himself as Jack Wade. He said he had been hired by the elder Hardin to do orchard work and to be on guard at night so that if Wes showed up he could be warned not to be seen near Comanche lest the entire family be killed.

Wes asked about Joe and was told of the hanging and the shooting.

"Could you take me to Joe's grave?" Wes asked.

Wade said it was within fairly easy walking distance. With Wes leading his horse, they walked stealthily to the grove of live oaks. Wes then sent Wade back to the house to talk to his father and ask whether it would be all right for him to stop briefly in the house and see the family and Jane and Molly.

Wes remained alone at the grave.

The new mound was muddy from the recent rains. Wes stood and looked down on it. For the first time, he, who had taken so many lives, realized what death meant.

The misty darkness closed in about Wes. He stooped, resting on one heel, and laid his hand on the heaped wet clods with the same brotherly touch that he had used so often in flinging his arm around Joe's shoulders. Time stood still and memories took the place of tears.

Wes's eyelids closed and scenes flashed into his vision so quickly and yet so clearly it was as if his life up to that moment had truly been but a twinkling of the eye. Always there had been steadfast Joe to depend on. When he had stabbed the boy in school, Joe had backed him up. After he had had to shoot old Mage, Joe had told him over and over that it was the only thing he could have done. While he was hiding from the Yankees and Joe was teaching school, he had felt safe just knowing Joe was near. Then when the Yankee soldiers did come and he outsmarted them and shot all three of the blue uniforms full of holes, Joe had worked harder than any of the neighboring men burying them and camouflaging their graves. And if it hadn't been for Joe's helping him at Round Rock he would never have eluded the state police and passed the course in law with Professor Landrum. Those long nights when he and Joe argued cases back and forth—Joe always stood for the letter of the law, and he always wanted the spirit of the law to count—were some of the best memories a brother could have.

Now, because of him, Joe was dead.

He had endangered Joe's life before, Wes suddenly realized. Indirectly many times, but he had done it outright when he had asked Joe to go to Indianola and sleuth out the plans of Bill Sutton. Joe had done that job well and the seemingly charmed life of Sutton had been ended. The audacity of those men of the Sutton gang to think they could insult and threaten his wife and child and escape his wrath! Without Joe's help it would have taken longer to get the prize of them all.

The incongruity of fate, Wes thought. All the agony, all the loss his family was now undergoing was not because of some great wrong he had done, but because Deputy Webb had tried to kill him just as Mage had done so long ago, and he had simply protected his own life. A right every man possessed. Yet because of that deputy, the mob had done this to Joe—and his cousins. Every single man responsible would pay for it. If they had wanted to kill someone for saving his own life they should have been smart enough to kill the right man—not innocent ones.

Deputy Webb and the other forty-odd men he had shot had received only what was their just due, he felt. He had done no more to them than they no doubt had already done to men less expert on the draw than Wes Hardin. But because

Joe had helped him preserve his life, his had been sacrificed. Here, Wes felt, lay the only man he had murdered.

And in the dark, back in his father's house were all the rest of those he loved best. He realized that because of his disregard of consequences he was not only responsible for his brother's death at the hands of a frenzied, bloodthirsty mob, but he was jeopardizing the lives of all his family. He desperately wanted to see his father, hear his mother's voice, and put his arms around Jane and the baby, to reassure himself that they were all right. A few weeks before he might have dashed to them, feeling he could outfight whatever threatened. But now the new mound at his feet held him. Wes had bumped into something he couldn't outshoot, outguess, outrun. Perhaps he could always keep himself invulnerable. He always had, but the mob had discovered his Achilles' heel, his family.

Wes was still standing, gazing down at the grave, when Wade called softly, "Johnny," and then walked up. He reported:

"Your pa says not to come about the house. He wouldn't let me wake up your wife for fear she might raise a fuss to come see you. He says if you're seen around Comanche your wife and baby and the whole family may be taken out and killed. Your pa says to make sure you keep away from here. He says to be sure to tell you not ever to surrender. . . ."

More swiftly and more quietly than he had ever done before, Wes mounted his horse. "Tell them I'll be in the Sandies," he whispered, and with only a few crackles of broken twigs on the soft, damp ground under his horse's hoofs, he disappeared into the night.

Wes found Gonzales County no haven of safety. Jim Taylor was still sick and holed up because of the gunning activities of the Sutton party. All of Wes's most stalwart friends except

George Tenelle were on the trail to Kansas. Wes managed to get a dozen men together and pitched an armed camp on Elm Creek near his home. These were loyal cohorts but they weren't bold, experienced, and dependable in the heat of battle.

Wes was so concerned about Jane and the baby that he risked a trip to Doc Bockius' old establishment at Sedan, which was being operated by others during Doc's absence, to see whether Jane had been able to slip out a letter. There *was* a letter from Comanche—from Ranger Captain Waller. He informed Wes that he was sending some prisoners (Scrap Taylor, Doc Bockius, Tuggle, and White) from Comanche to Clinton in DeWitt County and that if their guard was attacked Wes's father and brother Jeff, and perhaps Jane and the baby, would be held responsible.

The prisoners were delivered in Clinton without incident and placed in the courthouse under guard because the small jail was full. The enemies of Wes Hardin and the Taylors couldn't have asked for a better setup for what they had in mind. And they took full advantage. On a stormy night late in June a mob of forty men connected with the Sutton forces, surrounded the little courthouse, and demanded that the prisoners be turned over to them.

The man in charge of the jail facilities in the courthouse—Jim Wofford—stood on the courthouse steps, brandished his rifle menacingly and yelled out that he would shoot the first man who made a move. A man who had taken advantage of the darkness to worm to a position behind the jailer rammed a pistol into his ribs and warned: "You won't shoot but just once."

The four cowboy prisoners were led out barefooted and bareheaded into the night. Lightning flashed almost constantly in the low, dripping clouds and there was an occasional growl of thunder. A crowd of men on foot and on horses milled in the street. Joe Sunday, an enormously fat man, rode along the line of march. A tentlike slicker covered him and hung down over most of his horse. Between flashes of lightning, Sunday snatched Doc Bockius, pulled him up on the horse and quickly got him under the slicker; then Sunday took off with the rescued prisoner.

The mob marched the other three—all young kids—to a dripping tree near the cemetery and hanged them and left the bodies swinging the rest of the night.

16

Where There's a Will—

Texas, the state his forefathers had helped found and the state he dearly loved, had become a place of torment for Wes.

He had not dared lift a hand to help his cowboys for fear of reprisals on his wife, child, and family in Comanche. Two hundred members of the Sutton forces in DeWitt and Gonzales Counties, emboldened by the success of their rainy night's work in Clinton and still at white heat over the killing of Bill Sutton, rode the countryside constantly, trying to smoke him out. Although he had shot only one man, Charlie Webb, in self-defense at the beginning of this nightmarish ordeal, the vengeful mobs had taken the lives of eight men who were guilty of nothing except association with him. And, to top it all, the Texas Rangers were hot on his trail.

There was no one to whom Wes could turn. Jim Taylor was still sick and in hiding. George Tenelle, almost the only man in the Sutton-Taylor trouble to have attained middleage, was in the Sandies, but he was also hounded. Manning Clements,

Wes's most trusted cousin, was meandering up the long trail to Kansas with only a herd of cattle and perhaps recalcitrant cowboys to worry about. His brother Joe was dead. His father was forbidden to him. In the past, in time of crisis, they had all advised him, though he had ignored their advice, depended on his own judgment and done as he pleased. Now he *must* use his own judgment.

His judgment coincided with the advice his father had given him three years before. He could try to escape into Mexico. But the years had added to the danger and to the difficulty of that. He could not face life in Mexico or anywhere else without Jane. He would have to rescue his wife and baby.

He sent word of his decision to George Tenelle, and big George decided to follow suit, give up feuding and Texas, and find sanctuary in Mexico. He mounted his fleetest horse, Old Cibolo, for a dash to the border. A patrol of the Sutton party spied him and shot him to death in a cornfield.

George's bloody end changed the direction of Wes's plan of flight. In the middle of a moonless night he met his father-in-law, Neal Bowen, and hired him to go to Wichita and receive and sell the herd Joe Clements had driven up the Chisholm Trail. Then, employing every ounce of knowledge and ability that six years of hunted, precarious riding back and forth across his state had given him, Wes, with haste and ghostly quietness, slithered out of Gonzales County. He headed for a previous refuge—the home of his uncle at Brenham.

His uncle and cousins had just finished hoeing a fine cotton field and the crop of corn had been laid by waiting for the summer sun to turn the green ears golden. His aunt had two fryers sizzling in the black iron skillet on the hot cookstove thirty minutes after Wes, exhausted, dirty, and worried, came into her house. Time seemed to have stood still on the neat farm and Wes felt that only he had aged. After he told them of his plight and of the perilous situation of his family in Comanche, Wes saw an instantaneous change in his relatives. His Uncle Bob and his cousins bristled. His oldest cousin extended a work-hardened hand to Wes and volunteered to go to Comanche, bide his time, and slip away with Jane and Molly. Not all the daring Hardin blood flowed in Wes's veins.

While sweating out the dragging days, Wes made the acquaintance of a Brenham peace officer named Swain, who was a brother-in-law of one of Wes's cousins; this slight family link was sufficient for a warm friendship. So Wes had some protection from the law; moreover, Swain agreed to help him get out of Texas and into Louisiana.

Wes had one more dangerous undertaking—a trip back to Gonzales County to settle with Neal Bowen and get the money for the cattle; he would need this money. By the time he returned to Brenham, Jane and Molly were there. The reunion was joyous, although there was no time even for talking. Wes set out immediately on horseback for New Orleans, and a few days later the Swains followed with Jane and Molly. In honor of the man who had been so helpful, Wes adopted the name of J. H. Swain for the time of his exile.

Jane and Molly had never before tasted store-bought ice cream, and the family spent a great deal of time in the ice-cream salons of New Orleans, which Wes called "saloons." During ten days of fun and freedom in the old city, Wes sprouted a black, stubby mustache, his only effort at disguise. Since her husband was now known as J. H. Swain, Jane had to break her habit of calling him Wes, for that could be a giveaway; she called him John.

The most exciting experience for the land-loving, prairie-riding Hardins was a steamboat trip across the Gulf of Mexico. They landed in Cedar Keys, Florida, and went to Gainsville, where Wes bought a small saloon. On his second day as a business man he met the city marshal and became friendly with him.

Three days later Wes, glancing out the door, saw the marshal having trouble with several Negro men who were attempting to prevent his taking one of their friends to jail. A group of curious onlookers had gathered. The streak of the fanatic that was deep in Hardin's make-up quickly overpowered any idea of caution; he couldn't keep out of a fight, regardless of whether it was for or against law and order. He bolted out of the saloon, dashed up to the marshal and offered "as a citizen of Florida" to help him. The marshal deputized him to keep back the crowd. Thereupon, Wes pulled a pistol from a shoulder holster and held the surprised mob while the marshal jailed the prisoner.

Wes later moved his family to Jacksonville, where he bought cattle and sold them to butcher shops. Business was good, trouble stayed away from the door longer than ever before, and the family enjoyed normal living.

Wes subscribed to *The Galveston News* to keep posed on events in the home state. For a few weeks he and Jane read sensational stories about what Wes was supposed to be doing in Texas.

Senator Stephens of Comanche, with a fresh memory of what had happened in his town during the summer, introduced in the Texas legislature a resolution to pay a four-thousand-dollar reward for the capture of John Wesley Hardin. This passed both houses, and the reward, the largest ever offered by Texas, was posted; whoever caught Wes would come into this good-sized fortune.

Then the stories broke fast and furiously: *The Galveston*

News reported that Senator Stephens had received a letter from Wes Hardin threatening to kill him . . . A man positively identified as Hardin had been seen in Austin . . . Hardin had part of his old Taylor gang in Austin looking for the senator . . . Austin was on edge . . . The senator was in the center of attention. He was provided with a body-guard to protect him from Hardin.

All the time Wes and Jane were in Florida, and it was there in Jacksonville that John Wesley Hardin, Jr., arrived on August 3, 1875. For the duration of their exile, the baby, like his father, had to go under an assumed name, J. H. Swain, Jr.

Soon thereafter, Wes sensed that old demon, trouble. He was shadowed by two men; everywhere he went, one or the other of the men popped up. Wes was on such friendly terms with the sheriff and police that he risked asking them about the shadowing. The sheriff told him the men were probably Pinkerton detectives.

The scheme of the detectives was obvious: they suspected that J. H. Swain was John Wesley Hardin; they would make sure of this and then spring the capture and collect the four-thousand-dollar reward.

Wes quickly sent Jane and the children to the home of some of her father's relatives in Alabama, and then he fled, taking along a Jacksonville policeman who reminded Wes of Manning Clements—there was a bond and no questions asked. They went to New Orleans, where Wes intended to take a boat for Mexico, but the detectives stood between him and the docks. He and the friend doubled back eastward; on several occasions they had a chance to shoot down the detectives, but their idea was to shake them and head for Alabama.

One night Wes and the policeman jumped off a train at a small town on the Florida-Georgia line; they would hide out and catch the next train in the direction from which they had come. However, the detectives were on their heels; they had been on the same train and had also stepped off.

Wes and his friend hid in a large weedy area back of the depot. Within a little while they saw the detectives walking slowly toward them.

"This makes me just a little bit mad," Wes said.

"Hands up!" one of the detectives yelled.

They charged at Wes with their revolvers out.

He jerked out his gun, and with shots so close together they sounded almost as one he put a ball in the head of each detective. Then he and his friend took to the woods and made their way to the next town.

When they were out of danger, the Jacksonville policeman said, "Great guns, man! I never saw such quick shooting in all my life. It made me think of what I've heard about that wild man, John Wesley Hardin, in Texas."

"I've heard of him," Wes replied.

Their mission accomplished, the two went their separate ways. Wes's way led to Alabama, where he joined Jane and the children. They settled in the vicinity of Polland, where one of Jane's relatives, Neal McMellon, was sheriff; he was a man who believed in the adage that blood is thicker than water, and the secret of the Hardins was safe with him. Like some places in Texas, Polland was a sort of nest of kinfolks, and Jane's brother, Brown Bowen, showed up there. Brown had wandered about Florida and Alabama ever since the Christmas-time killing of Tom Halderman at Billings' store in 1872, and although he had married, he had never settled down in one spot. He worked occasionally at nearby Pensacola Junction over the line in Florida but spent a great deal of time with the Hardins.

Being broke and having to start all over after his adventure with the detectives, Wes fell back on work he knew well, buying, selling, and swapping horses. He made a living at this but was always looking for something better. By the spring of 1877, he was on the Stick River in Florida, some sixty miles west of Polland, trying to get a logging business started. This didn't go well at first, and it kept him away from home much of the time, making life trying for Jane. With two children to feed, and another one due very soon, she needed money and she wrote Wes at Milview, Florida, asking for twenty dollars.

He replied: "I would send you twenty dollars, but the money I have is scrip. But I will send you some money or some things to live on next week, if I live."

After explaining some of his business difficulties, he said in his note: "Jane, be in cheer, old gal, you know that it is a hard wind that never ceases. . . . Help a worn and weary brother pulling hard against the storm."

For the sake of safety, Wes and Jane had not written anyone in Texas and had not heard a word from any of their people. On April 28, 1877, a day when Wes had been away for three weeks, Jane was so lonely and blue that she decided to take a chance on getting some direct news from home. If Wes had been at home she never would have done it, but she wrote her uncle, Joshua Bowen, in Gonzales County. He replied promptly with disturbing news. The Sutton forces had killed Jim Taylor. There was talk all over the county that the Texas Rangers had information that Brown Bowen was in Alabama and that they were planning to have him arrested. He warned Wes, Jane, and Bowen to hide out as deep in the backwoods as possible.

"Everything has changed here under this New Constitution," he wrote. "They have got state Rangers nearly all over the state. They have got a book published with three thousand names and descriptive list of every man that has fled from justice in this state, and they are picking them in every direction."

Jane had no idea how costly the tidbits of news from home would prove to be.

Wes Hardin had not set foot in Texas in nearly three years, but he had left a growing legend there. A phantom John Wesley Hardin haunted the big state day and night. Reports like those of three years before about the threats against Senator Stephens of Comanche had never ceased. Every time there was a particularly bold shooting and the gunman was not identified, the newspapers were positive that Wes Hardin had returned—if, indeed, he had ever left.

On one occasion, when the State Savings Bank at Dallas was robbed, *The Dallas Herald* took the stand that, "It was the John Wesley Hardin gang, and if not Hardin, the James-Younger gang."

Scores of men who sought attention claimed to be Wes Hardin or else that they were buddies of his and had seen him lately. Often these stories were taken to police or sheriffs. One day Eugene McGee told officers Hamil and Spencer of Dallas that John Wesley Hardin was in the city. "Shook hands with Wes just a little while ago," he said.

McGee told the officers—in strictest confidence—that Wes would be in a certain house at the edge of town that night and that he would go with them to arrest him and claim the reward. The officers surprised a man at the house and shot him to death. He fell against a wall and crumpled down on his face. The men rolled him over and discovered to their horror that they had killed a peaceful citizen named J. Monroe.

One of the many Wes-is-right-here reports involved Ranger Lieutenant John Armstrong. Tipped that Wes Hardin was in a saloon, Armstrong strolled in and offered to buy the suspect a drink. The man accepted and walked to the bar with the

Ranger. When the moment seemed exactly right, Armstrong pulled his big six-gun and rammed it in the suspect's stomach. The man almost died of fright; he was one of the few Texans who had never even heard of John Wesley Hardin.

Armstrong was embarrassed and he had to take a lot of kidding; so, more to save face than anything else, he decided to convert the experience into a paying adventure. He asked to be assigned to the Hardin disappearance case and was given the job. Convinced that the best place for tips on Wes Hardin was Gonzales and DeWitt Counties, Armstrong moved to Cuero. He took in Jack Duncan, a Dallas detective, promising to share the reward should the project be successful.

Duncan was sent to the home of Hardin's father-in-law, Neal Bowen, to form a friendship and thereby try to sniff out information. Bowen was operating a small country store, and Duncan saw his chance: claiming that he wished to buy an interest in the business, he took up residence with Bowen while they negotiated. The detective couldn't have arrived at the country store at a more opportune time.

Jane's letter to her uncle had started something: her father had learned her address and had written to her. When she received this letter Jane had just become the mother of a baby girl, born on July 15, 1877, and named Callie, a Bowen family name. Since Jane was in bed, her brother Brown took over the task of writing their father without consulting Wes. Far down in the guarded wording he said: "My sister joins in sending love."

When the father received the letter from Brown, Duncan saw him read it and then hide it in an old trunk. At the first opportunity the detective slipped up the trunk lid, took out the letter and read the innocent-seeming "my sister joins. . . ."

A week or so later, Neal Bowen answered the letter and

went to the town of Rancho to mail it and to buy supplies for the store. Duncan went along. After Bowen had dropped the letter in the post office and gone into a nearby store, Duncan told the postmaster that he had mailed a letter and that he wanted it back to make alterations; he described the Bowen letter and the postmaster handed it over. Duncan found a secluded corner, read the letter, and remailed it quickly. It was addressed to J. H. Swain in Polland, Alabama, but inside were words directed to Wes Hardin. Duncan had the information he needed.

Now his job was to get away from the country store without arousing Neal Bowen's suspicion. He wrote Armstrong in a sort of code they had worked out, saying: "Come get your horse."

Armstrong played his part well. He appeared at the Bowen store and, wielding his six-shooter, made a big show of arresting Duncan and clamping him in heavy irons. Duncan was loaded into a wagon and hauled to Cuero, and Bowen felt that the brave Ranger had saved him from making a deal with a crook.

With this trick neatly turned, Armstrong and Duncan were on their way to Polland with a warrant for the arrest of John Wesley Hardin in Alabama. They were convinced they knew the whereabouts of their man, but there were still problems of gravest import.

The Rangers were not positive they could collect the four thousand dollars if they found Hardin and had to kill him; they had to return him to Texas alive in order to be sure of their pay.

How could Wes Hardin be arrested? It hadn't been done in many years. Wes had shot every man who had attempted to capture or kill him. No one could expect to walk up to Hardin, yank out a gun, and say, "Hands up." It might not be very easy even to kill Hardin unless it was with a safe shot in the back.

But yet there was four thousand dollars to be considered.

Upon arrival in Pensacola Junction, just across the Alabama state line in Florida, and only eight miles from Polland, they picked up a piece of unexpected information in a story that was going around the Junction. Two days before, Brown Bowen had been in a row with a man named Shipley and had come out second best; in a fit of anger Brown had shouted:

"Just wait 'til my brother-in-law gets back! He'll wake things up. He's not the peace-loving John Swain you think he is. He's the notorious John Wesley Hardin."

The Texans found Shipley, who was the local manager of the railroad, and he confirmed the story; moreover, Shipley joined in the investigation. J. H. Swain had just shipped some supplies from Pensacola to Polland and had bought a ticket on the next evening's train out of Pensacola. So the hunted man was in Pensacola. Shipley rigged up a special train and went with the Texans to Pensacola. That night they found Wes in a poker room. Shipley and a deputy sheriff, who happened along, joined the game, and Armstrong and Duncan watched from outside the room, hoping that liquor and high winnings might make Wes easy picking. Wes won heavily but he drank only lightly, and the setup never did look safe to the Texans. So their only hope was to catch Wes on the train the next evening. Their warrant called for arrest in Alabama, but they arranged with Shipley to have the train run quickly out of Florida into nearby Alabama if the capture were made.

Intricate plans involving many men and guns had to be made and then run off like clockwork if the attack on the train was to be successful. Accordingly, the Texans offered the sheriff five hundred dollars to help them arrest Hardin *alive*. The sheriff rounded up a score of deputies and special officers and borrowed from the police force. The army of officers gathered one by one at the station three hours before train time and hid at strategic points. Every man was assigned a specific duty at a specific time.

Wes, Jim Mann, a nineteen-year-old youth, and three other companions arrived at the station ten minutes before train time and went into the smoking car. Suspecting nothing, they took seats in the rear of the car and talked and laughed about the amount of money Wes had won at poker the night before.

At that moment the deputy sheriff who had been in the poker game and had lost more than one hundred dollars to Wes strolled down the aisle of the car.

"Why, hello there, Swain," he greeted. "Can't you stop over? I've got a roll here and if you can beat me you can have it."

"Business before pleasure," Wes answered. "I can't stop over."

The deputy chatted a moment and, before moving on down the aisle, shook hands with Wes.

In an instant, the sheriff and another deputy pounced on Wes from the rear and grabbed his arms. By his handshake the first deputy had put the finger on the right man.

Wes yelled. The deputy turned and pretended to help him but instead grabbed him by a leg, and Wes was spread-eagled in the aisle. He didn't have a chance to get out his pistol, for within an instant there was a pile of struggling humanity on top of him holding him by main strength.

Jim Mann jumped up and ran. He was shot to death.

Just then Armstrong rushed up and pressed the muzzle of his cocked pistol against Wes's forehead and ordered:

"Surrender or I'll blow your brains out!"

Blood was streaming from Hardin's nose and mouth. His

gray eyes blazed. "Blow away!" he stormed at Armstrong. "You'll never blow a more innocent man's out, or one that will care less."

Wes didn't surrender, keeping his pledge never to give up at the point of a gun. But he was overpowered and locked in chains. The train rolled out in a hurry for Alabama.

The scheduled stop in Polland was not made, for the Texans feared that friends of Wes might hear of the capture and meet them at the station and relieve them of their prisoner. Wes realized that his arrest, though a very slick piece of work, was not entirely legal. So when he was jailed for an overnight stay in Montgomery, he managed to get a lawyer and missed by a hair's breadth winning release on a writ of habeas corpus. But the Rangers received proper papers by telegraph, and Wes Hardin was their legal prisoner; they could collect the four-thousand-dollar reward.

Armstrong and Duncan there and then adopted the policy of never letting their prisoner out of their sight day or night. However, they were friendly with Wes. They were impressed by his coolness and poise. He didn't whine, accuse, or curse but displayed what seemed an unconquerable spirit. The Rangers permitted him to write to Jane—but with the handcuffs securely fastened—and to send her all the money he had.

Wes had sized up the Rangers and he had a certain respect for them. He wrote Jane that he was in good hands and that he had the Rangers' promise that he would not be turned over to a mob. He advised Jane to take the children to her father in Texas, but he expressed anger at one member of her family.

"Jane," he said, "Brown's bad conduct caused me to get caught."

But in the quickly scrawled note, Wes tried to be cheerful and to give Jane some hope. "What I have done in Texas was to save my life," he said. "They can never hang me nor penitentiary me for life by law. Do not give up. Where there is a will there is a way."

The train rattled on, taking Wes Hardin back to Texas, where, despite all his trouble, there was but a single murder charge against him—the killing of Deputy Webb in Comanche.

17

For Better or for Worse

No home-coming Texan had ever had quite such a welcome as that given Wes Hardin, and it hit him with a twofold impact.

Railroad officials telegraphed down the line to Armstrong that a vast throng was swamping the station at Austin and overflowing the surrounding yards and streets, waiting for the train.

When Wes heard of this, he paled slightly, for it sounded as if there might be a mob. The memory of the fate of Joe, his cousins, and his cowboys on those rainy nights in Comanche and Clinton haunted him. And then familiar emotion brought his color back and made him square his shoulders in an almost audacious manner. Although he was being brought back to Texas in shackles, he was gaining the attention of a multitude. In a perverse way it fed that same ego that had made him want to rule the roost of the schoolyard as a boy.

The presence of the crowd in Austin placed Armstrong in

the center of a double dilemma. He had his valuable and dangerous quarry almost at the doors of the jail, but down the glistening steel rails would there be those in that surging group who would try to snatch Hardin away to lynch him? Or would there be those who would try to rescue him? The Ranger decided to take no chances; he arranged for the train to stop briefly on the outskirts of town and then he whisked his prisoner into a waiting closed carriage. Down the back ways and side streets of Austin Wes Hardin was taken to jail.

The county jailhouse at Austin was one of the few in Texas strong enough to hold desperate men in and howling mobs out, and it was considered the official stronghold of the state. It took only seconds for Armstrong and Duncan, with the assistance of heavily armed Rangers waiting there for the purpose, to rush Wes into the most secure steel cell in the big rock building.

When county officials saw the commotion, they washed their hands of responsibility, announcing that if the state wanted to keep Wes Hardin in the Austin jail the state would have to be responsible. Seeking his share of the spotlight, Governor Hubbard promptly issued strict orders that every possible measure be taken to prevent either an escape or mob violence. Rangers stood guard within the building and more quick-eyed Rangers were assigned to a constant patrol of the grounds.

The finesse which had been employed to avoid the crowd and get Wes safely behind bars worked only to the extent that the increasing throng moved its location. The jail was surrounded by milling humanity. This situation, with all these Texans gathered there in the jailyard striving for a glimpse of one human being who had killed so many other human beings, was as paradoxical as Wes Hardin himself. To some of them he was a human rattlesnake and should be trampled on and killed; to others he was still the legendary boy wonder who had resisted occupation troops and Reconstruction decrees and had done more than any other one man to thin out the ranks of the dreaded state police. Quite a few women in Austin baked cakes and sent them to jail for Wes; others sent bouquets of roses. To them he was a young hero in trouble.

Words of encouragement as well as curses of condemnation penetrated the thick walls and barred windows. They came in large stacks of mail. Although day after day people continued to flock to the jail entrance and request permission to see Wes, the Rangers, understandably, permitted only a few within talking distance of him.

One of these was Manning Clements. He was out on bond and on the dodge himself, but he risked facing the Rangers to see Wes. Manning remembered how he had been released from Wild Bill Hickok's Abilene jail, and he now promised everything possible to help Wes get out—to try to break the jail, hire lawyers, or do anything else.

Newspaper reporters at Austin were amazed by the intense interest in the star prisoner. They chuckled over the remark of one visiting lawyer: "It seems to me as if Wes Hardin's jail cell is the busiest place in Austin, even busier than the governor's office."

And so the reporters clamored for interviews and made copy of every word Wes breathed and also every rumor that floated about Austin and the state. The estimate of the number of men Hardin had killed ranged from twenty-seven to seventy-five. The known total toll of the guns of this one man stood at forty-four.

A correspondent for *The Galveston News* managed to get the first full interview. Gazing at Wes through the bars, he asked: "What was your first trouble?"

"I don't think it would be proper for me to tell about my

killing anyone," Wes said, "but my first trouble was with the Yankees and the state police."

"How many scrapes did you get into in Kansas and the Indian Territory?" the reporter asked.

"I had no trouble there," Wes replied. Then as an afterthought, he said: "Read what you have taken down, if you please."

The reporter read it.

"Don't start it that way," Wes suggested. "It might appear as if I said I killed somebody. I don't want to deny and I don't want to confirm that I've killed anybody. Please don't start it that way."

The reporter reflected some personal feeling in his story. He wrote: "He is a very intelligent man."

It was through the newspapers that Hardin's mother learned of his arrest. Preacher Hardin had died several months before, still grieving over the hanging of his son Joe and the necessary disappearance of his son Wes. Mrs. Hardin was living on a farm at Bennett Station near Paris, Texas. She wrote Wes a long letter, the first in three years, telling of his father's death and of other family matters. There was word of the child she had been about to bear at the time tragedy struck the family at Comanche. She wrote: "Your sweet little brother, Barnett Gipson, that you have never seen talks about his buddie Johnny so much."

Like many another mother with a son in serious trouble, Mrs. Hardin never faltered in her belief that John Wesley was a fine, honorable man who had been badly treated. After recounting many of the things the newspapers had said about her son, the mother wrote: "Why, Johnny, I'm proud to tell strangers that I am the mother of John Wesley Hardin."

The mother offered more than words. She wrote: "I have the prospect of getting considerable estate from your Aunt Malinda

Lee's estate. So you can expect your ma to assist you in getting attorneys."

She and other relatives—the faithful Uncle Bob Hardin of Brenham and Barnett Jones, the cousin of the many escapades —pooled resources and retained four lawyers to defend Wes.

Within less than a month after his capture, he was taken to Comanche to stand trial for killing Deputy Webb. Twenty Rangers, a sheriff, and five deputies, all commanded by Ranger Lieutenant N. O. Reynolds, escorted him. This was no doubt the strongest guard—manwise, gunwise and shackle-wise—ever to accompany a prisoner in Texas. It resembled several trail-driving outfits grouped together. Lieutenant Reynolds and Wes traveled in a buggy drawn by a span of stocking-legged bay horses. Others of the guard, armed with rifles, shotguns, and pistols, rode horses. A lumbering chuck wagon pulled by two big black mules brought up the rear; it was laden with guns, ammunition, food, and camping equipment.

The Rangers tried to keep their movement secret, but reports of the escort's progress was grapevined well ahead, and people by the hundreds stood and stared and visited the noon and night camps. Wes tried to be friendly and he retained his dignity in the ignoble role that placed him on view much the same as a captured wild animal in a circus parade. He also retained his wit.

One excited country maiden called to him: "I wouldn't take a hundred dollars for seeing John Wesley Hardin. He is so handsome."

"My wife thinks so," Wes replied.

Upon arrival in Comanche Wes had to be carried into the jail because he was wrapped in so much steel he could not walk. Rumors of mob action were so prevalent that the Comanche sheriff deputized fifty citizens to guard the jail. The sheriff arranged his guard next to the jail with a ring of Rangers around the guard. Wes suggested to Lieutenant Reynolds that it might be wise to place the Rangers next to the jail to make sure that the sheriff's guard didn't break in and mob him. The lieutenant agreed and this was done. When whispers of a lynching continued, Reynolds announced publicly that if any man or group attempted to molest the prisoner during or after the trial the Rangers would "give Wes Hardin the two biggest guns in the arsenal and turn him loose."

Since there was so much talk of a mob and since the state had gone to such extreme measures to protect their prisoner, Wes felt sure that he couldn't get a fair trial in that county. The judge, on his own motion, could have given a change of venue, but he didn't; Wes was afraid, and he was advised that if he asked for a change of location of the trial and it were granted, he would be mobbed, despite the army of Rangers.

So the trial was opened in a hot little courtroom in a hostile town.

Bob Hardin of Brenham was there, but he was not permitted to see Wes except in the courtroom and then was not allowed to talk to him. Wes was neatly dressed in a dark suit with a white shirt that had stiff cuffs and a high collar. He was closely shaven except for a modest mustache. The month in jail had bleached a good deal of the tan out of his face. He retained his mild, boyish appearance. He held his manacled hands in his lap; the irons on his legs did not show while he was sitting at the bar.

The courtroom was crowded to capacity. Men packed the aisles. Hundreds of others jammed the corridor, and still other hundreds wandered about the building and grounds watching for chances to make their way in to the trial room. The general opinion, and the hope, was that the prisoner could get no less than death.

Wes had no witnesses to testify for him. Under a law existing at the time, a man accused of murder was not permitted to testify for himself. But as one by one the state witnesses strode to the stand, he used the only defense available to him: he held his steady gray eyes on the face of each witness.

State witnesses testified that Deputy Webb had indeed fired the first shot, but the state contended that he was provoked into shooting.

One state witness told of events leading up to the Webb-Hardin gunfight. He testified that when Webb walked up the street toward the Polk Wright Saloon, where he met his death, Wes Hardin saw and recognized him and, with a wink at Jim Taylor, said:

"Did you ever see anything working out so pretty?"

The jury, with D. L. Dodds as foreman, deliberated only a few hours. It convicted Wes of second-degree murder and fixed his punishment at twenty-five years in prison. A dozen Rangers stood with hands on guns when the verdict was read. There was no demonstration in the packed courtroom. Wes's lawyers asked for a new trial, which the judge denied; then they appealed the case to the Court of Criminal Appeals. Wes was wrapped in his chains again to return to Austin.

A vast crowd of men on horses and in wagons and buggies followed the escort for fifteen or twenty miles. Chained in the buggy with thirty pounds of metal around his neck, arms, and legs, Wes was uneasy, again remembering what a crowd like this had done to Joe. He feared that the men who were following planned to attack the escort and take him. On the second day the Comanche men disappeared and only the crowds in the small communities along the way lined the road to see the prisoner. Wes breathed more easily.

The entourage camped one evening on Brushy Creek in Williamson County some fifty miles north of Austin. One of the guards, John Harvey, rode down the creek in search of a spring. He found it and also a strange-looking man in camp there. He was small and dark, and he wore a dirty black robe with a purple sash. He told Harvey that he was a fortune-teller.

When Harvey mentioned this in camp, Wes told the Rangers that he believed somewhat in mystic powers and that he would like to have his fortune told. Lieutenant Reynolds sent Harvey back to the spring for the Gypsy. The dark little man gazed into Hardin's eyes, turned his cuffed hands palms up, and studied them. "You have had a hard life, young man," he said in a low, quavering voice. "You are going to the penitentiary for a long time. You will be a good man there and get out."

The soothsayer paused, leaving the impression that he had finished.

"Then what?" Wes asked.

The little man closed his eyes. "I see grave trouble ahead for you. When you get out you will kill two men. If you are not careful, you will be attacked from the back and killed."

A grim gray look came into Hardin's eyes.

The Rangers pitched several coins to the fortuneteller. They looked a little grim, too. They had heard many strange tales about their prisoner. One was that at night he had such dreadful dreams that he would spring up howling like a madman to grapple with some phantom foe or else cower whimpering. One of the Rangers—one who wrote a weekly piece for *The Galveston News*—had watched Wes in sleep nearly every night of the trip. He observed him more closely on the night of the fortunetelling, and the next morning he reported that Wes had slept more gently than any of the Rangers. At one time, the Ranger heard him murmur "Johnny," the name of his little son.

The Rangers openly admired Wes; this was perhaps because they admired daring and ability with guns and horses, and also perhaps because to some extent he was their kind of man. Many of the Rangers weren't the gentlest souls on earth.

Soon after his return to the Austin jail, Wes wrote his wife: "Dear, I had a treat of ice cream today by Lieutenant Reynolds who took me to Comanche. I thought of our visits to the ice cream saloons in New Orleans. . . ."

Jane had made her way to Texas and she hurried to Austin to see Wes. She brought the children with her and for a short while the family was together. Wes was glad that he could tell Jane about a letter he had received from his mother in which she invited her daughter-in-law and grandchildren to come and live with her while Wes's case was on appeal and, if worst came to worst, while he was in prison.

The bloom had begun to fade from Jane's cheeks, and there was anxiety in her eyes. But Jane was game; she and Wes had pledged each other to stick together until death.

A severe test of this pledge came suddenly. Rangers showed up at the Austin jail with Jane's brother, Brown Bowen. The letter he had written to Texas and the threat he had shouted at Pensacola Junction that resulted in Wes's arrest had also brought about his own downfall. He had been arrested in Polland, Alabama, on the old charge of murdering Tom Halderman. There was still strong feeling about this killing in Gonzales County because Halderman had been shot in the back. Little had Wes imagined when he engineered Brown's jail break soon after the killing that the day would come when they would be fellow prisoners.

Wes and Brown met occasionally in the Austin jail. Wes boiled when he saw his brother-in-law, whose carelessness was responsible for their dire predicament. Brown was cocky with Wes; he was sure he could beat his case because the killing had occurred six years before. When Wes tried to make suggestions to him on how he might break jail, Brown squealed to the guards, attempting to build himself up and to discredit Wes. These betrayals of confidence, which Wes had extended in the first place only because Brown was Jane's brother, reconfirmed his distrust of the man. In Wes's eyes, Brown had violated every part of the code of fair play and gentlemanly behavior. In his opinion, Brown had not only betrayed, but had committed the unforgivable sin of shooting a man who had no opportunity to defend himself. Wes's word had always been his bond; he held truth inviolate and any form of falsehood he repudiated with the contempt he showed cowardice.

Wes wrote Jane about Brown's behavior. "I've tried to help him, but he won't let me," he wrote.

Within a short time Brown was taken to Gonzales County for trial; he was convicted and sentenced to die by public hanging. The Court of Criminal Appeals soon affirmed the sentence. When Brown was returned to the Austin jail to await execution, he was a frightened man. He was also blackly bitter because he had been given a verdict of death, whereas Hardin had received twenty-five years in his trial at Comanche.

Now Brown's only hope to escape the gallows at Gonzales was to raise a doubt that he was the killer. Therefore, in an appeal to the high court for a rehearing and in pleas to the governor and to the public in newspapers, Brown claimed that he was innocent and that John Wesley Hardin had shot Tom Halderman.

Wes was amazed and infuriated, but he made no attempt to brand Brown's charge as a lie. When a newspaper reporter interviewed him on the accusation his only statement was: "I've never had the courage to kill a man in the way Tom Halderman was killed."

Brown's distraught father, old Neal Bowen, visited Wes in

jail. He had a fantastic plan. Wes was favorably known and liked in Gonzales County. He had powerful friends there. If he would shoulder the blame for the Halderman killing he could come clear in Gonzales County. Bowen had thought Wes almost invincible in Gonzales County.

Wes could scarcely believe his father-in-law—that the man would ask him to make a false statement even in an effort to save Jane's brother.

"You know," he said, "that I have no choice but to refuse."

Bowen walked slowly away. Embittered because Wes would not do the only thing that could save Brown Bowen's neck, Bowen went before the grand jury at Cuero and revived the 1873 Morgan killing. Wes had never denied this killing in front of a Cuero saloon; he had ridden home and emphasized to Jane that he had shot the man in self-defense. He had never been charged with the slaying, but now, on the complaint of his father-in-law, he was indicted for murder.

By letter, Wes kept Jane informed of the family struggle. In one note he said: "You can rest assured that Neal Bowen and Brown are not our friends but have done all they can against me. I am sorry for Brown's condition and yet it is only justice. . . . He has tried to lay his foul and disgraceful crimes on me."

Brown was taken to Gonzales and the scaffold was erected on the side of the jail. The execution was set for May 17. In a final desperate effort, Neal Bowen and his daughter Matt visited Wes in jail.

"Couldn't you make some statement, Wes," Neal Bowen pleaded, "that would save Brown?"

"Not an honorable one," Wes said. "I don't think you'd want me to make a false one."

Matt wailed and implored Wes. He turned away from her.

On the day before the scheduled execution, Matt was back at the jail. Wes refused to see her. She wrote him a note beseeching him to make a statement "on my account" and asked the jailer to hand it to Wes.

He replied to it, saying: "For your sake, I would do anything honorable. . . . I cannot be made a scapegoat . . . a true statement would do your brother no good and I won't make a false one."

Matt departed, weeping bitterly.

At the scheduled hour, Brown Bowen was led to the gallows at Gonzales. The streets were packed with thousands. Sheriff A. T. Bass and a minister stood on the scaffold with him. The nervous clergyman accidentally placed his hand on the trigger and the trap fell—almost taking the sheriff with it. The trap was replaced and within a few moments it was sprung, and Brown Bowen dropped to his death.

Old Neal Bowen took the body to the Bowen farm in Coon Hollow and buried it beneath the live oak under which Jane and Wes had pledged their love five years before. By this time, Jane could realize the awful truth of the warning Wes had tried so earnestly to give her that night so short a time, and yet so long, ago.

But in this grim family tragedy, she cleaved to Wes, turning her back on her own family.

Events to test whether Wes would do the same for Jane were building up rapidly.

He was hopeful that the appeals court would reverse his case and give him a new trial that could perhaps be held in a county other than Comanche; in this way, his case could be considered on its merits and not on the emotions of a mob. There was some reason for optimism. Billy Taylor had been given ten years for his chore on the *Clinton* in Indianola Harbor, where Bill Sutton and Gabe Slaughter were killed. The case had just been reversed and retried and Billy was acquitted.

However, there was at least one of Wes's old acquaintances who couldn't quite understand why he should try to get out from under a twenty-five-year term. He was Bill Longley. Big Bill had been sentenced to hang in Giddings, Texas. Shortly before the fatal day, he wrote letters to the sheriff who had arrested him; like the late Brown Bowen, Longley complained bitterly because he had been given death while "a man like Wes Hardin gets off with twenty-five years."

Other news of passing interest came to Wes in his cell at Austin: Detective Jack Duncan, who had helped put him in jail, was shot and seriously wounded by a woman in a house of prostitution in Dallas, and Sam Bass of Indiana was killed by Texas Rangers at Round Rock, where Wes had gone to school one day.

And then news in which Wes was desperately interested arrived: the high court had affirmed his sentence. In its opinion the court intimated that the decision was not wholly based on the Comanche trial but on "the enormity of the crimes of John Wesley Hardin and associates." In actuality he had been convicted and had his sentence affirmed not for killing Deputy Webb but because he was John Wesley Hardin and had cut such a bloody swath with his guns.

Again Wes tried to write cheerfully to Jane. He told her he would be taken back to Comanche for formal sentencing and then on to the penitentiary at Huntsville. "But I will have a dependable guard," he wrote. "Old Capt. Lynch will never get me."

Wes asked that the name of their baby be changed from Callie to Jane "in honor of her beautiful mother."

Then came his opportunity to cleave to his wife.

In the despondency of their mutual grief Jane and his mother had engaged in a torrent of heated words. Jane had gathered her babies to her and left. She was now penniless but not spiritless. She had found shelter in a neighboring home. She wrote Wes of this breach and added that their son was seriously ill.

His mother also wrote Wes about the misunderstanding.

Wes was worried and wondered whether he could play the role of a peacemaker.

The jailer rationed him only a single sheet of paper; so he had to write both Jane and his mother in one letter, knowing that each would read what he said to the other. Wes begged his mother to overlook any of Jane's shortcomings, saying "her troubles are great."

Then he asked Jane to forgive and forget and return to his mother. "Do so if you can honorably," he said, "but, dear, if it is dishonest—don't do it for me.

"I am satisfied that you both are to blame, but recollect never can I blame you for anything and whenever it comes to the point, you are my favorite above all others."

Wes might turn his back on his mother who had loved him, suffered for him, prayed for him, and the one he was asking to support his family of four, but never on Jane.

There was one other thing that sorely worried the jailed father. In a postscript, he asked:

"Jane, is little John W. H. much sick?"

On the brink of his journey to prison two letters were handed to Wes. He found that a man could derive satisfaction by taking the risk of seeing both sides of an issue and working at being a peacemaker. Jane and his mother wrote that they had ironed out their differences and were living together again.

Jane assured Wes that their little son was feeling much better and had played out in the sun that day. His mother added a postscript to her letter: "Johnny, you have such interesting children. I love them dearly."

18

Big Battles

When the grating steel door of the somber-walled penitentiary at Huntsville closed behind Wes on the bright blue day of October 5, 1878, his future had by no means come to an end. He refused to be a whipped man. Convicts in broad stripes and skull-close haircuts, which made their faces look enormous and brutal, gazed in awe at the man who had come at last to be one of them. Noticing this attention, Wes strutted a little.

He put prison officials on the spot the moment he arrived. They had the big prize of all Texas, a very unpredictable man, and he had to be held at all costs. Word was mumbled throughout the prison, especially among lifers and long-termers, that anyone who squealed on Wes and thereby prevented trouble or foiled a break would be royally rewarded with a pardon or a reduction in time.

Wes had no idea except to break out. For a man who had ridden the woods, the prairies, and the cattle trails as he had, freedom was the very breath of life, and in jail he felt suffocated, almost like a caged animal. Moreover, he wanted to be with Jane and their children and to relieve Jane of the burden of sorrow, shame, and poverty that had fallen on her thin shoulders. But more perhaps than anything else, he wanted to get out because he was convinced that he was being held illegally—at least unfairly. If there was such a thing as self-defense, the first law of nature, he had shot Deputy Webb in defense of his own life. Wes believed that he had been convicted of being John Wesley Hardin, not for shooting Webb, and there were no laws providing for such a conviction. To Wes, then, he had every right to escape, regardless of any measures of extreme violence he might have to take.

Within ten days he was set not only to break out himself but to throw open the entire penitentiary and release all the convicts who wished to flee—except those he wanted to keep behind the walls.

"All will be delivered," he told his conspirators, "except the rape fiends."

It was a grand plan in the Hardin manner.

Wes was assigned to labor in the wheelwright's shop. He noticed that every morning a squad of guards took guns from a small armory and marched about one hundred fifty convicts outside the walls to work; late in the day they returned and the guards stored their guns in the armory and went to the dining hall to eat. The armory was about sixty feet from the wheelwright's shop.

The plan was to tunnel to the armory and break through the floor soon after the guards had deposited their weapons; then with the force of arms take over every cell and portal of the prison. There would be enough men for this, for nearly a hundred convicts were in on the plot.

The tunnel was driven and the time set.

When the hour came, fifteen convicts silently assembled in

the wheelwright's shop. Wes moved toward the hidden opening of the tunnel; he would be the first to go in and also the first to leap into the armory and grab guns.

At the moment Wes dropped down to crawl into the tunnel, a dozen guards with leveled shotguns closed in on him and the others and marched them to solitary cells. Wes soon learned that nearly every long-termer in on the plan had reported it to officials, hoping for reward.

Wes was locked in an inky-black cell with a ball and chain attached to one leg, but even this dark hole didn't discourage him. He dickered with a guard and evolved the first steps in a plan to bribe his way out of prison.

The guard would take out sealed letters and mail them; in such letters Wes could say anything he wished, for they would not be seen by the prison office. The guard supplied writing material, which a prisoner in solitary was not supposed to receive.

Wes slipped a letter to Jane and in it established a code. He didn't wholly trust the conspiring guard and therefore he wrote in riddles that only Jane could understand. Moreover, he instructed her to answer through the regular channel of the prison office; if she received the slipped letter and it looked as if it had been opened she was to sign her name "Jane Hardin"; otherwise she was to sign in the usual way—"Mrs. Jane Hardin."

Jane quickly replied. She had received the letter unopened. Then Wes—in another slipped letter—instructed Jane to ask Manning Clements to raise money to encourage the guard as the plan progressed.

Upon release from solitary, after fifteen days on bread and water, Wes kept up the negotiations with the guard, but on his own he evolved another plan for a break—not an attempt to deliver the whole penitentiary, but just the men in his cell block. The heart of this plot was a trusty's pledge to deliver two pistols to Wes. A turnkey was set to open the locks at the right moment. The break was set for the evening of December 29th. Wes was so enthusiastic about it that he had to write Jane. In a slipped letter he told her of the big delivery that had barely failed.

"I guess you read about it in the newspapers," he said. Then he hinted buoyantly that another big deal was in the making. "Before long," he said, "I hope we can be in one another's embrace of love."

The next evening Wes was arrested. Again his conspirators had planned with him only so they could report it in hope of favors.

Prison officials had put up with all of the new prisoner's wholesale escape plans they wanted; it was time to give him the works.

Twenty men dragged Wes to a vacant room with a concrete floor. He was stripped and plopped down on his face. Two men tied his feet with a rope and held on to it; two others took care of his hands in the same way. A brawny man slipped out of his coat and stepped forward with the whip. He laid on the lash, each lick popping like a shotgun in an ambush. He gave Wes thirty-nine lashes, the limit, and his body was lacerated and bleeding from head to heel. The guards forced him to get up, and he was marched across the prison yard and locked in a dark cell where he was left without food or attention for three days.

When he was taken out, his body was covered with thick, running scabs and he was in a high fever and delirious. By January 9, 1879, he had recovered sufficiently to write Jane: "It is by the mercies of God alone that I now endeavor to communicate to you, my darling and true wife."

He said nothing of the flogging, but he did say that only the hope of seeing Jane again kept him from ending his troubles by killing himself. But the whipping didn't veer him from his determination to beat the prison. Negotiations with the guard got to the kernel of the thing. The guard demanded money. Wes had the promise of Manning Clements, who was in contact with Jane, that in one way or the other he would get the money.

One day while this deal was inching toward its climax Wes had a casual meeting with an old friend who was now a prison official. He was Captain Ben McCulloch, a one-time Texas Ranger. Wes had met him back in 1871 on the cattle trail; he had borrowed a horse from the captain when he was riding on the trail of Bideno, the Mexican who had killed a trail driver. Captain McCulloch was one of the cowmen who had admired Wes in Abilene.

The two talked of old times for a few moments. The captain was warm and friendly. "You know, John Wesley," he said, "I've been watching you. You've been convicted and sent to prison for twenty-five years, and you ought to know it couldn't do you much good to escape. The best way for a young man like you to get out of this place is to be good. By good behavior you can cut about ten years off your time, and while you're here you can give yourself a good education so when you get out you can make your mark. You've given a lot of trouble here, but if you want to try it my way, I'll see that you get a fair deal. Just think it over."

The captain strolled away.

Wes had confidence in this man, who had stood the gaff of the wild frontier without a single blemish on his name.

One of the things the captain had told him was revealing news: he didn't know that a prisoner could reduce his time by more than one-third by being a model convict. He also hadn't realized that a man could acquire an education in prison. Before he had plunged into a career of shooting, Wes had liked to read; he had been an exceptionally bright pupil in school, although he had found plenty of time for play.

The captain's friendly suggestion put him to thinking. He was a convicted man and he couldn't escape that, and there was little hope that any governor would ever pardon him. He could escape—he was convinced of that—and go to Jane; then he would be a fugitive again. Every officer in the land would be on his trail, and there could be no peace.

Wes was young, only twenty-six. If he could get out in fifteen years he would be only forty-one; there would be time for him to take up again his life with Jane. Then they would be free. If he took advantage of a prison education he could be a preacher, as his father had so deeply desired, or a lawyer; he could make Jane and the children proud of him. On the other hand, fifteen years would be an eternity to wait for Jane; it would likewise be an eternity for her to make a living for herself and the children, who would almost reach maturity in that time.

Only once before had Wes had the time to pause and take a long-range look at his life and the future; that was when he had considered postponing his marriage to Jane so he could go away and lose his identity as a gunman. Jane had changed that plan. This time the decision rested solely with Wes.

He weighed every consideration. This time he wanted to weigh the consequences.

A few days later he sought out Captain McCulloch and told the old Ranger he had made up his mind to make good in prison.

"You can do it, John Wesley," the captain said, "but it will be your big battle."

Wes wrote his decision to Jane, saying: "We are both young and I think and hope we can pass our latter days together in perfect happiness; then we can talk over our hardship and trials of life."

Officials who censored mail had a good chuckle over this. It was an old trick—a prisoner planting promise in his mail in an effort to throw his keepers off guard. So the word was passed on that Hardin was up to something again.

Wes was assigned to the shoe shop. He made an agreement with the supervisors that each day they would lay out the work expected of him and when it was finished to their satisfaction he would be given the rest of the day to read and study.

The suspicious supervisors almost doubled his work, but Wes always completed it and had time left for study. He first read the Bible and all the books on theology the prison had. With him, this was no ordinary jailhouse conversion. Religion in prison was weak tea compared to the dish his father had set out. So he studied theology as a scholar would and was soon superintendent of the Sunday schools.

Officials and guards were amazed and grew more suspicious by the day. They just didn't know of the bullheadedness of Wes Hardin. In the business of being good and studying, this bad boy was as wildly fanatical as he had ever been about any-thing—honor, chivalry, keeping a pledge, shooting, feuding, killing. He had it in his head to do it.

One day seven convicts with four loaded revolvers sidled up to him and outlined what looked like a sure-shot plan to es-cape. They wanted him in on it and offered him a pistol. Wes gazed at the gun. He itched to feel the familiar steel. He knew what he could do with that pistol.

He refused it, saying he had his own plans; he did not tattle on the convicts, who tried their break and failed.

Along with theology, Wes studied mathematics, science, his-tory, economics, and politics. He pored over a dictionary and developed an amazing vocabulary and the art of using words.

For a long time he tottered between the law and the ministry. In June of 1885, after almost seven years of good behavior, he received a letter from a sister telling him that their mother had died on June 6. The sister repeated Ma Hardin's last words: "My sky is clear."

Blackstone finally won over the Bible, and Wes concentrated on preparing to be a lawyer, reading every book he could get his hands on. He headed the debate team. Believing that politics and law would go well together, he studied political subjects with a passion.

The reading and study opened a vast new world for the champion man-killer of the nation and Wes still managed to live in a superlative degree: once he had been the most dangerous man ever to be locked in the prison; now he was the most studious and co-operative convict and was pointed out as a model prisoner. His letters to Jane reflected his learning and a new outlook on life.

Life for Jane was hard. She could not eat the encouraging letters Wes wrote. Her struggle was to keep soul and body together and to get food, clothing, and medicine for the children and, with them, face life as a notorious convict's wife. She had her big battle, too, and the challenge of it brought to the surface the vein of iron in this once shy girl.

She lived a few months more with Ma Hardin and managed to get along, but life there was something of an armed truce. Rather than bring the fight into the open again, she told Mrs. Hardin that she preferred to live near her old home and friends. Manning Clements, ever the friend, moved Jane and her little brood to his ranch in the Texas hill country near San Saba. Later Jane went back to Gonzales County; and there another old friend of Wes, Fred Duderstadt, helped her settle in a home near where she and Wes had first lived. He all but adopted the whole family.

But Jane was no dependent. She sewed, picked cotton, cleaned houses for neighbors. When Johnny at ten was large enough to assist, she operated a farm, doing nearly all the work herself, raising cattle, hogs, sheep. She milked cows and sold cream and butter; she raised chickens and sold eggs. She worked in the fields like a man. On Sunday she rested, wrote to Wes, and attended religious services; she joined the community church and sang in the choir.

In prison, Wes knew of Jane's big battle, but all he could do was encourage her. In his regular Sunday letters, some of them running to thousands of words, he advised her on everyday little problems. Once when the children were still very young, he wrote: "Tell Molly to be good to little Jiny [Jane] Also tell J.W. to not bite his sister M."

When each child reached the age of understanding, Wes wrote long letters in which he explained fully the life he had lived, going thoroughly into the Comanche episode which had sent him to prison. He told them that in the days ahead no stigma would be attached to his name or to theirs. "The blood which I have spilt," he said, "is of that kind which can never stain."

Soon the children were writing their father. He studied their letters and criticized them as if he were helping with homework. In one note to Jane he said: "Tell J. W. H. that 'sough' does not spell a female hog."

Upon reading several childish letters that were full of errors, Wes dashed off a note to Jane, saying: "Dearest, obtain a dictionary and have these children to recite lessons daily to you, both defining and spelling. Do not neglect this. Teach them to spell well by all means."

Jane taught the children that their father was a fine man and that, although away, he was head of the household. Many times the children wrote him for permission to do this or that.

When little Jane was big enough to lower her eyes when boys glanced at her, she wrote Wes at Christmas time and asked permission to dance at the holiday parties.

Wes replied: "Christmas will soon be here and papa hopes that you, your sister, brother, and mother will enjoy the festivities of that gala day, and papa doesn't care if you go to parties or respectable balls."

Wes saved most of his advice for his growing son. He exhorted the lad to be honest, chivalrous, and a gentleman. He urged him to stay away from race tracks and all gambling and never to use liquor or tobacco.

But he did advise him to buy a gun—for one reason only.

"Son," he said, "should any lecherous, treacherous scoundrel, no matter what garb he wears or what insignia he boasts, assault the character and try to debauch the mind and heart of either your sisters or mother, I say, son, don't make any threats. Just quietly get your gun, a double-barrel. Let it be a good gun; have no other kind. And go gunning for the enemy of mankind, and when you find him, just deliberately shoot him to death as you would a mad dog or a wild beast. Then go and surrender to the first sheriff you find."

Although a prisoner of the state, Wes remained a true Texan. He insisted that Jane teach the children to love the state. "Yes," he said, "Texas is the grandest state of all. There is none truer, braver, nobler than Texans."

He remembered the tales of his forebears, who had been stalwart Texans, and he repeated these stories for his children and encouraged them to be "peerless citizens as the Hardins were of yore."

Gradually as he studied and tried to help raise a family

from behind prison walls, a frightening realization came to Wes. He realized that there were overpowering impulses within him; he was convinced that he had a criminal mind which he could not always control no matter how hard he tried. What was more frightening was his fear that he might have transmitted his tragic traits to his children. He studied all he could find on heredity. The theory of kind-begets-kind was generally accepted and, therefore, Wes was fearful that his children might follow in his footsteps. This was the first time in his life that he had admitted himself to be a criminal with the impulse to kill at the slightest provocation.

He called to mind many lawless persons he had known whose children had also had criminal careers. He took up his terrifying conviction with Jane and pleaded with her to try to raise the children so that they would be like her instead of him.

"My knowledge of wayward, forward men and women is that they lead wicked, miserable lives and die wretched deaths," he wrote. "The gambler dies a blackleg. The prostitute dies a whore. The thief fills a thief's grave, and the sepulcher of the murderer is the assassin's sepulcher. This is the general rule. Their ways are hard, their days are sombrous and sad; their nights starless and sleepless, their hope for time and eternity has faded away and they await their terrible doom with trembling and fear because their end is dreadful and certain and terrific."

Then he came to the part that worried him the most. "Each of his kind begets children who make men and women of corresponding habits of vice and crime." In his letter to Jane on this topic he cried out that her biggest battle was to reverse this trend so that Molly, John W., Jr., and little Jane would not have the impulses, the impatience, and the mind of their father.

"If you can reverse this trend and guide our children in the right path," he said, "you will have won the battle of your life. You will give to the world the light of your example which will inspire hope in many a broken-hearted, bereaved mother . . . and this will be glory enough for me to compensate for all."

Wes remembered how he as a small boy had disobeyed his own strict parents, and he lived in mortal fear that his own children might disregard the teachings of their mother. He knew that they were at a great disadvantage: their father was a notorious killer and a convict, while his own father had been a minister. He feared that the son who bore his name might be expected to be like his father, even to being ready to fight and quick on the trigger. And, as the years dragged by, he kept this subject before Jane.

One day in 1891, Wes struck up with Captain McCulloch. The captain was grinning. He slapped Wes on the back and said: "You know, John Wesley, I've been checking up on your record, and it looks to me like you'll be out of here in two years or maybe a little bit longer. You're making the grade."

Wes was delighted. He had been in prison thirteen years. Now that his time was so short, comparatively, he didn't feel that he could wait two more years to see his family. He asked for a furlough, but despite his fine record it was denied. Then he started working on a scheme to get out and go to Jane, if only for a day.

He thought of the old indictment against him at Cuero, near where Jane was living. This was the 1873 case in which Wes had killed a man named Morgan.

Now this old case opened up a world of possibilities for Wes: if he could be tried in it, Jane and the children could attend the trial and he could see them. But as he studied the situation, Wes saw other contingencies. What if he were convicted of murder and given a long term? As a law scholar, he sized up the matter. If he could plead guilty to a charge of manslaughter, the minimum would be two years and the maximum five years. If he got a two-year sentence and could persuade the court to let it run concurrently with his present term, he could finish both of them in two years.

Wes wrote to a lawyer friend, Judge W. S. Fly, in Gonzales and asked him to look into the possibilities. The judge learned that District Attorney Davidson at Cuero was willing to take a plea of guilty to a charge of manslaughter in order to get the old case off the docket. The judge reasoned that under the circumstances Wes should get the minimum sentence to run concurrently with the term he was serving.

Judge Fly made arrangements for the trial to be held on January 1, 1892, in Cuero, which had replaced wild old Clinton as the DeWitt County seat.

19

Jane Hardin

The ironic return to Cuero in feuding old DeWitt County revived memories of the rough, bloody days of the Taylor-Sutton conflict and the nocturnal plotting in Mustang Mot. For Wes, who was facing the future and paying for the past, the most poignant memory coming alive that day was of a man who had sought revenge against him. With a subtlety characteristic of his madcap youth, Wes was turning that vengeance into a blessing. The case up for trial was the one in which Neal Bowen had sworn out the indictment when he was trying desperately to save his son from the gallows. That spiteful act of Jane's father fourteen years before was making it possible for Wes and Jane to be together after being apart so long.

Wes had been brought from prison in Huntsville and locked in the Cuero jail to await summons to the courtroom. Early that wintry morning he recognized a familiar, friendly voice at his cell door.

"Wes, are you in there?"

"Yes, Fred," Wes replied. "Did you bring Jane?"

Fred Duderstadt told him that Jane was waiting with his son and daughters and that the sheriff would allow them to visit in the cell if that were all right.

"It's not the place I'd like to meet them," Wes said, "but there's no other."

Presently the bolt in the lock clicked and the door squeaked open, barely wide enough for one person. Jane glided in. They gazed at each other as if transfixed.

"Oh, John!" Jane gasped and fell toward him. Wes grabbed her in his arms, lifted her off the floor and bent down and kissed her.

The children came in one by one and stood, silently watching their parents in their long embrace.

When Wes released Jane he gazed in amazement at his three children. He embraced each one, starting with Molly; then he looked at them long and intently and said, "I can't believe it. They have grown up!"

Wes had last seen his children in the Austin jail. Jane had sent him pictures but he hadn't realized that they had changed so much. Molly was almost nineteen years old. She was a beautiful, vivacious girl with soft olive skin, kind, sparkling brown eyes, and dark hair. Her full lips were shaped so that it looked as if she might be smiling all the time. She seemed more at ease than her brother and sister.

John Wesley, Jr., was a sturdy, lean boy almost seventeen years old, the age Wes had been when he had started on the Chisholm Trail to Abilene; he looked a great deal like Wes as he had been then. The lad was tanned from farm and ranch work and his hands were big and tough. After a few moments his son reminded Wes of someone—his Uncle Bob at Brenham.

Molly and her brother could remember their father, but little Jane could not; she had been only a year old when Wes had gone to prison. She was now almost fourteen and a delicate young image of her mother—that is, as her mother had looked when Wes was courting her in Coon Hollow.

Wes couldn't keep his eyes off his wife. She wore a new blue dress and dangling earrings because she knew Wes liked them. But her new clothes didn't hide the tiredness of her body; she looked as if her very bones were tired. Her brown hair had turned an iron-gray, the flash had faded from her eyes, and her cheeks were hollow, although now flushed a rosy pink. She was frail and slightly stooped.

In contrast, Wes looked young, solid, and robust; there was not a gray hair in his head. His eyes were bright with no sign of a prison stare. He was cheerful and optimistic and kept the conversation going, although for several minutes Jane and the children seemed at a loss as to how to act or what to say.

Within just two years, Wes told them, they would all be together again with a bright future before them—that is, if everything worked out right. A determined look flashed over Jane's face. She had not lost her spirit. She told Wes that nearly all the people of Gonzales and DeWitt Counties were talking about this trial and that Cuero and the courthouse were already packed to capacity.

"I've heard that you are to plead guilty," Jane said. "Is that so?"

"Yes—to manslaughter."

Then Jane protested strongly, reminding Wes that he had insisted to her that he had shot Morgan in self-defense and that therefore he was not guilty and should not stand up and say he was.

Wes explained the situation—how a guilty plea could clear up the case and make him a free man within two years.

But still Jane was not convinced. She urged him to change his mind and never say he was guilty when he was innocent, no matter what the advantage. Several things she said sounded as if they were quoted from the letters styled in the long words and sententious philosophy that Wes had written from prison.

"But Jane, darling," Wes said. "I have promised to do this thing so I could see you and the children. My word is out."

Then Jane agreed, with obvious misgivings. She had been loyal to Wes through the most trying tragedies of their hard lives and she would continue to be so, yet she preferred to face whatever music there was rather than turn her back on a principle.

Soon the prison guards arrived and called Wes to the courtroom. Duderstadt had returned with the guards. The Hardin children would stay with him during the trial.

Jane walked with Wes to the courtroom and sat close beside him. The eyes of the throng centered on them. A jury was quickly selected and Wes entered his plea. There were no witnesses. District Attorney Davidson briefly outlined the case. Wes's attorney, Judge Fly, pointed out that the indictment was old, that the shooting was in self-defense and that John Wesley Hardin had proved himself a reformed man.

Then Wes rose and a hush fell on the courtroom; all the people leaned forward to see and hear the man who had been considered a terror in their county twenty years before. In this first appearance as a lawyer, Wes exhibited poise, and in a clear and steady voice, he made an eloquent plea for a minimum sentence that would run concurrently with the rest of his long term so that he could clear up his record and start life anew with his family. Jane gazed at him with wonder and pride.

The jury required less than five minutes to reach a verdict —guilty as charged with a recommendation for a two-year sentence.

The judge promptly passed sentence to run concurrently with Wes's present term.

Wes rose quickly and in an emotion-packed voice thanked the court and each juror.

Jane's face glowed.

The trial was over. While standing at the bar, Wes, the lad with the one-time quick trigger finger, had glimpsed out of the corner of his eye many of his old friends and also some old half-forgotten enemies. He had made good with words, though. Even the reporter from *The Galveston News* noticed. He reported:

"Hardin has been reading law and to judge by the remarks he made to the court and jury, under the circumstances, he has been quite a student and may yet make his mark."

Back in prison Wes launched the work on the next phase of his future, that of obtaining a full pardon at the end of his term so that his civil rights would be restored. He was now a trusted man and almost a privileged character. Penitentiary officials were proud of the man who had once come very close to shooting wide all its gates for an almost complete coup. His duties were easy and he could therefore look to his future. His petition for a pardon was a tremendous job, for he had to give a complete factual history of the shooting, mobbing, and trial at Comanche and fortify it with statements by witnesses.

He knew, however, that a pardon would depend to some extent on politics, and his interest in that subject was keen. Wes liked big, loud Governor Jim Hogg, a liberal, a friend of the poor and downtrodden, the first native Texan to be governor; he would be the one to pass on the proposed pardon. Wes had his family send him the Gonzales County newspapers so that he could keep up with politics and other local events.

In one of these papers he saw a startling item—Mrs. J. W.

Hardin had been ill, but was up again. The next news, which came by letter, was that Jane was critically ill. Wes fired one letter after the other to his children, pleading with them to do all possible for their mother and to keep him informed. In one note he said: "Any serious mishap to your lovable mama would be to each of you, as well as to myself, a calamity irretrievable and irreparable."

The calamity came on November 6, 1892, when Jane died at the age of thirty-six. She was buried in the lonely, live-oak-studded Asher Cemetery not far from her old Coon Hollow home. The children went to the Fred Duderstadt ranch to live.

Wes was distraught for weeks. He realized that the future for which he had waited and planned so long was gone or, at least, vastly changed. Jane had been the greatest influence in his life; his devotion to her and their plans for the future had made prison life bearable. She had been the soothing influence, the anodyne, which had eased somewhat his terrifying conviction that his children might inherit the traits that had made him a violent rebel and killer.

After walking about in a virtual daze for months, Wes gained control of himself and returned to the task of working up the application for a pardon.

On the first anniversary of Jane's death, he transmitted the long, hand-written document to Judge Fly and requested him to forward it to Governor Hogg, with or without the judge's recommendation.

Then on February 17, 1894, the prison door opened and Wes walked out a free man—really free for the first time since he was fifteen years old. Within three months, he would be forty-one years old. The fortuneteller at the spring on Brushy Creek had proved correct in one prediction: Wes had been a good man in prison.

He boarded a train for Gonzales. When the train puffed into the station Wes noticed that several persons had gathered there. He paused briefly on the top step of the coach and his eyes swept the crowd. Except on the occasion when the state police had escorted him from Austin to Gonzales in 1872, this was the first time he had ever been in the town without his guns.

Fred Duderstadt stepped forward, grabbed his hand, and led him to a nearby tree where two horses were tied. They were soon riding toward the Sandies country.

On the way, Duderstadt invited Wes to stay at his ranch two or three months, help with the spring work, visit old friends, and "sort of get your feet back on the ground." Wes gratefully accepted.

"I'd like to go to the cemetery as soon as possible," he said.

"We'll do that the first thing in the morning," Duderstadt replied.

It was late in the day when the two men approached the ranch. Wes's children dashed out of the house and raced to meet them. Wes leaped off his horse and hugged all three of them at the same time. Duderstadt sat on his horse and looked down solemnly at this family reunion, no doubt wondering what the fates now held for Wes Hardin and his grown-up children.

The next morning the Hardins and the Duderstadts drove in a wagon to Asher Cemetery, a lonely, isolated little plot in a large pasture with only a dim, winding road leading to it. A few weather-worn headstones rose above the grass. The morning shade of a live oak on the eastern border of the cemetery fell across Jane's unmarked grave, a grassy little mound which the children had kept free of weeds. Birds twittered in the trees.

With his children beside him, Wes stood there, a gaunt, silently grieving figure, and looked down at the grave.

It was at about this same time, in early spring, twenty-two years before that Jane and Wes had sat under the big live oak in Coon Hollow, only a few miles from Asher Cemetery, and made their decision to face life together and to share each other's troubles. They had lived together only six violent years, half of them as fugitives under assumed names. But through all the hard years of separation they had remained close together in thought.

Jane had been the only person Wes could ever trust completely. She had stood by him through the bloody days of the old feud. She had been brave during the ordeal at Comanche and had fled with him when there was a price of four thousand dollars on his head. With her three small children and with almost no money, she had managed to follow him to Texas after his arrest in Florida. When he had been forced to refuse the aid her brother, Brown Bowen, had requested of him, Jane had stood firmly with Wes against her own family. She had disagreed with Wes's mother and his brothers and sisters, but not once had she ever found fault with Wes.

Life had been wonderful with Jane during the short time they had lived in the little house near Coon Hollow and later in Florida and Alabama. In every way Jane had lived up to her pledge to love him until death. Wes had never ceased loving Jane as he did the night he killed a good horse in a hundred-mile ride so he could be with her.

Jane had remained true, faithful, and brave during his long years in prison. With her own hands she had eked out a living for herself and their children. And she had raised them right —inspired them to be good, honest, Christian children. She had found time during the trials of a hard life to write him encouraging letters every week. These letters and the knowledge that Jane was out there waiting had made prison life bearable and kept him planning for the future that he and Jane wanted so much. All his plans—his reformation, his education, his decision to become a lawyer—had been built around the hope of life with Jane after the prison door opened.

She had stood by his side at his trial in Cuero—the last time he had seen her. She had been care-worn and ill but still beautiful and spirited.

And then on the eve of the long-anticipated future, Jane had died. The dream of being a free man had come true, but the main part of the dream was here in this lonely little cemetery. How, Wes wondered, could he live without her? She had been the light of his life.

Without turning his head, he said to all the others gathered close beside him, "About everything good I ever hoped for is buried here."

Throwing his arms around his three children, he turned and walked slowly away with them.

20

Hard Against the Storm

Wes Hardin had not been forgotten. And there were also some things *he* had not forgotten, although the years had blotted out many of the reasons he had once found for fighting. But the name he had made as the fastest man in Texas on the draw would stick to him like his shadow.

A tangible piece of testimony indicating how well he was remembered turned up the second night he was at the Duderstadt ranch. A man rode up and called him out to the road from the front porch, where he and Fred had been quietly talking. The rider handed Wes five hundred dollars and the reins of a saddled horse he was leading. Before Wes could ask a question, the visitor told him the money, horse, and saddle were his without obligation. They were the gift of a man who wanted to be remembered to Wes only as a friend and one who had known him in former days.

Wes put the horse to good use. He was back in the Sandies country, which he loved, and within a few days he was doing what he liked best: he was in the saddle on the range chasing cows. The sun was in his face, rope burns on his hands and the acrid odor of the sizzling branding iron on live cowhide in his nostrils. He felt the familiar weight of a pistol in a holster at his side, for it was still customary on the ranches to carry firearms.

The range was no longer open, but the Duderstadt pastures were large and the barbed-wire fences were not too restrictive. The cattle Wes punched were not the tough old longhorns he had herded up the Chisholm but red, surly-eyed Durhams and a few clean-faced Herefords.

Day after day Wes and his son rode the range together. Johnny was an excellent cowboy. He could cut out a big calf, snake his lariat on it, and drag it out to the branding fire. Often he took turns with other men at flanking the calves and holding them down while the hot iron was applied.

Wes watched the boy closely. He noticed that Johnny sat a horse and twirled a rope just as he had when young. Since Wes had not taught the boy these arts, he figured that Johnny must have inherited his knack at them. Wes was gloriously proud of his son, but, as he had written Jane, he didn't want the lad to be a chip off the old block. He was thankful that the boy still reminded him of his Uncle Bob.

But Wes discussed no fears, or the stark past; instead he was light-hearted. Often he let Duderstadt's young son, Tom, ride on his horse with him. Little Tom adored Wes and wanted to see him shoot. His own son, Johnny, had heard all his life of his father's shooting abilities but had never seen him in action. Both boys had this chance one day when several cowhands from neighboring outfits congregated near the Duderstadt ranch house.

They bantered Wes to try his hand with a pistol. He told

them he had practiced very little and might not be able to hit the side of a barn. Duderstadt pointed to a white knot the size of a saucer on a tree.

"Wes," he said, "let's see if you can run by on your horse and hit that knot."

Little Tom's eyes danced.

Wes rode off fifty yards and turned. The tree would be on his left, and since he would be shooting with his right hand, he would have to hold the pistol across his chest. He put his horse into a run, with hoofs thumping and mane and tail flying. Just before he was even with the target he whipped out his pistol and fired six times as the horse plunged past the tree.

The men and boys rushed over to check the result. They counted six bulletholes in the knot.

"Gee whiz!" young Tom Duderstadt exclaimed. Johnny Hardin grinned.

Then Wes really hit the bull's-eye with a long shot. On a Saturday in March Duderstadt rode to Gonzales on business and returned in the afternoon with a thick, heavy letter for Wes. After carefully slitting the envelope, Wes slowly drew out a legal-looking document.

It was a full pardon for his two convictions; it restored his civil rights and re-endowed him with the responsibilities of citizenship. Here was his bill of accounts to the State of Texas marked paid in full. The black years of shooting and prison were wiped out. Instead of fleeing from the law as he had done so often, Wes could at last help select the law-enforcement officers.

Any other man who had been sent to the penitentiary on the basis of the "enormity of his crimes" would have been happy to have won release without any thought of pardon. But when Wes had dreamed of freedom he had not imagined a half-freedom that would restrain him from all the privileges that other men enjoyed. He didn't want to be out of prison only to find himself a hobbled horse.

The pardon was victory; in a sense it was a tribute to that something in Wes that set him apart from other violent men of the Western frontier—sparkling ego or a strong belief in the survival of the fittest. Of all the gunmen, Wes had been considered the most dangerous, the most wanted, the most capable with a gun, and the one with the greatest number of notches thereon. But he alone had emerged a free citizen with a clear name and the promise of a future. This was perhaps because, even at his worst, Wes had held tenaciously to a certain set of principles which made him consider himself more a gentleman of guns than a gunman. The pardon in his hands was the vindication he had promised himself, his wife, his daughters, and his son.

The pardon had been relayed from Governor Hogg by Judge Fly, who had written Wes a note admonishing him to start over and lead a useful life. He wrote:

"Did you ever read Victor Hugo's masterpiece, *Les Misérables?* If not, you ought to read it. It paints in graphic words the life of one who had tasted the bitterest dregs of life's cup, but in his Christian manhood rose above it almost like a god and left behind him a path luminous with good deeds."

Wes folded the letter and the pardon and put them back in the envelope.

This was the past; the future was ahead. . . .

That first early evening of the future found Wes again sitting on the front porch; he didn't like to stay inside unless he had to. His eyes feasted on the far horizon. Molly came and sat beside him. He noticed a large pink ribbon in her hair and the scent of rosewater in the air.

"And why are you so dressed up, Molly?" he asked.

She smiled. "Charley's coming over tonight."

"Charley?"

"Yes, Charley Billings. He's been so busy riding after cattle he hasn't had a chance to come over. But he's coming to-night."

Wes remembered the Billingses well. "I know he's a fine young man," Wes said, "but I'm sure there's nothing serious."

"Papa," Molly said quickly, "there *is* something serious. Charley and I are going to get married. He wants to meet you."

Quick as a flash, Wes forbade any such plans and told Molly that he had dreamed for years of sending her to college.

"But, Papa," she protested, "girls my age are not starting off to school. I'm twenty-one."

Wes shook his head. "Well, anyhow this Billings boy is not well enough educated for you."

Molly's face flamed. "He is, too," she snapped, "and we are going to get married."

"I forbid it."

"It will do no good."

Wes looked at her a moment and said: "Molly, you remind me of me."

He could see in the flushed face of his pretty daughter at least a touch of the Hardin obstinacy. Almost the finest thing that could happen to them had happened that afternoon, the arrival of the pardon, yet the father and daughter had just exchanged their first angry words. With a sad smile, Wes gained control of himself and talked persuasively, fatherly, to Molly, pleading with her not to marry in haste but first to try living with him and the other children in a home of their own. Now that his civil rights had been restored and he had the gift of five hundred dollars to tide him over for a while, he intended to obtain a license to practice law and open an office in Gonzales.

Molly agreed to the idea of moving to town for a while, but she urged her father to meet her fiancé. This was what Wes wanted. It looked like an ace in the hole; he was still fully aware that his name had struck fear into the hearts of many men, and his disapproval could very likely make Charley Billings shudder and agree.

Charley walked unsuspectingly into this meeting. He was excited and embarrassed, and his ruddy face was all the redder for it. But he didn't bat an eye when Wes advised a long delay in any wedding plans. With Molly by his side, Charley stood up to Wes, saying that he and Molly were in love and that he saw no reason to postpone their plans.

Commenting later to Fred Duderstadt, Wes said: "To say the least, the boy didn't turn and run. He's no coward, and I admire him for that."

A couple of weeks later Wes and the children moved to Gonzales, a quiet old town of about two thousand population. They rented, furnished, a small gray house with a bannistered front gallery on a tree-bordered street. After so long a time, Wes was again the head of a house. He looked and acted a great deal as his father had at his age. His hair had grown out and also a mustache, both streaked with gray, but there were no chin whiskers. Wes dressed soberly and neatly in a black suit. He was mild, mannerly, and hospitable. Like his father, he expected obedience of his children. He shunned gambling places, and he didn't drink.

On Sunday he and his children dressed in their best and walked together to the Methodist Church. Soon after the family had settled in Gonzales, an evangelist known as Brother Lowery conducted a revival in the town, with services every evening. The windows of the small sanctuary were raised as high as they would go to admit every little vagrant breeze, for the late spring weather had turned unseasonably warm. Wes had been attending the revival regularly and one night he arrived quite early. The minister and Wes drifted to an open window and talked awhile. Lowery was astonished at Wes' knowledge of the Bible and theology. He told Wes so. Wes smiled. "My father was a minister," he said.

During the service, the time came for a prayer from someone in the congregation. Brother Lowery looked out over the bowed heads. "Brother Hardin, will you lead us in prayer?" he asked.

Wes stood up. There was an almost audible gasp from the townspeople, but it subsided quickly. Wes had heard his father pray many, many times. His father would have been proud had he heard his son.

Wes formed one of his warmest friendships with a man he met at church, Deputy Sheriff F. M. Fly. The deputy was a bachelor and usually attended church services alone. Wes often asked him home for Sunday dinner, and they whiled away the afternoon discussing local events or walking about town.

On weekdays Wes spent nearly all his time downtown, conferring with attorneys on the procedure for getting a certificate to practice law and renewing friendships. He probably had more friends in Gonzales than anywhere else, for here he was remembered favorably for his hard fight against the state police. He enjoyed walking around the courthouse square, speaking to acquaintances and tipping his hat to women. He saw the old jail where he had once sawed his way to freedom. He still bore the scars from the deep cuts the bar stubs had cut in his body when Manning Clements had pulled him through the window in his escape. With his sense of the heroic and historic, Wes felt a sort of reverence for Gonzales. Around its square were some of the oldest buildings in Texas. The town often called itself "the cradle of Texas liberty," for the first battle of the Texas Revolution had been fought there; and it was Gonzales alone that had sent reinforcements to the besieged Alamo—the "thirty-two immortals" who had marched there to die with Travis, Bowie, and Crockett.

Wes went often to the sheriff's office to chat with Deputy Fly. Among others, he met Sheriff R. M. Glover and Deputy Bob Coleman. The sheriff's office was an unofficial gathering place, a sort of spit-and-whittle club, for old-timers who had retired to reminiscence and dominoes and for men who liked to talk politics. This was a political year, and at least one big issue made argumentative conversation: the insurgent Populist Party, which battled an imponderable known as "economic and social injustice," had gained a foothold in Gonzales and had the support of a waspy little weekly newspaper, *The Drag Net*, which had the front page motto: "We Admire No One in Particular."

Wes listened to the political discussions but had little to say.

One afternoon at the sheriff's office, some of the old-timers brought up the famed battle Wes had fought with two state policemen in Smiley, the fight in which one officer was killed and the other, John Lackey, had lost his teeth to a Hardin bullet and had escaped by diving into a lake at the edge of town.

As a boy in rompers, Deputy Fly had been deeply impressed by the stories he had heard of that fight. After listening to this latest discussion of the episode he told Wes that John Lackey still lived in Gonzales and operated a blacksmith shop.

"Is that so?" Wes said. "I'd like to see old John. Let's take a look for him."

Wes and deputies Fly and Coleman went to the tumbledown shop and found the old Negro hammering away at his anvil, still minus the teeth he had lost in the fight at Smiley. In pleasant conversation, Wes mentioned the Smiley incident. Thereupon Lackey's eyes shone, and in a boastful manner he told how he had "really mixed it" with Wes Hardin, not mentioning the disastrous result.

"Have you ever seen Hardin since that day?" Wes asked.

"No, never laid eyes on him since."

"Well—" Wes repeated almost exactly what he had said to Lackey twenty-two years before—"you're looking right square at him now."

Lackey was terrified. He trembled and dropped to his knees. "Mister Wes," he pleaded, "you wouldn't shoot a pore old man just for lying, would you?"

Wes smiled. "Get up, John," he said. "We're friends."

When Wes applied for his license to practice law he felt the first sharp sting of being an ex-convict. The procedure was for the district judge to appoint three lawyers to examine the applicant orally and pass on his qualifications. The judge in the Gonzales district didn't like the idea: should he take action to make Wes Hardin a member of his profession? The politics of it might not be good, but on the other hand, the judge was hardly as naïve as Charley Billings; he didn't wish the enmity of Wes, and he finally appointed the examining board.

Wes passed the examination without difficulty, and he hung out his shingle—John W. Hardin, Esq., Lawyer—at the street entrance of the creaky stairs leading to the second floor of the Peck and Fly Building on the west side of the courthouse square. His small office was not pretentious—a secondhand table, a few chairs, and one law book—but he was in business.

There was no rush of clients to the new law office, however. His first case was in justice-of-the-peace court in defense of a transient Mexican, named Cortez, who had been charged with petty theft. Several friends of Cortez and all the courthouse hangers-on crowded into the tiny courtroom.

The crux of the case rested on identification—that is, if witnesses could identify Cortez as the culprit, he was sunk. The first two witnesses pointed out Cortez as the man.

Wes then resorted to strategy. He was convinced that all Mexican men looked alike and that the witnesses had been able to identify Cortez because of the clothes he was wearing. He asked the court for a ten-minute recess. During that time he hurried Cortez and another Mexican into an adjoining room and had them change clothes. Returning to the courtroom, he asked three Mexicans to sit with Cortez at the table.

When the trial resumed, every witness continued without hesitation to identify Cortez, and Wes lost his case. It almost broke his heart, but he laughed with those who chuckled over the attempted cleverness which had failed to work.

But what was as discouraging as the loss of that first case was the stubborn fact that very little law business came his way. People were congenial enough, but when it came to seeking the service of a lawyer, very few wanted to do business with a man of Wes's old reputation. Wes felt this deeply. The economic struggle was tough, almost sufficient to make a man a hot-headed Populist. The five-hundred-dollar gift was dwindling away and the few small fees helped very little.

At home, the reaction of his daughters to the new life was not what Wes had anticipated it would be. Molly was lonely for Charley and homesick for the Sandies. For a few weeks she smiled and struggled to give the impression that she was content. But finally she could stand it no longer; her unhappiness away from the life she had known and loved became so unbearable that she returned to the Duderstadt ranch and visited often in the homes of Charley's relatives. Little Jane then missed Molly and her friends in the country, and she begged her father to let her "go home" for a while. Wes sadly granted her wish. This left only him and his son together. Johnny didn't like town ways, but he wanted to stick to his father.

Wes grew discouraged and despondent. The realization that his children had grown beyond any need of him and longed to manage their own lives left him with a feeling of emptiness. Always before he had been in the forefront one way or another. But life out of prison in a vastly changed world had turned out to be drab and disheartening in a sleepy little town.

Then Wes woke things up in Gonzales. A political issue ignited fiery sparks in him, and he let them fly in the traditional Hardin manner.

W. E. Jones was given the Democratic nomination for the office of sheriff in 1894. He had held that job once before, back in 1872 when he was appointed by Governor E. J. Davis, who had tried to run Texas with his state police. Jones had been sheriff at the time Wes had sawed out of the Gonzales jail.

Deputy Sheriff Bob Coleman took the Populist nomination to oppose Jones in the forthcoming election. Coleman was not widely known in the county and had once been tried for murder in DeWitt County, but had been cleared. However, he was a Populist and represented those who lived on sowbelly and sorghum, while Jones was considered by the insurgents to be of the old-line class of complacency and plenty that feasted on fried chicken and coconut cake.

For two days after the candidates for sheriff were announced, Wes stuck to his law office, writing furiously. The next morning, he met Deputy Fly on a street corner and asked him to read an article he said he had written for *The Drag Net*. Fly had the surprise of his life.

In the statement, Wes claimed that Jones, as sheriff in 1872, had known of his escape plans and had made it possible for him to saw out of jail. Moreover, he charged that after his escape, Sheriff Jones had protected him from arrest. With an attitude of righteous indignation, Wes took the stand that a man who had done what he accused Jones of having done was not fit to be an officer of the law, that he had been corrupt and probably would be again.

"I wouldn't publish it, Wes," Fly said, returning the paper to him. "I wouldn't say anything about it."

"Why?"

"Well, a lot of people won't believe it. A lot of others will think you should be the last man to tell it if Jones was enough of a friend at that time to fix it so you could escape."

There was a flash of the old gray in Wes's eyes. Here was a situation he had faced before, one which offered him the choice of compromise and going along or sticking to his life-long principle of black is black and white is white, right is right and wrong is wrong. When Brown Bowen had been under sentence of death, Wes had flatly refused to sign a false statement that could have saved his brother-in-law's life. Now one of his most trusted friends had suggested that he suppress what he considered a true statement—because of the possible consequences.

As far as Wes personally was concerned, the consequences were much greater this time. He was just out of prison and struggling hard for a comeback; to plunge into a violent political campaign, which would certainly drag in the tragedies of the past, could only hurt his chances for that comeback. And there were his children.

But how could he stand by tight-lipped and permit a man he

considered corrupt to win the office of sheriff and thereby become the law of a whole county?

Wes had known peace officers. He had known them from the occupying soldiers during Reconstruction and the hated state police to Wild Bill Hickok, to Deputy Charlie Webb and on down to the present. He had known many of the "legal gunmen." He had been harassed by officers. He had known badge-wearing men who were susceptible to corruption and capable of the lowest tricks, and this he had stood against even in his days as a gunman. To his way of thinking, being an outlaw wasn't such a bad thing if the outlaw didn't try to appear to be a saint. To Wes an officer who turned his head to keep from seeing certain things—or who winked at certain things because it was politically expedient—was ten times worse than an outlaw or a notorious ex-convict.

When Wes had decided to reform, he had gone all the way; a man had to be either within or without the law, and there was no middle ground.

Wes had made up his own mind to write the statement accusing Jones, but he had asked Deputy Fly to read it before publication, thinking his friend would approve it and applaud his stand. So he was stunned when Deputy Fly advised him to keep quiet.

"But listen, Fly," Wes said, "I've been to the pen. Many a man who was as much of a law violator as I ever was has lived here, posing as a reputable man and enjoying the free, respected life while I've been paying for mine in the pen. I've served my time and have come back to be a law-abiding citizen. There's only one way to be a law-abiding citizen and that is to respect every law; you can't enforce some of them and wink at others. I know this fact on Jones, and, as a good citizen, it is my duty to tell it."

Fly, thinking Wes was still rankled over the old state police and Bill Jones's one-time connection with their administration, begged him to wait a few days and think it over. Ever since his boyhood, Fly had admired Wes. He now felt that, at best, Wes's chances to make good were slim. He wanted to help him.

"A thing like this should have long and careful thought and consideration," Fly said.

Wes thanked his friend, but, as of old, he depended on his own judgment of right and wrong. He walked straight to *The Drag Net* and had the article published.

The blast set off excitement in every precinct in the county. Gonzales was aghast. Newspapers over the state heard the howls from the "cradle of Texas liberty" and there were big headlines: "John Wesley Hardin Heard from Again." The man who had spent many idle hours in his law office and at the courthouse was the talk of the county. The Populists had found a fighter who could hit hard and wasn't afraid to do it, and many of them flocked to Wes. However, such high-sounding generalities as "economic injustice" and "the privileged class" were soon forgotten; likewise, candidate Coleman was almost overlooked. Wes Hardin was the issue. He was back in the limelight trying to get his man.

Jones, who had been prominent in the county for many years, doubtless would have ignored with a snort of contempt any other ex-convict, but he couldn't ignore Wes. The interest *The Drag Net* statement had stirred up couldn't be passed over lightly. Jones came bristling back in *The Gonzales Inquirer*, which was supporting Democratic candidates. He denied every charge and made some of his own.

Wes shoved his law book aside and converted his office into political campaign headquarters. He came out openly for Coleman and promised to "expose Jones and his kind."

Many men in the county were aware that Wes knew perhaps more than anyone else of the intrigues and acts of violence in the old feuding days. Since Wes had made the charges against Jones, no one knew what he might reveal of the blood-and-thunder past. There were things about those bitter years that simply could not be told without wrecking friendships, ruining reputations, and probably leading to killings.

Seeing what was happening, and also what might happen, Deputy Sheriff Fly and other close friends of Wes went to him and implored him to withdraw and say no more. They emphasized that their plea was for his own good, that he could ruin his chance for a wonderful comeback by risking everything on a sheriff's race that really didn't matter.

Wes listened quietly, but he had the stance and the look of a man who might be in a gunfight at any moment. "Look," he said, "some law-breakers are sent to prison and come back ex-convicts. Some men who wear the cloak of righteousness and respectability wink at sin and corruption but pose as upright citizens, and they never see a prison. I have paid for mine. I pledged myself and my now dead wife that I would be a law-abiding citizen, and I intend to keep the pledge."

When the friends left, Wes sat down and turned out a statement which poured more fuel on the political fire as well as showing that he was about as adept with syllables as he had ever been with six-guns.

"Some say I have cut my own throat," he said. "I say I am here to pursue life in the paths of peace. I want your friendship, but only on honorable terms. . . . Yes, I desire your friendship, good will, and confidence much, but however much I crave your support, if I have to obtain it by doing a cowardly or ignoble act, my wish will remain forever ungratified. . . .

"Someone has said, 'Man is the noblest work of God,' but I suppose the sentiment expressed refers to an honest, brave, sincere, and enlightened man, one that dares to do his duty as he understands it, regardless of consequences. To say the least of it, this is the kind of man that I admire, but I have a natural loathing for a misanthrope, a poltroon, a traitor, whether he be a Judas in God's heavenly company, an Arnold in the immortal Army of America, or Bill Jones as sheriff of Gonzales County in 1872."

As many had feared, animosities that had long been sleeping were aroused. Old skeletons were rattled out of closets. Wes went to see old John Lackey and solicited his support in lining up the Negro citizens for Coleman. At almost the same time, supporters of Jones called on Lackey to stir up the Negroes against Hardin and Coleman. Thus old wounds of the days of Reconstruction were reopened.

There were Hardin partisans ready to shoot at the drop of a hat, and there were Jones partisans anxious to do the same thing. As a result of the turmoil, nearly every place of business in Gonzales bristled with guns. Sheriff Glover was uneasy, but he knew that if he did anything that could be interpreted as taking sides his action might set off a riot.

"I don't know just what to do except watch and wait," he told Deputy Fly. "I'm positive that if a single shot is fired we'll have a feud that will make the old Sutton-Taylor trouble look like recess at school."

Out at the ranch Fred Duderstadt watched the storm with mounting concern. He knew Wes could take care of himself, but something could happen to Johnny. Therefore he rode into Gonzales leading a saddled horse. He found Johnny at home, but Wes was out campaigning in the county.

"Johnny, pack some duds and come back to the ranch with me," Duderstadt said. "I'm 'way behind since you've been in town. I need you."

Johnny's face brightened when he saw his favorite horse

standing in front of the house. He had been homesick for ranch work, but he saw through Duderstadt's offer. "Wish I could go to the ranch," he said, "but Papa needs me right now. He's fighting mad over this sheriff's race, and I've got to stick with him, no matter what happens."

Duderstadt took on the fatherly role he had played for this boy. "I know how you feel, Johnny, and I don't blame you, but the best way you can stick to your pa is to come on out to the ranch with me. You stay here and something happen to you or if you got mixed up in this mess it would kill your pa. Now, listen, Johnny, I *know* what I'm talking about. You've got to trust me in this."

Johnny was in a quandary. He trusted Duderstadt implicitly, yet he had another loyalty. "I trust you," he said, "but I can't go without talking to Papa about it."

Duderstadt and Johnny went to the law office and waited until Wes returned late in the afternoon. Wes was tense. He had a thousand things he wanted to do that day to turn votes against Jones, but he listened to Duderstadt and Johnny, and he agreed that Johnny should go to the country and stay away until after the election.

"If you want me for anything, Papa," Johnny said, "I'll be here as fast as a horse can bring me."

Johnny shook hands warmly with his father and he and Duderstadt rode to the ranch. Duderstadt wouldn't permit Molly or little Jane to go to town, fearing they might be insulted and thereby bring the long-silent guns of their father into action.

The public statements grew so vitriolic that the newspapers declined to print them. Jones wrote an article denouncing Coleman and Hardin as liars, thieves, cutthroats, and murderers. He charged that the scheme was for Coleman to be sheriff in name only and to appoint Wes Hardin his chief deputy so that Wes could legally tote a pistol and force his will on the people of the county. When the papers refused to touch this, Jones had thousands of circulars printed and distributed all over the county.

The claim that Wes sought a job as deputy set off a world of speculation. Wes Hardin, the law in Gonzales County! The thought of it was fantastic. Wes had first seen the county when he was a boy fugitive heading for Mexico. He had stayed in the county and fought through the bloody years. To come back from fifteen years in prison and within a few months pin on the badge of the law—well, no man of his notoriety could have a more fanciful dream. Just to win the election without any thought of a job as deputy sheriff would be an amazing victory, one that would give Wes prestige not only in the county but all over the state.

During his last five years in prison, Wes had studied politics and all the colorful campaigns that had rocked Texas in the past. The Texas technique had been to make noise, cry out against corruption, inject the spectacular, and shoulder the cross of the downtrodden. There were men in Gonzales County—men who were as close friends of Wes as Fred Duderstadt had been through the years—who said that while in prison Wes had made up his mind to combine law and politics with the full intention of becoming governor of Texas.

Wes hotly denied the charge that there had been any deal with Coleman for him to be deputy sheriff. He declared that he desired no such honors but wanted only to be a peaceful citizen and a practicing lawyer, that he was in the political fight only because he wanted "an upright, honest sheriff who would protect the people of the county."

Wes had never done anything halfway and he was in his true form. He swore that he would not live in a county in which Bill Jones was sheriff and that he would leave immediately if Coleman were defeated. Having made that pledge, he doubled his efforts to discredit Jones. He wrote friends and relatives who had left the county, or had been run out, asking them to recall the old days and give him information that would hurt Jones.

One of these letters went to Jim Clements, a cousin and old trail partner who had moved to Sterling City, Texas.

Wes explained his position and said: "If you know anything that will reflect upon his [Jones'] character as an officer, please write me plainly. I am after him to defeat him for office and in case I fail I will move." He added this postscript: "He expects to be elected by the Negro vote—but I think he is badly beaten."

The election was on November 6, the second anniversary of Jane Hardin's death.

The day was cold and rainy, and Elm, Clear, Salty, and other creeks in the county were running full. But the men flocked to the polls in greater numbers than ever before. That night all the returns were in except from the Sedan precinct, which was thirty-five miles from Gonzales and had been cut off from town by high water. The count was so close that the votes at Sedan could decide the contest.

The next day it was reported that the presiding judge at Sedan was two miles out of Gonzales with the all-important returns. This presiding judge was Doc Bockius, the mysterious little man who had once quit his store at Sedan to work as a Wes Hardin cowboy and had barely escaped with his life.

Wes and Coleman mounted their horses and headed out to meet Doc. Hearing of this, Jones and his brother Gus likewise rode to find Bockius. Sheriff Glover and Deputy Fly saw this action and decided that anything might happen now; however, they told the crowd at the courthouse that the Sedan returns were expected shortly.

When Wes and Coleman met Doc Bockius he refused to tell them the results, saying he was honor bound to report only to the county clerk. He rode on. Soon he struck up with the Jones brothers. "I'm taking the returns to the county clerk's office," he told them. "If you want to know how Sedan voted, go to the courthouse."

When all the votes were finally counted, Bill Jones had 2,054 and Coleman had 2,046. Jones had won by only eight votes.

Everything considered, this was a tremendous victory and a vote of confidence for Wes. No one had thought he could make such a showing. For a man of his reputation, to support an obscure candidate in an offshoot political party in a county that had been traditionally Democratic and to lose by only eight votes was nothing short of a political miracle. It was a loss, yet it was something of which Wes could have been proud.

But, characteristically, he had gone all out. He had burned his bridges behind him, setting fires that could not be extinguished in years. Ever since Comanche, and even before that, Wes had lived in terror of mobs. It turned out that eight Democratic citizens in his home county had been the mob that "got" him; as the old saying goes, he had taken enough rope to hang himself, and there hadn't been enough votes on his side to keep the knot from being tied neatly around his throat. Wes had sworn to leave the county if Bill Jones won. His word was out on that. And there were people who intended for him to keep that word. Among them was Gus Jones, brother of the sheriff-elect.

On the second morning after the votes were counted Wes met Gus Jones in front of P. Levyson's store.

"Wes," Jones said, "this county isn't big enough for us both to live in. I was born here and reared here and I'm not going to leave."

Wes had a pistol within inches of his right hand. He was no more afraid of Gus Jones than he was of a coon and could shoot him down as easily as he had put six holes in the knot on the tree at the Duderstadt ranch. Although thoroughly angry, Wes knew that if he involved himself in a killing his past was against him and that it could only heap trouble on his daughters and son.

"Gus," he said, "you know good and well I'll be out of this county long before Bill Jones takes office as sheriff." He whirled and walked away. It was the first time in his life he had ever turned his back on an invitation to trouble when he was armed. For once, he had considered the consequences.

21

Starless Nights

When a man kills he has to live with those whose lives he has taken. He can never escape their presence or the gaze, gossip, and judgment of the living who know he has killed. At least, that was the way with Wes Hardin. Sitting beside a sputtering lamp in the small gray house that now seemed desolate and deserted, he read a description of what happens to the wayward and the killer:

"Their ways are hard, their days are sombrous and sad; their nights are starless and sleepless; their hope for time and eternity has faded away and they await their terrible doom. . . ."

Wes had written the words himself—to Jane from prison at the time he had feared he had a criminal mind and had beseeched her to keep their children from being like him. In packing his law book and other belongings for his move away from Gonzales County, he had come upon a huge stack of old letters which Jane had saved for him; in the stack—written in his own words and those of his family and friends—was a story. While sorting through the letters and pausing now and then to read one, he decided to write the story of his life and of Jane's hard struggle. Mentally he would ride and shoot in the past he had failed to live down. He packed the letters in his trunk.

Wes made a quick trip to the Sandies—to the Duderstadt ranch to tell Johnny and the girls good-bye. Molly had set her wedding for December 16, and Wes gave her his blessing. He and Johnny rode one afternoon over the wide, familiar range and Wes advised his son to stay with the land. The boy promised he would if his father would likewise make a promise: to call on him if he needed him.

"Son," Wes said, "if I ever think it best to send for you, rest assured that I will."

In a short conversation on the ranch house front porch, Wes expressed his undying gratitude to Fred Duderstadt for his staunch friendship.

And then he moved to the home of friends near old Riddle-ville, where he had married Jane, in neighboring Karnes County, there to start his writing chore. This work wasn't as easy as he had anticipated, and he sweated a week before he had the first page written to his satisfaction. He started sipping a toddy occasionally in order to bolster his will to stick to the job.

Early in December Wes received a note from his brother, Jeff Davis Hardin, who lived near Junction in the Texas hill country to the west of Austin. Jeff told him some friends there needed the services of a lawyer and that Junction might be a good place to open an office. Wes made a final visit to Asher Cemetery, then traveled to Junction. Shortly after he opened a law office in the picturesque hill town on the Llano River he was involved in another strange adventure.

His brother Jeff told him of some cousins he had never seen who lived in the nearby community of London. Christmas was at hand and the holiday spirit was taking hold. This was Wes's first Christmas season out of prison, and he was lonely; this loneliness plus the old Hardin love of visiting kinfolks led him to hire a horse and ride to London to see the cousins. They introduced him to a young lady, Miss Callie Lewis, the daughter of a substantial landowner and stockman.

Wes was attracted to her at first by her name; it reminded him that his baby daughter had been known as Callie until the name was changed to Jane just before he had gone to prison. Callie Lewis was only a little older than young Jane Hardin. Wes was still handsome, and he retained his gentlemanly manners when in the company of women. The sprinkle of gray in his hair and mustache gave him a distinguished appearance. Callie was fascinated by the famed John Wesley Hardin—and more so when Wes confided in her that he was writing the story of his life. Callie invited him to visit her.

A week later Wes hired a horse and buggy and drove out to London to see Callie. He met her father, Captain Len Lewis, and her mother. It turned out that Captain Lewis and Wes had several mutual friends in the cattle business and also that the captain had been an admirer of what he called "Wes Hardin spunk." So the men were soon deep in friendly conversation.

However, Wes didn't forget Callie. He took her on a ride in the moonlight that evening and asked her to marry him. Callie was completely surprised and told Wes she would have to think it over.

Driving back through the hills to Junction that night, Wes spotted a coyote loping across a grassy glade. On an impulse, he pulled out his pistol and fired, killing the animal. The sudden report of the gun frightened the horse and it bolted.

The quick jerk threw Wes across the seat and crashed his face into the buggy bows. The horse sprinted into a run and high-tailed it down the hilly road half a mile before Wes could regain his balance and stop the runaway. The bump into the bows bruised the left side of his face and laid him up for a few days.

During this time, Jeff Hardin stopped by to see Wes and heard of the new romance. Jeff joshed Wes about "robbing the cradle" and marrying a chunk of land and money. But this didn't deter Wes. On January 1, 1895, he wrote Callie, telling her about his runaway and urging her to give an answer "to my proposition." Callie replied immediately that she didn't like to answer such questions by letter, but preferred to see him "I think Papa would like to see you," she wrote. "So come as soon as you can. I will be looking for you."

Wes and Callie were married on January 8 by Justice of the Peace F. Wahrmund in the Kimble County courthouse at Junction. Only Callie's parents and a few close friends of the family were witnesses. Captain Lewis formally gave his daughter to Wes.

News of the wedding spread like wildfire over Junction and the county. The ranching and business families had a custom of giving a grand ball when there was a wedding of notable people. This wedding called for a really big one and a county-wide ball was quickly arranged. All the furniture was removed from a large room in the courthouse and a string band was hired. The elite, or the coconut-cake group of the county, all dressed in their Sunday best, assembled at the courthouse and awaited the bride and groom. Wes and Callie would lead the grand march; it was to be followed by a waltz to the tune of "Over the Waves."

All was in readiness at the appointed hour. The fiddlers had their instruments in tune and their bows in position to saw down on the first note the instant the honor guests appeared. The minutes dragged by. Men consulted their watches time and again. Questioning eyes were turned politely on the bride's parents. When an hour had passed Captain and Mrs. Lewis disappeared. They went to the friend's home where Wes and Callie had spent the time after the wedding while awaiting the grand ball. They found Wes bending over Callie, talking persuasively. She was sobbing. Something that Wes couldn't explain had happened.

When he and Callie had stepped out of the house to go to the big party they met Jeff Hardin and his wife, and the four had chatted. Jeff had chided Wes again about the youthfulness of his bride.

The first thing Wes knew, Callie burst into tears and ran into the house. Wes followed and tried his best to soothe her. When the parents arrived, Callie asked them to take her home.

The arrival in her own room did not improve the bride's condition or change her mind. She demanded that her husband of a few hours get out and not come back. Wes was dumbfounded. He humbly apologized to the parents and left. He remained in the vicinity several days and inquired often of Callie; then he moved to nearby Kerrville and plunged into the work of writing his book.

Callie's parents took his side. They tried to persuade their daughter to go to Wes. They wrote him often and expressed their admiration and friendship. In one note, Captain Lewis said: "I believed you to be a gentleman when I gave you my daughter. Now I know you are a thoroughbred gentleman for the treatment you gave Callie at Junction."

Finally, after three months, the mother all but gave up. She wrote Wes: "Sometimes I think that Callie will come around but if you want to get a divorce I would not object, but I would like it if you and Callie could live together."

Wes didn't see his bride again. He never did know exactly what caused Callie's behavior, and her parents didn't either. Her mother made a guess, telling Wes: "I believe that if you hadn't met up with your brother when you started off you and Callie would be living together now." From beginning to end, the romance was an amazing one indeed. The young girl had been infatuated by this man of legend and gentlemanly manners and swept off her feet. On Wes's side the affair with Callie had presented him with an opportunity again to have a home and at the same time marry into a prominent family that he admired. Regardless of whether he had considered the fact, the marriage would certainly improve his economic standing. The surprising end of the romance did not cause any immediate desperate action. During the three months of correspondence with Callie's parents he worked day and night on his manuscript and brought the story up to the time when he had met and killed Deputy Webb in Comanche.

Early in April of 1895, at about the time all hope ended for a reconciliation with Callie, Wes heard what amounted to a clan call; at least it was a distant echo of the fury of the cowboy and feuding days in Gonzales County. At Pecos in far Western Texas, Jim Miller had been shot and severely wounded by G. A. Frazier. Miller had been extremely close to Wes's late beloved cousin and pal, Manning Clements. Miller and his friends wanted Frazier sent to the penitentiary or killed. Having heard that Wes was now a lawyer, and knowing of his other abilities in former years, they had sent for him.

Wes went to Pecos and once again found himself among killers and desperate men. While the case against Frazier was in the process of development, he went on to El Paso and rented a room, there to wind up the work on his book. He couldn't have gone to a tougher, more dangerous town in the nation. Nearly all the rest of Texas had passed its wild-frontier stage and had settled down to relative peace and order. Many of the killers, cattle rustlers, and outlaws who couldn't quit their old game had drifted from quietening places to El Paso, which, because of its location geographically, was a sort of sanctuary of sin. Any hunted man could dash from its city limits across the Rio Grande into Mexico and there, in Juarez, enjoy protection against Texas and United States civil authorities. Just over the Texas line stretched the vast territory of New Mexico, which was raw and lawless and fifteen years from statehood; it furnished El Paso a full quota of the homicidally inclined. There were factions among these fractious citizens, each scheming to get the upper hand. In fact, El Paso was so infested with undesirables and fugitives and so alive with intrigue and conflict that the city had a noted lead-slinger, Jeff Milton, as chief of police. Old John Selman, the slayer of the desperado, Bass Outlaw, and several other men of violence, was a constable, and his son, John Selman, Jr., was on the police force.

El Paso was the kind of place Wes had pleaded with his son Johnny to shun; it was full of the sort of dives that he had advised his son never to enter. When he had come out of prison a reformed man he had planned never to darken the doors of such places again. But circumstances often alter cases. Wes had not been able to establish any real sense of belonging with his children, for they had grown away from him. His participation in politics, for what he considered a principle, had not only shattered his dream of a career as a lawyer in Gonzales County but had separated him still further from his family, and led eventually to his second marriage, which had failed completely. If any of these things had been successful, he doubtless could have settled down and, as so many had predicted through the years, made his mark. But his plans and efforts hadn't worked out that way. Instead, everything had led inexorably to El Paso, and there Wes found himself, alone and friendless, exposed to all the lures and excitement of the outlaw life. It was natural enough that he should be susceptible to them.

When word that John Wesley Hardin was in town spread through the perilous precincts of El Paso, bad men who were friendly enough to pal around together exchanged knowing looks and recited to each other tales they had heard of the Hardin genius with guns. Chief Milton was so wary that he added to his arsenal and warned his force that Wes Hardin was by all odds the most dangerous man in America.

On his first night in El Paso, Wes made the town—the gambling halls and the saloons. In every place he went the tough men, many of them of considerable repute, came close to bowing and scraping before him. They set up the drinks; they lost to him at games; they displayed a desire to be on friendly terms with this great gunman. There was still the old envy of reputation among gunmen, the lesser lights yearning for the glory of the star.

These men in El Paso didn't realize Wes hadn't pulled a gun on a man for twenty years. They knew nothing of his reform, education, and good resolutions while in prison and were not aware of the dream he had dreamed for his family. They judged him solely on his old preprison reputation, which had never been equaled.

Therefore, it was almost a phantom Wes Hardin who came to El Paso; but the phantom soon came alive. Wes realized at once that he was respected and feared, even by the most dangerous. He realized, too, that in the smelly atmosphere and the din of the saloon and gambling house where bad men congregated he had no peer. In a place where ability and readiness to shoot brought respect, Wes didn't need a pardon

from the governor or the vote of the good citizens of Gonzales County. Here he was the kingpin on his own; it was like
old times. Like Abilene in '71? Not quite. In Abilene he
had been a glorified boy filling a man's shoes, a deft, cocky
kid with the spunk and speed to disarm Wild Bill Hickok.
Moreover, in the old days he had worn a halo of heroism for
his fight against occupying troops and the state police.

But in El Paso Wes represented no righteous cause; the glory
was gone and only the grimness remained. In El Paso he was
simply a gunman.

For months, in working on his manuscript, Wes had been
going back over his career and reliving the old life, glimpsing
both the glory and the grimness. However, his story had been
dispassionate, a straightforward narrative in which he had
made no attempt to overheroize or to excuse himself. Battle
by battle and bullet by bullet he had told of all his escapades.

And now in El Paso he had come in his story to the
Comanche tragedy. Nothing else in his life had affected him
so deeply as the lynching of his brother Joe at Comanche.
And the Comanche incident had been the breaking point; not
only had it brought grief and shame to his family, but it had
sent him to prison.

As fate would have it, at the time Wes was busy reliving the
events at Comanche, he learned something that brought poi-
son to every pore: J. C. Jones, who had been at Comanche
at the time of the Hardin family's troubles, was now the El
Paso city jailer. Through the years Wes had thought that
Jones had been involved in some way in the mob action
against his family.

Again the impulse to kill, to even accounts, surged within
him. His pen dripped venom. After telling of the killing of
his brothers and cousins in Comanche, Wes broke into the
sequence of his narrative with:

"While I write this, I say from the deepest depths of my heart that my desire for revenge is not satisfied, and if I live another year, I promise my friends and my God to make another of my brother's murderers bite the dust."

The gathering of all these stormy elements hit hard. Wes was almost at rock bottom physically, mentally, and financially; his eyes were bleary and he was nervous. But, with all this, he still tried to keep up the distinction of being a practicing lawyer, with his room as an office.

One day an unexpected client called. She was a young lady named Mrs. Martin McRose, a bosomy blonde with heavy lips, blue eyes, and rouge-dabbed cheeks. She was in trouble and needed the assistance of a lawyer. Some time ago Chief Milton and other Texas peace officers had chased her husband across the Rio Grande and had sent word to him at Juarez that, if he returned, he would be jailed or killed.

McRose was wanted on a number of serious criminal charges. He had left his young wife in El Paso with some three thousand dollars in cash. Now Mrs. McRose wanted Lawyer Hardin to help her get her husband safely out of Mexico and then protect him from the law in El Paso.

Wes treated Mrs. McRose with the genteel courtesy a client deserved, and he promised to look into possible legal action. However, after several conferences with Wes, Mrs. McRose showed plainly that she was attracted to him, and she soon lost interest in getting her husband back across the Rio Grande.

Three of McRose's main henchmen were hemmed up in Juarez with him, but he had a score of confederates who were on the loose and could circulate freely between Juarez and El Paso. They watched for chances to outmaneuver the police, kill Wes Hardin, or do anything else reckoned to assist McRose. So the city was an armed camp. No one had ever described more vividly many of the persons involved than

Wes Hardin himself in the old letter about "starless nights." Eventually, on June 29, McRose did attempt to slip back to El Paso. As Chief Milton had warned, he was shot to death before he reached the Texas side of the river. This left the woman on Wes's hands. He saw her often and she was known as "Wes Hardin's woman." Wes continued to devote a good deal of time to his writing and he was almost through with his manuscript.

In the early part of August Wes had to go to Pecos for a couple of days to see about legal matters in his case there. During his absence Mrs. McRose grew lonely and went on a binge. While very drunk she walked San Antonio Street waving a pistol. Policeman John Selman, Jr., arrested her and she was fined fifty dollars.

When Wes returned to El Paso and heard of this, he was infuriated. He accused Policeman Selman of being disrespectful to a lady.

"If I had been here," Wes said in an angry tone, "you wouldn't have done it."

Wes brooded over this for several days. The fact that anyone would molest a woman known to be his special friend was something of an affront to his standing as the most dreaded man in El Paso, and a lawyer as well. Wes was sliding downhill rapidly: he was so edgy that he fussed with Mrs. McRose; she ran to the police and claimed he had threatened to kill her. However, Wes and Mrs. McRose made up; then he began worrying about her, fearing that she might not be safe in El Paso. He persuaded her to leave and put her on a train bound for Phoenix.

The next day Wes received a telegram from Mrs. McRose in a New Mexico town. In it she said she had a premonition that something terrible was about to happen to him and that, therefore, she planned to return to him. The premonition troubled Wes.

Nevertheless, he stuck to his writing that day, which was August 19, 1895. Early in the evening he told friends that with one more day's work his story would be ended. The prospect of having the long, nerve-racking job off his hands made him jovial. But a little later while walking along San Antonio Street near the Acme Saloon, Wes saw Constable John Selman, the policeman's father. He upbraided Selman because his son had arrested and fined Mrs. McRose. Wes was extremely rough, but Selman, although he had been noted as a man of steel nerve, took no chance on a draw against the Hardin reputation. Selman was badly shaken by the encounter and told a friend, E. L. Shackleford, that Wes had threatened to kill him and also his son because of the Mrs. McRose affair.

Wes strolled into the Acme, which happened to have only a handful of customers that night. He drank lightly and tried his hand at a few games. He was in a good humor. A few minutes after eleven o'clock he matched a dice game with H. S. Brown, an El Paso grocer. When the game was under way Wes stood with his back to the front door, which, for a man of his repute in El Paso, was about the equivalent of suicide.

A few moments later, old John Selman appeared in the saloon door. He took careful aim and shot Wes in the head. He kept shooting. Wes crumpled to the floor dead.

Word that Selman had killed John Wesley Hardin crackled over the saloon section of the city and soon the Acme was jammed.

Dozens of men stood and stared down at the body. Lying there on the saloon floor with blood spreading from the wound in his head, Wes Hardin was still true to his complex character: he was the center of a raging controversy, the essence of which involved honor. Constable Selman claimed he had shot Wes in the eye and that the bullet had come out at the back of his head. Chief Jeff Milton strolled in, took one look at the body and, with a snort of contempt, refused to take the constable's proffered hand because, Milton said, the man on the floor had been shot from the back.

A coroner's inquiry was called hurriedly. Two pistols were found on the body. Groceryman Brown claimed that the shot had come from the rear and that Wes had made no attempt to reach for a gun. Three doctors examined the body and wrote a report saying that death had been caused by a bullet "that entered near the base of the skull posteriorly."

According to this eyewitness and expert testimony, the Brushy Creek fortuneteller had been right on another of his predictions: Wes had been killed by a shot from the back. However, the seer had missed completely one point—that Wes would kill two men after release from prison. Maybe he had yearned to shoot jailer Jones and policeman Selman, but in his seventeen months as a free and pardoned citizen he had not killed a single soul.

Selman may have thought that the blood he "caused to flow was not of the kind that leaves a stain," but the history and legends of the State of Texas had been indelibly marked by the daring and violent actions of this man who had described a flaming pattern of vengeance. He tried to take judgment into his own two-gunned hands, and he likewise coolly foresaw what his own dreadful end would be.

The preacher's son killed more men than any other man of the West. To the end he remained an unfathomable mystery, the extreme of the period of the furious frontier and the tragic era of the Civil War and Reconstruction in the most recalcitrant of the defeated Southern states.

He was a rebel's rebel.

He despised man-made bans as he did injustice, falsehood, cowardice, compromise, and all half-gods.

In the fine balancing of history, it is possible that Wes, numerous as were his deeds outside the letter of the law, saved more lives than he took. The most savage reign of terror and wanton murder Texas ever had was in the time of the state police force. Texans feared and hated it, but Wes was almost the only man who fought it openly and aggressively from the first. There was never any doubt that his single-handed fight did more than perhaps anything else to discredit the police force and finally to bring about its downfall. This made way for the re-establishment of the Texas Rangers and the eventual arrival of law and order in a state that had been torn by upheaval so long.

With all the good and bad in his unique life, he measured on a gigantic scale a fault common to many men—he preached the good life and often practiced the bad. But in one thing he was steadfast: the love of family he never violated.

Even in his last dark days Wes made a final attempt to protect his children from his own willful ways. The identification card in his pocketbook listed Fred Duderstadt, his old and trusted rancher friend in the Sandies, as the person to be notified in case of an accident. A few hours after the killing in the Acme Saloon, police telephoned Duderstadt. He knew and understood the reason his name was on the little card. Carefully he explained to Johnny and the girls about their father. He reasoned with them that, since Wes had died violently and under a cloud in El Paso, their father wouldn't want his body returned to Gonzales, where it would serve to reawaken old animosities. So even in death the word that Wes had given that he would stay out of Gonzales County was kept. He was buried in Concordia Cemetery in El Paso with no kinfolks present.

The death of Wes Hardin was headline news for a day or so. One reporter mentioned that he had a son somewhere in Eastern Texas; otherwise his family was not involved. Another newspaper commented that the small engraved plate on the casket bore the words: "At Peace."

In the span of his forty-two years, the wide, grassy prairies and the tree-shaded valleys of Texas had grown peaceful, as peaceful as such a vast stretch of country ever could be—except for one faraway corner, the stormy spot John Wesley Hardin had picked to end the story of his life.

Acknowledgments

Many persons contributed to the engaging work of searching dark and long-forgotten corners for the information contained in this story. Among them is F. M. Fly, who was still serving as justice of the peace in Gonzales in 1956. He was a wide-eyed lad when Wes Hardin was battling the state police, and a deputy sheriff when Hardin returned to Gonzales from prison. Judge Fly kept tucked in his mind many Hardin stories and legends, and he gave me the benefit of his keen memory.

Descendants of Wes and Joe Hardin made available scores of letters and documents and family lore; the letters, written by Hardin, his friends, relatives, and acquaintances, were not meant at the time for public perusal and therefore contained intimate detail that could not be found elsewhere.

Then there was the manuscript which Hardin had almost completed on the day of his death. Nearly every episode described in it could be checked against official records and other authentic sources, including letters and documents, even though written reports of many major events in the 1860's and 1870's are scarce, quite a few early-day courthouses having been burned and the scanty records with them. In order to get a clear picture of the geography of this story, I covered all the trails of Wes Hardin in Texas, Oklahoma, and Kansas. I spent time at Comanche, had a good look at Round Mountain and the area thereabouts, and acquainted myself with the trail Wes Hardin and Jim Taylor rode to Austin and on to the Sandies country. I visited the live oak under which Wes and Jane made their desperate decision and where Brown Bowen lies buried; I saw the place where Wes and Jane lived immediately after they were married; I browsed about old Sedan, Mustang Mot, Asher Cemetery. I went to El Paso to reconstruct the scenes there and even inspected the Texas prison.

It is impossible to list all who assisted in collecting and checking information, but my gratitude is hereby expressed to all. Special thanks are due the following:

Mr. and Mrs. E. D. Spellman of Burnet, Texas, who put me on the track of much Hardin information that had never been revealed before; Dr. Llerena Friend, historian and librarian at the Barker Texas History Center at the University of Texas; the reference staff of the University of Texas Library; John A. Hudson of the newspaper files divison of the University of Texas Library; Miss Alice Green, librarian of the Amarillo Public Library; the El Paso Public Library and its friendly staff; C. L. Sonnichsen of El Paso, author of *I'll Die Before I'll Run* and several other outstanding books on the Southwest; Fred Gipson, widely known author of Mason, Texas; Miss Sue Flanagan of San Angelo, Texas; and John Willey of William Morrow & Company, New York, a fast and effective man on the editorial draw.—L. N.

Index